Follow the Ribbons Missy

Ann Cofield

Charleston, SC
www.PalmettoPublishing.com

Follow the Ribbons, Missy
Copyright © 2021 by *Ann Cofield*

All rights reserved

Paperback ISBN: 978-1-63837-471-8

Dedication

To Jill Faulkner, who gave me a leg up on her horse and said, "Pick up the reins. This is how you learn to ride."

I was a horse-crazy nine year old youngster living in Oxford, Mississippi down the road from Rowan Oak, William Faulkner's home. Jill's cousin, Vicki, who knew my passion, said, "I know where there are horses."

Jill, my only regret is not thanking you for this life-changing moment. Little did I know, when I looked between your horse's ears, what my destiny would be! 'The good you do, lives after you' is truly spoken.

My friends, pick up the reins and ride through life, always remembering to thank those who gave you a leg up!

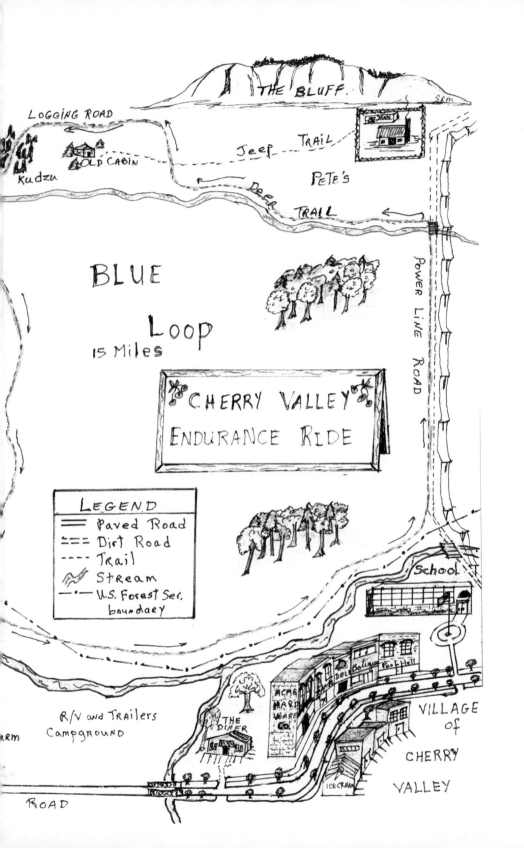

Chapter One

Blue Ridge Mountains, last Friday in June ~ 1990's

Tremors of fear chased up Moria's spine. *Maybe I'll just ride to finish. Why should I race?* She took no notice of the sheltering pines and hardwoods on the roadside or the last rays of the sun lighting the way to their next endurance ride as the horse trailer travelled down a steep, dusty road to camp.

"Hey, this is new." Jackson pointed to strips of orange flagging tied to a tree. "They've moved the finish line a good distance before the turn into camp."

"Guess they remembered last year when Rainbow swerved into the driveway and I fell. This'll be safer for everybody."

"You can do this," he encouraged, and turned the truck into the organized chaos of the ride.

Moria pointed toward the tree line. "I see Maxine's saving us a place," unfastening her seat belt and reaching for her boots. "Looks like Jeremy already has their camp set up," noticing their four-horse living quarters trailer. The bay, Catch On Fire, and the gray, Arctic Cat, whinnied to welcome the new arrivals.

The roadway stretched along the river, bordered by a freshly mowed meadow. Higher up, the Blue Ridge Mountains stood watchful over the acres of trailers spread out across the field.

Jackson drove through a moving mosaic of blended colors. Riders led their horses—a flashing array of bays, chestnuts, grays, and more—down the lane to the vet check. People trudged along dressed in rugged attire, a testament to a hard day's work. Most riders and crews wore dirty jeans or overalls, smeared with grime, spots, and streaks. Many wore bright tee shirts earned at the rides they'd attended. In wearing these shirts, they were reminded of the past, the thrill of success, the agony of defeat.

Maxine removed the empty water buckets that held the parking space and called, "All clear."

Jackson backed the Peace in the Valley trailer in, saying, "Did anyone try to steal our spot? Need I ask?"

Maxine shook her dark curly hair. "Are you kidding? They know me, and most of them know the Cherry Valley Riders are a team. Come on, we need to get to the vet check."

Moria jumped out of the truck and headed to the back of the trailer. "Maxine, if y'all are settled, would you help me get the horses out?" The two geldings peered sideways for a glimpse of freedom from the rough ride.

Rainbow Chaser stepped carefully to the ground and whinnied for Silver Dollar to follow him. Moria handed his lead rope to Maxine and returned through the empty stall, untied the grey and backed him out. Silver gave a shrill whinny and shook himself. *I'm here. Let the games begin.*

The two women walked the horses away to let them graze and renew their gut sounds. Maxine pressed her ear to Silver's side and listened. "Sounds good," she said with relief, upon hearing the familiar gurgling.

Moria nodded and bent over to feel Rainbow's legs, checking for swelling from the trip. Maxine ran her hands down Silver's legs and gave him a back scratch. "These dudes are going to be fine tomorrow. They're sound and well-conditioned, for sure."

Moria frowned. "Thanks, but in my opinion, every ride's a crap shoot."

Maxine turned toward the corrals to see Jackson and Jeremy heading to the vet check with Catch On Fire and Arctic Cat. "Well, let's look at the bright side. At least we have hookups. Guess that's one reason people like this ride. Plus, we have your girl Sarah and her friend Will to crew for us. Too bad they have to go back to college this summer." With those words, they joined Jackson and Jeremy.

As the Cherry Valley riders stood in the vet line with their horses, conversations swirled around them.

"I heard they changed the trail."

"I think my horse's shoe is loose."

"I saw the Peace in the Valley trailer here."

"It's going to be hot and humid tomorrow."

Moria listened to the conversations as she watched Catch On Fire trot out, with Maxine running beside her.

"That lady with the chestnut gelding won the Championship ride last year."

"Yeah, but I heard she's afraid to race. She only did it to sponsor the little girl."

Moria bit her lip, remembering her fear.

Silver and Arctic Cat cleared the check and the volunteer motioned for Rainbow and Moria to move forward for the exam. She handed her card to the scribe and stepped to Rainbow's head. The vet checked the horse's pulse, hydration, possible girth rubs, or other injuries, felt the legs for heat, checked the back for soreness, then motioned for the trot out.

"Good to go," the vet called to the scribe as Rainbow finished his trot with a long, sure stride.

Moria smiled and rubbed the horse's neck as she and her friends left the vet area. "Good job, buddy. The sun will rise, and we will go. We gotta road trip coming on."

Maxine said, "The chips are down, Missy." Moria frowned in response. They returned the horses to the corrals, checked the hay and water, then the four friends hurried across the field toward the meeting site.

Twilight settled over the endurance camp as other riders and crews left their trailers, heading to the pavilion for dinner and the ride meeting. The Cherry Valley riders walked in silence, perhaps gathering their wits to focus on the coming day.

Moria kicked a dirt clod. "I'll be glad when the ride's over."

Maxine looked closely at Moria's face. "Hey, what's got you all sideways? If you're not up to being a front runner, don't do it. You could ride middle of the pack with Jeremy and me."

"I'm not backing out. Not since I won last year."

A small voice whispered to Moria, *and why did you win?* Moria clinched her fists and buried her gaze in the grass, remembering *Jessie needed a sponsor for the Junior Division Championship. Trainer Doris Weaver was a hard case, and her broken leg changed my life.*

A light breeze blew through the camp. Moria shivered and looked up at the mountains sheltering the valley. Music from the pavilion played one of the endurance riders' favorite songs, "The Gambler." *Is this the ride where I walk away? I just don't have a good feeling about tomorrow. Am I afraid ... of falling ... of not winning? It used to be so easy, 'To finish is to win.' just because I won the ride, do people expect more of me? Guess you gotta know when to hold 'em and know when to fold 'em.*

Maxine caught up with Jackson and Jeremy. "Jackson, you better work some magic on your girl tonight. She's getting cold feet about the ride. Something's going on."

Jackson turned and walked back beside Moria, putting his arm around her. "Hey, where are your boots, Missy? Better lace 'em up. Tomorrow's a big day."

She blinked the tears away and tossed her hair over her shoulders. *What to say? I don't want to drag Jackson into my worries.* "No problem, it's just another ride."

He stopped, spun her toward him, pulled her close and tipped her face to his. "No, it's not just another ride. You think you've got to prove yourself all over again. You won because you sponsored Jessie. She and Doris pushed you to run, not because you wanted to win. Remember, it's not just about you. It's about the horse, too. You're a team. Get it?"

"I got it. Let's move on. I'm hungry."

After the meal, people's voices quieted. Children playing around the pavilion were motioned to sit still. Crickets chirped and night creatures scurried in the nearby woods. An owl hooted and Moria felt an unknown presence awaiting her on the trail.

The ride manager's greeting and instructions were brief. "Fifty-milers will do the blue loop first with a fifteen-minute vet check up on the mountain. There's plenty of water from an abandoned well. Yes, we had the water quality checked," he added, noticing some concerned looks. "Crews for fifties take Road 16 to the mountain vet check."

"Twenty-five milers, your loops are orange and yellow. You will share parts of the Blue Trail. Watch for the ribbons where the trails split."

The manager winked at Moria saying, "The finish line is a quarter mile farther down the road before you get to camp."

"'Preciate that," Moria answered with a wave of thanks.

"Good luck, riders. If the deer don't eat the ribbons, you'll be fine."

The Cherry Valley riders returned to the trailers to organize for the next day. Jackson pointed down the road. "Here come Sarah and Will. Hope they've got plenty of water. Let's double check their crewing stuff."

Sarah came over to give Moria a hug. "Good night, Mom. Good luck tomorrow. Ride like the wind, or maybe a breeze."

Moria, laughed "Yeah, or maybe a tornado. Who knows? Thanks so much for coming to help us." Looking across the field at their two tents, she added, "Are you sure y'all are safe down there by yourselves?"

Sarah glanced at Will, "We're safe. See you in the morning." With those words she and Will waved and headed toward their tents.

Moria opened the door to the living quarters of the Peace in the Valley trailer. *This space is truly my peace.* She took a deep breath, stretched, shed her shirt and jeans, then leaned over the sink. A few swipes of soap and water cleaned away the worst of the day. A dab of lavender fragrance, Jackson's favorite, finished the job. "Bring it on, buddy, I'm a-waitin'." Looking out the window, she watched him give the horses more hay, water, and check their legs one last time. *What did I do to deserve this awesome cowboy?*

Although it was only ten o'clock, all was quiet. A full moon shone over the camp, casting shadows which created horses larger than life. Unconcerned, they whinnied softly to each other, or squealed if another approached their hay. A dog barked down the lane. Night birds flew from tree to tree, their wings flapping softly in the evening.

Footsteps sounded nearby, perhaps someone on a last trip to the Porta Potty. In a trailer across the lane, another favorite song, "My Wish for You," reached into the night. Smells of fresh cut hay, campfire smoke and well-oiled leather added to the pine-scented evening air and comforted her heart. She turned from the window and drifted off to sleep.

Later, Jackson climbed into bed and pulled Moria close.

"Is it morning yet?" she mumbled.

Jackson kissed her softly. "Not yet, Missy. Sweet dreams."

~ ~ ~

Dew covers the morning grass. Moisture drips from the horses' blankets. Lights come on in the trailers and a long, eventful day begins. The rattle of feed buckets being filled, the smell of coffee brewing, and voices in the early dawn remind the riders that a mission is at hand.

Horse and rider teams walk and trot up and down the road to warm up. Horses taunt each other with tossing heads and shrill whinnies. Riders shift their eyes back and forth, perhaps considering the competition of the day. Moria keeps Rainbow close to the front runners, not wanting to get caught behind slower riders when the horses bound away.

The timer stands on a high weed-covered bank and shouts the count down for the start, "Three, two, one. The trail's open. Have a safe ride." A cloud of dust floats into the trees as horses gallop down the road. With the dust fly the dreams and misfortunes of the day.

Moria's body tenses as she gathers Rainbow's reins and looks ahead. *You can do this*, coaches the mantra in her mind. Seventy horses, a herd of colors with manes and tails flying in the misty morning, surge down the red clay road. Colorful outfitted riders appear as a scattered box of crayons, blending with the collage of running horses. Tears well in Moria's eyes from the wind, or maybe the sound of hoof beats challenging her to own the day.

Will meets Moria and Rainbow as the two approach the first vet check on the mountain. She jumps off and loosens the girth. "Would you go ahead and check his pulse? I think he's pretty close to sixty-four."

At the crew truck, they remove the saddle, cool the horse briefly, check the pulse again, and head for the vet line. Rainbow clears the check and Moria leads him back to the truck.

Will asks, "Did y'all water on the trail?"

"No time. We're good."

Looking doubtful, he says, "Do you want to offer him food or water one more time?

"This is a short stop. Time to go. They're calling my number. Don't worry. Thanks for your help." Smiling, she pats the horse's neck. "Good boy, let's do this." Remounting, she waits with the other riders.

Now there are five front runners timing out together, including Moria. Will gives a thumbs up and waves goodbye.

Moria rides out across the ridge, drafting along behind the other riders. Endless stretches of mountains, tinted with shades of blue and freshened with the green of spring, shelter the valley. Sunlight through the pines dapples the trail and gray granite boulders hug the mountainside.

Moria's mind wanders. *I'm such a poser. I don't belong here ... pretty soon it might be my turn to lead ... maybe I should stop to pee ... they would know ... I'm afraid to race.*

A deer bolts across the trail.

The first horse spins, throwing his rider. Close behind, the next two horses whirl, crashing into each other. These riders fall, land on their feet and manage to keep hold of their reins. The horse in front of Moria leaps into the bushes, dumping his rider as they tangle in vines. The rider frees the frightened horse from the under brush and they scramble back onto the trail.

Rainbow skids to a stop and spins a one eighty. Moria loses the reins, somersaults off backward, and hits the ground.

The rider climbing out of the bushes grabs Rainbow's reins.

Pretty certain she isn't hurt, Moria stands up and brushes herself off. "Y'all go on."

"You're sure?" he asks, handing her the reins and remounting his horse.

"Yeah, I'm going to take it easy the rest of the way."

The other riders thunder on down the trail toward camp.

Moria remounts and they walk down the trail a few yards. She rubs her eyes and shakes her head. *Maybe I have a concussion.* Feeling sorry for herself, she meanders around the bend. Hoofbeats sound behind them. Rainbow tenses, his ears prick back and forth. Dancing sideways, he takes off toward camp, flying over rocks and debris, listening to the horses behind him. "Oh, shit!" Moria snatches up the slack reins, tightens her grip and calls to her horse, "Nobody's going to pass us. Let's catch those front runners!"

Her vision seems to be on fast forward as a blur of trees rush by. She pushes Rainbow hard for the next few miles, catching up with the front runners just before camp.

Moria and her competitors approach the vet check. The five riders jump down and toss the reins to their crews.

Sarah takes charge of Rainbow. "Mom, you don't look so good. Better get something to drink. We don't want to be scooping you up off the trail. Let's get this guy ready for the check."

Moria rubs her eyes. "Yeah, I took a spill but I'm okay."

Sarah looks doubtful but knowing Moria and her determination to finish the ride, said, "Here's your water. Why don't you sit down? We'll take Rainbow through the check."

"How's Maxine doing?" Moria asks, reaching for the bottle Sarah offers.

"She's still on the Blue Loop, keeping a steady pace. But bad news for Jackson. Moria drops the water bottle. "What? Is Silver okay?"

Just then, she sees Jackson approaching. Looking at his stricken face, she runs to him.

"What happened?"

"His pulse wouldn't come down in time. He's recovered now. The vet said he was carrying too much weight, but he's alright. I wouldn't hurt him for the world. Well, guess I should have gone to the newbie's meeting."

Hugging him, she says, "Honey, I'm so sorry. We can handle this."

Taking Rainbow's reins from Sarah, Jackson shrugs and hurries over to their crewing station under the tent.

Preparations for the vet check follow a practiced routine. Saddles, bridles and other tack are cast aside. Crews cool the horses with sponges and water. First the legs, chest, and stomach. Then, the back and neck in that order, so the cooling blood will not rush to the horse's feet, pool in the hooves, and cause them to be lame. Be careful with cold water on large muscles, which can cause cramps. Finally, they scrape the water off, which is hot by now, to let the horse air cool. Moria grabs the stethoscope to check the pulse and heads for the vet check. She stays in the vet line to hold her place while Jackson walks Rainbow Chaser around to keep him relaxed.

"Next," calls the vet attendant.

Jackson hands Moria the reins. "He didn't want to graze. Something is going on."

Moria answers with a frown, "He's fine. He's always fine." She turns away, presenting her horse to the vet. Standing at Rainbow's head, she faces to watch the vet, and holds her breath.

"Not much gut sound, and he's getting a little dehydrated," the vet announces. "You're going to need to bring him back for a recheck."

The other front runners are headed back to their crew stations. *They passed the check ... I'm going to be behind.* Looking away from her competitors, Moria takes the lead rope and heads toward the crew truck, shaking the rope to make the horse hurry. Rainbow stops, paws the ground, doubles up, sinks to the grass and begins to thrash back and forth.

Moria leaps out of the way and the last thing she remembers is a roaring sound in her ears. Gold, green, blue, and chestnut colors spin out before her as she falls to the ground. Blackness takes her to another world.

~ ~ ~

The long road back to Cherry Valley Sunday morning after the Ridge and Valley Ride wound like a shadowed ribbon through the Blue Ridge Mountains. Tall pines sighed and whispered in sadness for yet another trial in Moria's endurance riding life.

She slouched down in the seat, crossing her arms. "I'm so sick of shit happening at every endurance ride we go to. Maybe we should just quit. This ride's such bad luck. You know, the first time we went, you got lost, and the storm wrecked the trails. Then last year, I had the accident at the finish line. Poor Rainbow, he caught it this time."

At the fourway stop, Jackson turned the trailer toward the River Road and home. "And whose fault was that, Missy?"

"Uh, guess I did override him. A concussion for me, no award, and a vet bill for two hundred dollars when Rainbow had the colic attack. God willing, he's going to be okay." Moria gazed out the window. The abandoned fields matched her spirit. Taking a deep breath, she sighed and said, "So we both spent a lot of money for expensive lessons... don't override your horse and don't carry extra weight. Maybe I should take up barrel racing."

Jackson sensed this was not a time for false praise or scolding. "We're almost home. I'm looking forward to a good dinner at The Diner after we get the horses settled." His answer was her brief smile.

The rig bumped over the wooden bridge. Lost in thought, Moria looked between the iron rails at the water below. Her angst about the rides floated along with the foam and detritus in the rushing stream. *I love endurance riding. There's more to this than winning... adventures, friends and most of all, the horses.*

She wrinkled her forehead and rubbed her hands over her face. *Rainbow, I'm sorry. I know better ... it's not all about me. What would I do without you?*

Wanting to distract Moria from the recent past, Jackson asked, "You think Will is going to be Sarah's forever guy?"

"Who knows? She's pretty smart, and her dad's keeping an eye on things."

"Well, you're lucky Fredrick's paying her tuition. At least, you won't be talking in your sleep and calling his name. I was about ready to slap you upside the head. Remember the day we came home from a ride and there sat Fredrick on the steps? I didn't know whether to run, pray, or shake his hand."

"At least he made amends for causing our lives to be so chaotic with his drinking. He is a good dad, and he's a hundred miles away," she answered.

"By the way, how's your head?"

"Better. The EMT said to take it easy for a couple of days, and if it gets worse, go see a doctor."

~ ~ ~

As they reached the farm, a breeze blew through the cedars lining the driveway and they swayed in unison as if to wave a greeting. Two gray streaks ran toward them. Dixie and Hero, beloved Weimaraners and guardians of the farm, leapt into the air alongside the truck, barking with glee. *Where y'all been?* Lighted windows from the restored Victorian cottage signaled, *all is well. Welcome home.*

Sarah and Will came out on the porch, meeting them at the driveway and walking ahead to open the gate. Sarah pushed back her tousled hair. "Glad y'all had a safe trip. We've been here a couple of hours. The barn's clean, but I wasn't sure what you wanted to do for Rainbow and Silver's feed."

Moria unloaded the horses, handing Rainbow's lead rope to Sarah. The horse shook himself and looked toward the pasture.

"Thanks for getting things ready. We stopped about three hours out from camp at a country gas station in the middle of nowhere. The horses grazed and both drank some water. Then, we just had three more hours to go. When we stopped for food, we checked them again. Let's turn them out for a few minutes. We can watch them and unload some of the stuff."

Both horses found their favorite spots and rolled, scrambled up, shook off loose dirt, and commenced to graze.

Moria and Sarah entered the trailer, pulling out blankets, extra feed, buckets, and various items such as electrolytes, lineament, leg wraps, boots for horses and people, leftover food, dirty clothes, bedding, and more. "No more rides till Fall," Moria said, looking at Rainbow and Silver one more time to be sure they had no ill effects from the trip.

Jackson walked over to unhook the trailer. With raised eyebrows, he said, "In a week you'll be checking the ride schedule and planning a trip to who-knows-where. Me? Remember, I have a job without a three-month vacation."

"No more trips this summer," she answered, separating the piles: house and barn, wash or clean, throw away, and buy more. "Hmm, where's my notebook? I need to make a Tractor Supply list."

Jackson handed her the notebook from the truck cab. "Come on, let's get to The Diner. Jeremy and Maxine are waiting."

"Mom, we're going to skip dinner and head back to school. It's not too far and we've got a busy day tomorrow."

Moria gave Sarah a hug, saying, "Wish you could stay longer. Drive safe and thanks again for your help. Will, don't be a stranger."

~ ~ ~

Jackson turned into the gravel parking lot at the restaurant, a quaint old farm- house restored to its original turn of the century architecture and known to serve the best country food for miles around.

The lot was crowded with cars parked under the ancient oaks. Some customers sat in rocking chairs on the wide porch, chatting with neighbors and strangers alike.

"Good thing Jeremy and Maxine got here early and saved a table. Let's eat before all those biscuits are gone."

Greetings were exchanged all around as everyone seated themselves. The cane-bottom chairs were pulled up to the round pine table. Darla, hurried to the table and began taking orders. She poured sweet tea into Mason jars and a communal sigh of contentment escaped the thirsty diners.

Moria propped her chin in her hands and looked at the group, tears in her eyes. "What can I say? Y'all are the best. Thanks for all the help this weekend. I owe you, but hopefully not for the same reason. You know what I say so many times, my plan is not always God's plan. Maybe this was another lesson in patience, with some courage thrown in." She lifted her chin, smiled and wiped the tears away. "Guess I'll have this summer to think about it."

Jackson reached for Moria's hand, gave it a squeeze and winked at her. "Maybe you need to put your boots on, Missy."

Wordless, she turned her head into Jackson's chest and launched into an epic meltdown as the events of the weekend caught up with her. Others at the table did not seem surprised.

Giving Moria a hug, Jackson handed her a paper napkin to blow her nose. "Enough already, here comes our food."

Maxine broke the drama. "At least you didn't fall on the floor and have a true Southern hissy fit." Everyone laughed, knowing it could have happened.

Some of the restaurant patrons glanced their way with curiosity. A few people did look concerned and one elderly woman, Miss Ella from the neighborhood, came over to the table, laid a hand on Jackson's shoulder and patted Moria's back with the other.

"Bless your heart, Miss Moria," she said with a smile. "Remember what Scarlett said, 'I'll think about that tomorrow. Tomorrow is another day.'"

Taking Miss Ella's hand, Moria sniffed and then began to laugh. "Oh, yeah, and I got a better man than Rhett."

As her friend turned to walk away, Moria called after her, "Thank you, ma'am."

"You know, I love Miss Ella, she's a true part of Cherry Valley."

The group joined hands and bowed their heads. Maxine began, "Thank you Lord for returning us safely home to ride another day. Bless this food to the nourishment of our bodies."

"Amen" echoed around the table.

Moria reminded Maxine, "I can't believe we have to go to a county school workshop next week."

"Well, it is optional to attend, and they offered us incentive pay or two extra personal days." Maxine grinned and looked at the group. "You can guess which one we took." She lifted her glass and announced, "Cheers.

Two more personal days for endurance rides and may we all finish and one of us wins!"

On the way home, Jackson said, "We need to go by Rodney's and pay him for taking care of my rodeo string.

"Sure. Let's see how his weekend went."

The grizzled cowboy stepped out onto the porch greeting them with a beer in his raised hand. "Y'all come set a spell."

As they settled on the porch with ice cold beers, Rodney asked, "Wal, how'd it go?"

Moria gave a brief version of the weekend, assuring him that she and the horses were fine. "How are plans for your summer camp?"

The cowboy took off his battered straw hat, scratched his head and drawled, "Wal, I'm not having camp this year."

Moria leaned forward in her chair, not sure she'd heard his answer. "Are you sick? What's going on?"

Rodney grinned. "Made a better deal."

"You won the lottery?"

"No." Pleased to have their undivided attention, he said, "My sister from Atlanta is keeping two kids all summer while their parents go to Europe. The parents wanted them out of their neighborhood for a while, somewhere in the country where they don't know nobody. Guess the kids must'a got in trouble. She didn't say. All I know is that they paid us a boat load of money to keep them."

Being an attorney, Jackson looked a little dubious. "Why didn't they just go to camp somewhere? What are y'all gonna do to entertain them?"

"Rita, my sister, has to tutor them some. The kids know how to ride, so I'm gonna turn 'em loose with a coupl'a ponies and a compass."

Jackson couldn't help laughing. "On a serious note, as an attorney, will your liability insurance cover this 'arrangement'? How old are they, anyway?"

With a smirk on his face he answered, "Old enough to be a problem. I think. Rita said they're about fifteen and twelve. Hmm. Hadn't thought about that kind'a trouble. Hold on. I'll get my policy. Maybe you can take a look at it. They'll be here tomorrow."

The screen door slammed, punctuating Rodney's news, as he went inside. Moria looked at Jackson, noticing worry lines on his forehead. "What? You don't think this is a good idea?"

Jackson peeled the label from his bottle and studied it as if the answer would appear. "I don't know. He's a good guy. I just don't want him to get between a rock and a hard place. For all his horse experience, he's not too savvy about some things, like teenage girls."

Moria laughed. "Or, crazy like a fox. A lot of money for a little work."

"I just don't want the fox to bite him," Jackson replied, as Rodney returned.

" I owe yu for takin' a look?"

"Not a thing. I'll get back to you tomorrow. Thanks again, for taking care of the horses," Jackson answered, paying his friend and waving goodbye.

Returning home, Moria and Jackson went down to the barn as the setting sun spread a soft summer light over the valley. The dogs rambled ahead, plowing through the underbrush in search of varmints, real or imagined. From the bottom of the pasture, the horses alerted, racing to the gate. The last rays of the sun cast an aura of light shining silver and gold around the running horses as they skidded to a stop.

Moria opened the gate and laughed with relief and delight, seeing their treasures back to normal. "Let's give them one more look. Check for anything we've missed."

Jackson stepped into the tack room and handed her a grooming box. "I'm getting more bran mash and electrolytes ready." The two riders worked silently, savoring the peaceful evening.

Moria rubbed Rainbow with the curry comb, inhaling that special horse aroma. Then, she leaned her cheek against the horse's neck and whispered, "It just doesn't get any better than this. Thank you, buddy. You gave me a pass on this one. Lesson learned."

Rainbow turned his head and snuffled into Moria's sleeve. *Until next time.*

Later, the couple walked arm in arm toward the house. The curtain on the loft window moved slightly. Jackson laughed, "Well, looks like the furballs are waiting for us. At least I have a truce with those wily cats now."

Pounce pulled the curtain aside with his paw and began to purr when he saw Jackson reach in his pocket. The cat growled with pleasure. *Oh, yeah. He's got the treats.*

Pandora licked a golden paw and began to wash her face. *Get over yourself, Pounce. He just pretends to be friendly, so you won't pee on his boots or jump on his back when he's busy with Moria. Don't kid yourself. He doesn't really like cats. Remember the first time we met him? He said, and I quote, 'Cats belong in barns,' as he dumped you out of the chair.*

Ignoring Pandora, Pounce fluffed his gray fur and moved to the edge of the loft. His green eyes glittered and his body quivered in anticipation of his cowboy's return. As Jackson entered the hallway beside the loft, Pounce gathered himself ready for the invitation. Jackson stopped, turned his back to the loft, patted his shoulder and said, "Launch!"

Pounce flew into the air, landing on the Jackson's shoulder. Jackson leaned over for Pounce's dismount as Pandora padded daintily down the stairs to receive her treat. Jackson ruffled their heads, "What a pair," he laughed.

Moria came up behind Jackson, tapped him on the shoulder, purring, "Can I jump on your back? Do you have any treats left?"

"Do I? Come on for the five dollar special." Turning his back to her and patting his shoulder. "Launch." She jumped on Jackson's back and he trotted toward the bedroom, stopping at the foot of the bed.

She reached around for his belt buckle. The jeans pooled at his feet as he swung her around to face him. Another buckle hit the floor.

Kicking the clothes aside, Jackson took Moria in his arms, whispering, "Okay, teacher. Show me what you got." His dark eyes focused on her face as he ran his hands through her hair.

Thunder rolled in the distance. Lightning flashed across the sky, illuminating the dark room. A breeze lifted the curtains, brushing them across Moria's back.

With a sigh, she brought his face to hers. *My lifeline for solving the equation, one plus one always makes two.* "I love you, mister."

The bedroom door, slightly ajar, framed Pounce's excited face. He growled to Pandora who stood close by. *They're taking their clothes off. Jackson's touching her. Do you think they'll make a litter?*

Pandora could pretend disinterest no longer. *Let me see.* She pushed against Pounce, the door banged against the wall and the two startled cats tumbled into the room.

Moria fell back on the bed as Jackson whipped around, slapping his forehead. "You furballs get out," he yelled, and the frightened pair scrambled away.

Slamming the door after them, he reached for Moria's hand." Come on, Missy, let's start over in the shower. Help me remember where we were."

Rain sluiced against the window panes. Steam filled the room as two images entwined in the fog-shrouded shower stall and so began an unforgettable night.

Later the two lovers lay among the sweaty sheets as the storm passed over and moonlight shone through the trees.

Moria rolled over and snuggled up to Jackson, running her hand through his wet hair. "What a great ending to our weekend. Peace in the Valley Farm, for sure." No answer as Jackson took a deep breath of welcome sleep.

Chapter Two

The next morning Moria paced back and forth across the weather-beaten cottage porch as she waited for Maxine. Dixie and Hero climbed out from under the porch to join her, sprawling their long selves in her path.

"You goobers, I see you." With those words Moria sat down on the stone steps and motioned the dogs to her. Rubbing their ears, she said, "This is going to be a hot summer. Stay out of trouble, you hear?" Dixie rolled over and put her head in Moria's lap. *Yes, ma'am.* Hero gazed off toward the road, making no commitment about his plans. Both dogs jumped to attention upon hearing the rumble of Maxine's truck and bounded off the porch to meet her.

"Hey, you guys, watch it." Maxine called out as she opened the truck door. The dogs stopped their antics and sat with bright eyes and drools, awaiting their treats. "God forbid if I ever forget the leftover bacon," she said, giving them each a bite.

Grabbing the porch post and pulling herself up, Moria groaned aloud. "Drapersville, here we come. You know, it's going to be painful sitting in the workshop all day. My legs are killing me."

"Yeah, me too. Did you get a therapeutic shower last night? It does help those sore muscles," Maxine said, and rubbed her thighs and shoulders. "That Jeremy. Riders always know where it hurts and how to make it better."

"That's the truth," Moria agreed with a smile.

A required trip through Dunkin' Donuts started their journey. As they wound through the foothills, climbing higher with each turn, Moria sipped her coffee and looked down into the valley. "You know, we ought to explore more of our valley first chance we get. Seems like we're just riding the same old trails, and I know there are other areas out there available to us. Maybe you can get some help with that GPS doodad you bought. It's a waste of money not to use it."

Continuing up the mountain, Maxine's truck followed the narrow, twisting road as if on a mission. "Sounds like a plan. Maybe the new ranger can help me, and we should get some updated maps if we're going to explore the National Forest. By the way, I heard Jada bought two new horses. To be so smart, you think she'd take better care of her critters. Remember last year? Blackjack pulled a tendon, and just before the Championship Ride she bought that mare, White Trash. That poor thing nearly died from dehydration, and now White Trash has a foal. She'll probably call it Ho Baby. And there's more. The new horses are, get this, Chaos and Mayhem."

Moria burst out laughing, spewing her coffee all over the dashboard. Out of a strangled cough, she gasped, "Sorry," and reached for paper napkins.

"No worries." Maxine laughed. "Now, I've got to pay attention. We're on the downhill drag, literally."

The valley spread out before them. Tiny houses, that could have resided on a Monopoly board, clustered amongst the hardwoods, so treasured in the Blue Ridge Mountains. The town of Drapersville had managed to retain its country atmosphere while offering a Piggly Wiggly, locally owned drugstore, a clothing store, lumber yard, various other small stores, including one for feed and tack, several churches, and a quaint brick school.

"Well, today I guess we're teachers again, at least for this week," Moria said as they walked toward the school. "The horses need a rest anyway. I want to be sure Rainbow doesn't have any more colic spells and Silver needs to get over carrying Jackson's heavy saddle bags."

Maxine opened the schoolhouse door. "I heard that the speaker is from California and his expertise is behavioral management. Maybe we'll get some ideas on how to better handle the horses," she joked.

"Huh?" Moria answered, then grinned. "Yeah, that's a thought. Also, we're going to get certified in CPR. Who knows? We might have to use it for somebody on the trail."

"Or even in the classroom," Maxine answered as they took their seats and tried to get comfortable with their aching muscles.

~ ~ ~

On the drive back to Cherry Valley that afternoon, the two women talked about their day and concluded that they might even have learned something.

"Don't forget we have to stop by Rodney's so I can return the insurance papers," Moria said.

Soon they pulled into Rodney's driveway beside a blue, older Dodge Caravan with a Georgia tag. "Guess they're here. Sounds like everyone's out back."

The two women headed toward the barn and corrals, stepping over various tractor parts, dead potted plants, a pile of empty feed bags and other unidentified rubbish. As they came around the corner, Moria called, "Hey, you've got company."

The group of four, who had been leaning on the fence petting the horses, turned at the sound of her voice.

Rodney waved his hat, calling, "Come on over. Meet my summer family."

Rita appeared to be in her fifties and sporting a new straw hat with fringes of grayish-red hair peeking from underneath. She turned to greet the women with a smile. The two young girls looked at Rita. She gave a brief nod and they smiled and waved.

Moria handed Rodney the papers, which he stuffed in his back pocket.

"Thank ye, ma'am Guess everything's okay."

Putting his hand on Rita's shoulder, he introduced her. "This is my sister I told you about. He gestured toward the girls. "This young'un is Sassy." She gave a bright smile, as bright as her spiked orange and pink hair. "And her sister, Mousey," who gave a nod and turned around to pet the horses. Rodney faced his guests and continued, "These are my good neighbors, Moria and Maxine. They live just down the road and have horses, too. Maybe they'll take y'all on the trails one day soon. Their horses need to rest because they rode 'em fifty miles last weekend."

Sassy rolled her eyes, "Oh yeah. In your dreams."

Moria looked sideways at Maxine, who smiled and leveled a gaze directly at Sassy. "Yeah, we did. How far have you ridden?"

Sassy, taken aback by Maxine's bold approach and Rita's stern look, hesitated. "Well, not that far, I guess."

Maxine continued, "We're going to do some trail exploring this summer. You, Mousey and Rita are welcome to come with us. Rodney told us you girls can ride."

"Rita, what about you?"

Rita smiled, "I've done some riding. We'd enjoy it. And you, Mouse?"

The young girl looked down, her lank, light brown hair falling over her face as she dug her toe in the dirt.

Rita answered, "That's a yes."

Rodney motioned to Moria and Maxine, "Come on over and get a look at my new critters." He pointed towards two ponies standing away from the other horses. "This here's a Mustang. The guy I bought him from said this dude was broke." He laughed, "Guess we'll find out. This other one's a mix. Don't know 'bout him." The bay pony eyed the group warily, flicking his ears and moving closer to Mousey, who climbed over the fence to stand beside him.

Rodney grinned, "Wal, guess that settles that."

Alarm flashed through Moria. "Wait a minute, Rodney. What's your plan for these kids to ride? I know you better than that. You'll just to turn them loose on the ponies?"

Sassy's eyes lit up. "Sounds like fun."

Unconcerned, Mousey had her arms around her pony and buried her face in his mane.

"Naw, they're gonna have to spend some time in the round pen with me and the ponies. Rita and I'll take them out on the trail a few times before they ride with you." He gave Moria a wide smile and a wink. "Miss Moria, you know me better than that. I knowed I'd get a rise outta ya."

Moria, feeling stressed by now, looked at Maxine and nodded toward the truck. "We'd better be getting on home. Nice to meet y'all. Let us know when you're ready to go out with us. Rodney, you rascal, have a good day."

Maxine added, "Come over any time. I'm just down the road. Good to meet everybody."

As the two women drove away, Moria let out a heavy breath. "Something's going on with those kids. We need to have a heads-up here, especially if we take them out on the trail."

"Yeah, I agree. Rita seems nice. You know, I think she's more than a babysitter. Did you notice her walk? She's got that 'don't mess with me' military look."

~ ~ ~

The remainder of the week unraveled in a flurry of scribbled lecture notes and restless teachers, anxious to get on with their summer plans. "Free, free at last!" Moria cheered as they left the parking lot of the Drapersville School on the final day of the course.

"What are you all doing for Fourth of July?" Maxine asked.

"No plans. There's work to do on the farm that we've put off till later. I guess later has caught up with us."

"Why don't we go dancing at The Juniper Tree? Fireworks are being shot in that big field next door to the bar. We can watch from the parking lot and there's going to be plenty of food."

"Sounds like fun. There's always adventure at The Juniper Tree."

Maxine began to gather up her items from the workshop. "What are you doing tomorrow?"

"Nothing, if I can help it," Moria laughed. "Maybe Jackson will let me have one rest day before we start the farm work."

"We could take a ride."

"Looking forward to it, but not at the crack of dawn."

"Sure. We could go check out the bridge and see if there's any more damage since last time we looked. At least we've got the grant to get it fixed now. We need to get it repaired this summer before we lose our resources. Maybe this will be a project for Jackson and Jeremy.

Moria headed the truck up Maxine's winding driveway toward the blue-roofed white farmhouse. She looked out over the fields as Arctic Cat and Catch On Fire galloped along the fence beside them. "What a pair, a bay and a gray … perfect."

Jeremy came out of the house and waved. Maxine got out of the truck and Jeremy motioned for Moria to come inside, too.

"Thanks," she said, "I need to get home."

"Aww, come in for a minute. I want to show you something."

Maxine and Moria walked onto the porch as Jeremy opened the door, stepped aside with a flourish, and ushered them into the house.

Maxine's response, "Wow!"

Moria followed behind her. "Double wow," as Jackson stepped out of the kitchen, wearing an apron from The Diner.

The dining room table, covered with a white linen cloth, held settings for four. The best china, candles, champagne in an ice bucket, and fresh summer flowers created a finishing touch for the meal.

Grinning with success, the two men pulled chairs out for their wives to sit.

"To what do we owe this honor?" asked Moria.

"Well, there are several reasons to celebrate," Jackson chimed in. "First, we and the horses all survived the ride. Second, you two have gotten your teachers' training workshop behind you."

Jeremy added, tipping Maxine's face toward his, "This is our first wedding anniversary."

Maxine's mouth flew open. "Oh, no! *You* remembered and I forgot. How did that happen?"

"Because you're horse crazy?" Jeremy replied, giving her a kiss to remind her of the evening to come.

Enticing smells drifted from the kitchen. Moria laughed as she reached for her napkin, "Smells like The Diner, in a good way."

Jeremy and Jackson headed for the kitchen and Jackson said, over his shoulder, "The Diner is our new best friend."

The table was covered with all their favorites, right down to the pecan pie.

Later Maxine said, "What a great surprise to end our day. Uh, I think I need a nap."

Moria echoed her friend's compliment, adding to Jackson, "Guess we'd better get home to take care of the critters."

Jackson smiled and took Moria by the hand. "No, Missy, chores are done. We're going for a moonlight ride."

"Are you kidding?" She looked out the window at the gathering dusk and back at Jackson.

"Not kidding. Come here." He led Moria to the back porch and there stood Rainbow Chaser and Silver Dollar, saddled and ready to go. Catch On Fire and Arctic Cat perked their ears up, also tacked up and ready for an adventure.

"I even brought your boots and helmet. Get those boots on, Missy. We're hitting the trail tonight."

The four friends headed up the dirt road. Light from a waning moon wrapped the countryside in a trusted light. Shadows of the horses and riders shifted along the road, accompanying them on the ride until they turned into the forest.

They proceeded in single file up the steep climb to the ridge. The sound of the horses' breathing in sync with their pacing, the scurry of night animals, and the wind ruffling the leaves gave peace to Moria's heart.

She leaned forward on Rainbow's neck, locked her fingers in his mane, dropped the weight into her heels, tightened her legs on his sweating sides and let her horse do his job.

Shafts of moonbeams travelled down through the pines and onto the trail, reflecting off worn granite stones. Hundreds of lightening bugs glimmered through the forest like jewels, a free gift to the riders.

They reached the ridge and stopped to let the horses and themselves catch a breath. Maxine wiped her forehead and announced, "We're going to race across the ridge."

Moria cringed and frowned at Maxine. *Why now, when we're having such a great ride?*

As if reading her friend's mind, Maxine's eyes returned the look. "Because it's what we do, in case we meet a challenge someday."

Knowing she was outnumbered, Moria gathered Rainbow's reins, took a deep seat and said, "Let's go."

Aware of Moria's fear of racing and falling, the four riders led out with Jeremy in front. Maxine, Moria and Jackson followed. As the horses picked up the pace, wind blew Rainbow's mane into Moria's face and her auburn hair streamed out behind her, a banner of courage.

I can do this. I'm not afraid, the mantra drummed in her mind.

Pounding hooves and the sound of scattered rocks echoed into the night as the riders cantered along the familiar trail. Soon, they broke to a trot and then a walk. Jeremy dropped back behind Jackson and Maxine now led. The horses worked off each other, straining at the bit to move on. After the Cherry Valley riders had covered about two miles and reached the descent, Maxine dropped back behind Jeremy, saying to Moria, "Okay, Missy, take us down."

Moria took hold of the neck strap, shortened the reins and peered ahead into the night. She listened intently for the sounds of deer and other animals on their night travels through the woods. All seemed quiet. She nudged the chestnut horse to move forward into the deepening tree cover. Proceeding down the switchbacks seemed like a simple task. *Why am I making such a big deal about this?*

And then she knew. An owl flew low across the trail. Its huge wings flapped to lift it higher to safety. Rainbow spun a one-eighty but Moria did not fall. The horse now faced the descending group. They pulled up sharply as their horses also spooked.

Moria smiled and gave a thumbs up as everyone got their horses under control. "Let's ride."

The riders soon reached the valley and made the turn toward home. Moria, still in the lead, said, "Why don't we cross the creek at the bridge. Then we won't have far to go."

The others agreed, and Moria kept the lead. They trotted and cantered for several miles on a stretch of level trail beside the stream. As the friends reached the crossing, they slowed to a walk and entered the water just below the bridge. The horses snuffled in the current, pawing to cool their undersides, and then drank.

The bridge, an ancient structure, spoke of times past in the forest. For a moment Moria was sure she saw a horse and buggy enter the covered bridge. She blinked and took a deep breath. Then the vision faded returning her ancestors to their world.

Jackson rode up beside Moria and said, under his breath, "I thought I heard a horse and buggy go over the bridge just now."

Moria winked at him, "Yes sir, you did. Welcome to the South." Her mind flashed back to her Wyoming trip and the visit to Jackson's old homestead. She remembered seeing the ghostly figures as they went about their daily tasks and welcomed her to the family by their visual presence.

Jackson smiled in return. "So, I guess I'm one of the family now."

A growling sound came from somewhere in the darkness.

Moria frowned and looked toward the bridge and then at Jackson. "Or maybe not."

A black bear and her cub scrambled out from their hiding place. In one motion, the horses bolted up the bank. The riders, who had dropped their stirrups to rest their legs, grabbed manes, saddles and reins, to get control of their mounts. The four horses became a herd, fleeing the predator. Never mind the riders.

Not too far down the trail they were able to get their startled mounts under control. Maxine rode up beside Moria. "You okay?"

Moria laughed, "Now I know why we learn to race … there might be a challenge someday … or night. I think I have adrenalin drooling out my ears."

"I believe I could use a beer, or two," Jackson said, breathing hard from the escape. He leaned down to pat Silver's neck and said to Moria, "We need to give Rodney a heads up about the bears. I know they've been riding all over the place these past few weeks. I met those girls and Rita the other day when I helped Rodney with some fence work. The young'uns were riding in the pasture, so I only got to talk to them for a minute. They seemed to be regular kids, but I guess we'll find out sooner or later."

"Let's hope it's not sooner or later," Moria answered.

By now they had reached the farm. Jeremy dismounted, opened their pasture gate and the riders walked toward the barn. "You're welcome to leave the horses here overnight."

"No problem. Thanks anyway," Jackson answered, "Missy can drive the truck. I'll sit on the tailgate and pony the critters. Let's unsaddle and get going. It's past my bedtime. Jeremy, I think we can go into work a little late tomorrow. You all got some anniversary celebrating to do."

Jackson and Moria took the horses to their pasture and turned them loose. Moria said, "Guess there's no purpose in washing them down tonight," as the two horses rolled and were enveloped in a cloud of dust. "I can do it in the morning."

The security lights came on as the couple approached the house. Pounce pulled the curtain aside and peered out. Turning to Pandora, he said, *I don't think there's gonna be any excitement tonight. They look whooped. Wonder where they went? We'll have to ask Rainbow and Silver.*

Chapter Three

Fourth of July greeted the morning with a picture perfect postcard of Cherry Valley. Sun and sky painted the land with a brush of blues and golds, shadows and clouds. Moria opened the barn gate, saying to the dogs, "You hooligans, go find some rats." The horses raced across the pasture and stood by the feed room door, ears laid back, shouldering each other out of the way until they were settled and munching away.

"Might as well do a little cleaning," Moria announced to the animals, and soon all the items in the tackroom were piled in the aisle. Just then, her cell phone rang.

Jackson said, "Rita called and wanted to know if it is okay to come over. I think she wants to look in your school closet for stuff that might help with tutoring. She's bringing the girls."

Moria explained her dilemma. "Tell her that's fine if you can come down and guard what I've pulled out of the tackroom so the horses won't get into it. You won't even have to do anything" *because I want to arrange it my way.*

When Rita and the girls arrived, Jackson went down to the barn. "Come in. Glad y'all stopped by," Moria said. "Let's see what I've got that might help you," and she began to rummage through her school closet. "We can go over to the middle school, too."

Sassy and Mousey wandered around the room looking at pictures and other mementos. Moria noticed that they were not at all interested in the school closet. "Would you girls like to go down to the barn? Maybe Jackson will let you groom the horses."

"Sure," Sassy answered as she and Mousey raced out, slamming the door behind them.

With a worried look, Moria faced Rita. "Sorry, I forgot to ask. Do you mind if they go to the barn?"

Rita smiled. "They've been pretty good, almost too good. We've done a lot of riding to keep them occupied. They'll be fine at the barn."

Meanwhile, Jackson settled down on a hay bale to watch over Moria's unfinished task. Mousey came around the corner of the barn, smiling.

"Hey, Mr. Jackson, I came down to help you." She moved closer.

"Sure, I can find something for you to do. Where's Sassy?"

"Oh, she's at the house." Mousey took a few steps closer.

Jackson, not paying attention, leaned over to reach for some grooming tools. As he straightened up, Mousey jumped in his lap, put her arms around his neck and attempted to lay her head on his shoulder. "Will you adopt me?"

Startled, Jackson threw the brushes down, leapt up and dumped Mousey in the aisle. The youngster began to wail and roll around.

"You little …"

"Bitch?" Sassy said, coming around the corner with a grin.

Jackson helped Mousey up and glared at Sassy, "What th—"

Sassy walked over, sat down on the tack room steps and motioned to her sister, "Come here."

Continuing to snivel, she sat down beside Sassy, who smiled, saying, "We need something."

Hands on hips, Jackson stood before the two girls, staring in disbelief. "What!"

Sassy continued, "We need a burner phone and some pot."

Jackson yelled, "Who are you? Some kind of midget drug dealers? Enough. We're going to the house."

"So we can tell Miss Moria and Rita how you molested my sister?" Sassy's eyes turned hard as she stood and faced Jackson.

Perhaps his grim expression reminded her of some past trouble. She took a step back.

Jackson picked up a riding crop, whipped it against his leg. "Move it. When we get to the house, you all better have some answers."

Sassy stalked ahead of Jackson, who smacked the whip against bushes, a constant reminder of who was in charge. Mousey trudged along behind, rubbing dirt-caked hands over her sweaty, tear-stained face.

Moria and Rita looked through the glass-topped door to see an unbelievable picture, the crying girls and Jackson's irate face.

Moria flung the door open against the wall. "Good grief! What's going on?" she called out, her face a picture of shock and dismay.

Rita, right behind her, glared at the girls as they entered. She pointed them toward the sofa. "Sit." Then looked at Jackson. "There seems to be a problem."

"These brats want some pot and a burner phone." Jackson ran his hands through his hair, looking at Rita with a question, "Who are these kids, anyway?"

Moria stood speechless, staring at Jackson. *This is a side of him I've never seen.*

Sassy managed to appear remorseful and Mousey covered her face and sobbed.

Not answering, Rita pulled a kitchen chair to the sofa and sat in front of the two miscreants. "Look at me. Do you want to finish your time in Juvenile Hall?"

"No ma'am," they answered, realizing they were way out of bounds.

Rita continued, as if they were having a normal conversation. "What's this business about pot and a burner phone?"

Sassy had regained some composure. Wiping her tear-stained face, she sat up straight and looked Rita in the eye. "We miss our friends and we've gotten used to smoking a little pot."

"Well, I gathered *that* from the reports and that's how you got yourselves in this mess in the first place. Girls, this is serious business. Remember when we talked to the FBI? I thought they made it clear that you could get hurt or even killed. Why do you think we keep the van packed at all times?"

The girls nodded. Mousey said, "Yes, in case we need to leave in a hurry."

Rita paused to assess the youngsters' demeanor. Satisfied that she had their attention, she said, "Ladies, what do you have to say for yourselves?"

The girls looked at Moria and Jackson with solemn faces. They walked to the couple and Sassy reached out her hands. "We're very sorry we've caused trouble in your day. It won't happen again."

Mousey knelt before them, clasped her hands and looked up with contrite eyes. "Please forgive me. I'm so sorry." A tear slid down her cheek.

The girls returned to the sofa. Moria smiled at them. *Drama queens.* "Everybody makes mistakes. Just remember to mind Miss Rita. This sounds serious."

Jackson frowned, saying to Rita, "You know, we'd like more information in case we need to help y'all. Besides, we could end up in danger too."

Rita moved over to the couch and sat beside the girls. "Fair enough. I'm a US Marshall. These girls are in protective custody until a trial in the Fall where they have to testify." Sassy stared straight ahead. Mousey gazed at the floor, twirling a strand of hair around her fingers.

Rita turned to Moria and Jackson. "You do need to know what's going on. I have the care of these children until the trial. They witnessed a murder and can identify the shooter. In fact, they already have, through a window at the jail. She paused a moment. "I'm going to let them tell their story."

Mousey began to cry again. Sassy took her hand and said to Rita, "All of it?"

"Yes ma'am."

Sassy looked sad, as if a movie replayed in her mind. Then locking her gaze on the couple, she began in a soft voice, "Oscar killed our friend's father." Then in a stronger voice, filled with determination, she announced, "We're going to get that devil." She glanced at Rita who nodded for her to continue.

Sassy gathered her thoughts for a moment. "We were allowed to walk to school. Mousey and I got in the habit of going to the convenience store for snacks and then cutting through the woods to school. Last fall a guy parked his van near the store, smiled at us and …," she searched for words. "So, Oscar and his friend Karl robbed the store and Oscar shot the owner."

Rita placed her hand on Sassy's shoulder.

"The whole story."

"Okay. Oscar and his friend gave us cigarettes and one day asked us if we wanted something better. We made a bad choice. That's when we … chose the pot."

Rita smiled.

"Yes," Sassy repeated, "a bad choice."

Mousey echoed in a tearful voice, "A bad choice."

Sassy continued. "One day we were in the store restroom and just as we opened the door to leave, Oscar and Karl rushed in. I guess they thought we were gone. Anyway, we saw Oscar shoot our friend's dad. Somebody else had come into the store and was knocked over as those guys ran out. The man recovered and went over to check on Mr. Green and called the police. He told us to stay where we were because he was trying to help the owner."

Sassy wiped her eyes and Mousey began to moan. "Then, the cops came. It was terrible, the blood, the first responders … and our parents. We never got to go home. They took our phones and the phone Oscar gave us.

"We heard the police talking. They said Oscar wrecked the van and was in the hospital. Karl stole Oscar's phone and got away. Miss Rita came to the store and picked us up. My mom was hysterical and went to the safe house with us to spend the night. My Dad went home to get some of our things. The next day we left and came to Cherry Valley. When Oscar recovered and got put in jail, Rita took Mousey and me back to Atlanta to identify him through a window. The end."

Mousey added, "We felt really bad because we didn't get to go to Mr. Green's funeral, but we sent flowers."

Moria could tell the reality of these, and coming events, had not completely filtered into the children's minds.

Sassy paused, closed her eyes, and put her head on her knees. "I can't talk any more. I need a therapy dog."

Moria handed Cokes to the two girls. "Well, you have therapy ponies. They'll have to do."

Mousey smiled, "Oh yeah, the ponies. Maybe we can ride this afternoon."

"No," Rita answered.

Moria gathered up the school items and handed them to Rita. "Thanks girls, for sharing your story. Remember what Christopher Robin said to Winnie the Pooh: *You're Braver than you believe; Stronger than you seem; And Smarter than you think.* We're here for y'all, anytime."

"Thank you," the girls said in unison, and soon they were dozing on the sofa. Jackson and Rita sat down at the table and Moria brought out a pitcher of sweet tea.

Jackson turned to Rita. "There's more to the story?"

"Yes, these girls come from an affluent family, busy parents making good money, but they're trusting the school and the neighbors to raise their children. This never ends well. Sometimes choices can come at a high price."

"So where are the parents now?" Jackson asked, adding sugar to his tea.

Rita grinned, "About twenty miles from here. They've rented a house and can work from home or do whatever they have to do. They are not allowed to have contact with the girls, not even a phone call. Word on the street is that the family's gone to Europe. Sheriff Bramblett is on the lookout for strangers prowling around the local area. Well, now that I've livened up your day, I'll take my charges and go home. Thanks for the materials. We're going to have our noses in these books for a while, and thanks for your support, Jackson." Then, with a laugh, she added, "I wouldn't be surprised if Mousey's parents would be glad for you to adopt her, and Sassy, too."

Rita woke the drowsy girls. Jackson opened the door and ushered them out with a smile. "Get out of here, you scoundrels."

He collapsed on the couch and Moria headed to the kitchen. "What about some lunch? Too bad, we missed the Fourth of July parade this morning. Who knows what else this holiday will bring?"

Jackson came into the kitchen with open arms. "I have a better idea. What about a nap?"

Moria heard her stomach rumble. *I'm really hungry.* "Not even a choice. Let's go." Taking her cowboy's hand, they trotted toward the bedroom.

Pounce peered down from the loft, then pushed Pandora toward the stairs. *Come on, there's gonna be entertainment.*

Pandora yawned and stretched, *It's just like listening to the radio. We can only imagine. You go. I'm taking a nap.*

~ ~ ~

Late afternoon sun woke Moria. She rubbed her face and turned over. "What time is it?"

Jackson sat on the edge of the bed, putting on his boots. "It's time to feed the horses and get down to The Juniper Tree. I hear there's a barbeque to start the evening. Don't want to miss that."

Moria heard her stomach complain about missing lunch. "I'm on it. Let's go. Uh oh, I'm afraid to look at the aisle and the stuff from the tack room." She opened the gate and looked around the corner of the barn. "Guess the gods were watching over us."

Soon the couple had everything back in order. "Here come our unicorns," as the horses raced toward the barn. "Maybe we'd better put them up tonight. We're too far from town for them to hear the fireworks, but you never know who might be coming down the road throwing firecrackers. Come on dogs, in the tack room." Hero and Dixie dropped their ears and produced sad faces as they jumped up the steps, knowing their night was over.

Chapter Four

The Juniper Tree parking lot corralled cars of all makes and models, motorcycles, and trucks. The bangs, bumps, and scratches on the faithful vehicles told stories of folks who awaited whatever adventures the night would bring.

Trees sheltered tents set up with tables covered in patriotic decorations. Lighted lanterns glowed in the darkening night.

Jeremy waved Moria and Jackson toward the tables already occupied by many of the horse people from Cherry Valley. "Looks like the gang's all here," Jackson commented.

"Yeah, there's Jada in all her glory, holding court over her minions."

"Jealous?" Jackson replied.

"No." Moria huffed. "She's just so … much."

The tables were laden with barbecue and all the trimmings. Waitresses, dressed in red, white and blue sequined cowgirl outfits served liberal amounts of drinks. The band struck up the first song of the night, "God Bless the USA." The revelers sang along, some standing and swaying to the music, others calling for another beer.

The band continued with some of their favorites. The strains of "Country Roads, Take Me Home" brought Moria and Jackson to their feet as they swirled into the dancing crowd. Moria leaned into Jackson, arms around his neck as he held her close. *He smells so good and I'm so lucky and happy.*

Later, while the band took a break, the dancers sat down a for few minutes, refreshing themselves with drinks and seconds on the food. Jada made the rounds of the nearby tables, running her hands over the guy's shoulders and tweaking their ears. No one complained.

As Jada reached Jackson, Moria gave her a hands off glare. Unconcerned, the determined woman leaned into Jackson and lingered as she rubbed his shoulders and winked at Moria, who smiled and tipped her hat. *Too bad, bitch. He's mine. You had your chance.*

Returning to her table, Jada waved her arms to get everyone nearby to listen. "What about a toast to a brand new endurance ride?" She paused, enjoying the startled looks from her friends. "Get ready for The Cherry Valley Ride!"

"'Scuse me, have I missed something here?" Maxine asked, a forkful of sweet potatoes halfway to her mouth.

A *God help us* look passed between Jeremy and Jackson.

Jada, sensing their confusion, continued, "It'll be fun to put on a ride."

"She said ...," as Maxine finished the thought.

"How hard can it be?" said the nemesis of the endurance world, tossing her long dark hair back over her shoulders.

Seeing the determination and excitement in Jada's face, Maxine laughed, "Well, I guess she's going to put on a ride."

By now, most of those in ear shot had recovered from the pronouncement. They, too, saw a mission in progress.

The Cherry Valley riders pounded their bottles on the table, echoing each other. "Ride. Ride. Ride."

Jada's husband, Richard, pulled her down into the chair beside him and whispered in her ear.

She listened intently and then jumped up, announcing, "Richard says whoever's interested can meet at our house tomorrow. Most of you know where we live."

With a grin, Jada waved to the waitress for another beer.

The grim smile on Richard's face was testament to an epic misinterpretation of his words to Jada.

Fireworks exploded, punctuating Jada's proclamation, accenting the sky with colors and sparkles. Folks also were reminded that it's an honor to live in the USA, especially in Cherry Valley. And now they're going to have a new ride!

Jackson took Moria's hand and motioned Jeremy and Maxine to his truck. As the four climbed into the back and settled down, Moria put her head on Jackson's shoulder. Fireworks blazed across the sky delighting the viewers.

She turned to Maxine. Wordless, they looked at each other and burst out laughing. Maxine said, "Guess we better help her, or no telling what will happen."

~ ~ ~

Early the next morning, Jeremy and Maxine pulled into Peace in the Valley Farm to meet with their friends and discuss Jada's fireworks from the night before.

"Hey, I even cooked breakfast," Moria announced, setting platters of scrambled eggs and bacon on the table. Walmart muffins and coffee completed the meal.

Maxine started the conversation. "We're gonna have to help her with this ride, if it really happens. Otherwise, it'll look bad for all of us."

Jackson frowned. "Missy, don't let this cost us anything. Richard can foot the bill if the ride doesn't make enough money to cover expenses."

Moria nodded, "Maxine and I are going to write up an expected cost to put on a ride and be sure Richard gets it. I hope he's at the meeting today. We don't have to be there until eleven. It looks like a lot of people are interested."

The two guys left for work, and the girls settled down to make a list for Richard. Moria brought a legal pad to the table.

Maxine opened her laptop and began to type. Her voice accompanied the tapping of the keys. "Approved ride date, camping site, water source, vets, timer and volunteers, places for the volunteers to stay, Porta Potties and a generator to pump water from a creek." she paused, "Oh yeah, a marked and measured trail not to mention awards, and possibly food and all the permits. I'm sure there's more."

Moria jotted notes then stopped, saying, "We don't even know how much most of this will cost. We need to talk to some ride managers and get their budgets. There's a job for the ride manager."

~ ~ ~

As they started up Jada's winding driveway, Moria looked out over the wooded hillside. "No ride site here. They keep the horses in a small barn with paddocks. The horses can also run wild through their fifty acres. What is she thinking? Maybe we should turn around."

"And let the worst-ride-ever happen in our neighborhood? I don't think so." Maxine replied.

The large, timbered house cast a shadow over the parked cars, as if holding them in place. Jada opened the door and with a welcoming grin said, "Glad y'all could make it. Come on in."

About fifteen local riders sat around on the well-appointed deck, chatting and enjoying sandwiches and sweet tea. Moria smiled to herself, seeing catering boxes from The Diner over in a corner. *There you go, Richard. This is just the beginning. Hope you've got some deep pockets.*

Richard sat at one of the tables with his laptop, pecking away, oblivious of his surroundings. Jada clapped her hands, conversation stopped, and the group focused on their hostess. "Y'all know I'm one of you, a dedicated endurance rider." Several people glanced at each other, remembering her disregard for her horses. "Well, it's about time we show our friends, far and wide, what we've got." She waved her arm out toward the forest. "Beautiful mountains, excellent trails, and dedicated horse people to put this ride together. I've made a list of what I need people to do."

The riders became attentive as the reality of Jada's words set in. The volunteers' response was scuffling feet and flickering eyes. They knew this would surely interfere with their daily lives. Maxine whispered to Moria, "Trouble in paradise, already."

Jada began to read the list. "Rodney, I'd like for you to be in charge of the trails. Maybe Lacey and Sheldon from Over the Mountain Saddle Club can help you.

Rodney raised his hand. "For fifty miles?"

The saddle club people looked worried. "Lacey answered, "We don't know much about the trails except to ride them, cut face branches or pick another way if the trail gets bad."

"Perfect. You'll do great. There's your help, Rodney." Jada put a check mark by that item and moved on.

"Moria, we can camp in your pasture."

"What? A hundred people, trucks and horses in our pasture? You've got to be kidding."

Jada ignored Moria's stubborn answer. "It will be perfect. Close to the trail, flat space, plenty of water ..."

Standing up, hands on hips, Moria leaned toward Jada, "Just hold on a minute. I need to run this by Jackson."

Annoyed, Jada frowned. "And, why do you have to ask Jackson?"

Blowing her breath out in disgust, she answered hotly, "He's my husband. We're a team. Get it?"

Moria's raised voice got the attention of the others, who waited to see what would happen next.

Jada, startled by Moria's response, replied, "Well, it's your property. You should have the say-so."

"News flash. We own the property *together*. You just *don't* get it."

Seeing that she wasn't getting the agreement she wanted, Jada said, "Just ask him and get back to me."

Several of the riders got up. One said, "Thanks for having us. I'm not sure I'll have time for this project. Maybe I can help the day of the ride." The others nodded thanks and shuffled out.

Jada sat down, crumpled her papers and threw them over the railing. "What a bunch of slackers."

Richard gave a sigh of relief. "Try again next year. Maybe folks need time to think about it."

Moria took a breath, glanced at Maxine, who gave a thumbs up. "Jada, let's start over. A lot goes into putting on a ride." She handed Richard the list.

Shaken by her failure, Jada glared at Moria. "So, you're an experienced ride manager?"

With a straight face, Moria answered, "No, but I pay attention to what's involved and can only imagine what it costs."

Turning to Richard, Moria said, "Why don't y'all investigate. Talk to some ride managers in our region. Then decide if you want to tackle this. Get back to us and we'll work with you, and I'm sure others will too. Give this a little time. Remember, it was only last night this idea was born. Beer and fireworks were a good start."

Richard began to type. "What are you doing?" Jada asked.

"American Endurance Ride Conference. Seems like we should get a ride manager's packet to start with."

As Moria and the remaining riders left, she said over her shoulder, "Keep in touch."

Jada nodded, "Will do," and went over to sit by Richard, as they began the long and winding journey of managing an endurance ride.

Moria returned home and sat down in the porch swing to ponder the situation with Jada's desire to be a star in a currently dim universe. "I can't sit here all afternoon. Maybe I need to clean the house and do some laundry." And so went the rest of the afternoon until it was time to feed the horses.

In the feed room, she looked into the empty barrels, then heard Jackson's truck on the lane to the barn. Opening the gate and shooing the horses away she said, "Oh, thank goodness you went to the feed store. I got a little distracted today."

Jackson laughed, "Tell me something new."

When they finished the chores, Moria said, "Let's sit a minute. Gotta tell you about my day."

"This sounds like a front porch tale," Jackson replied, taking her hand and heading to the house.

Moria fetched a couple of beers and the two settled in the swing. She took a deep breath and Jackson pulled her close. "This sounds like a two-beer story. Let's have it." He leaned back and put the swing in motion. Dixie and Hero lay close by, listening to their people's mouth noises.

The story unfolded in Moria's worried voice. Jackson listened without interrupting, "Good job, Missy, about protecting the pasture. So, end of story?"

"'Fraid not. Jada is determined to do this, and I think Richard will go along with her to keep the peace."

"Would you bring me that second beer, if you don't mind," Jackson asked, and began to scratch Hero's ears. An evening breeze rustled the leaves on the maples and oaks shading the front lawn. The cedars along the driveway swayed as if to say, *Peace in the Valley Farm is going to have to take a deep seat and a faraway look to survive the Cherry Valley Ride.*

Popping open their second drinks, Jackson tipped his girl's face toward him, kissing her softly and then with stronger purpose.

"Hey, mister, are we done here?"

"Well, no. Two things. I haven't had a chance to tell you. Jeremy and I are taking a week off to haul my rodeo horses to south Georgia. There's a regional event in Valdosta. Depending on how it goes, I'll either sell the horses or maybe lease them out. The roping dudes are worth some money. They need to go somewhere and do their jobs. The others are good, too. Second thing, if you're involved in putting on a ride, I would rather it be here on our farm. I don't want you at Jada's mercy."

"What? You want the ride here … at Peace in the Valley?" Moria's feet hit the floor and the swing jerked to a halt. Jackson fell forward, saved from the floor by Hero, who was standing by Jackson's knee.

"Surprised?" Jackson asked, putting the swing in motion again.

Moria uttered one word, "Why?"

"You and I, and Maxine and Jeremy, will have the most work to do if this happens. I trust y'all not to lose the farm in this process. I can get an event clause on our homeowners' insurance, AERC has insurance, and Richard will be responsible as co-manager with Jada to sign on the dotted line."

"Did you think this through while I was talking?"

"No, Richard called me. We talked and he's taking full financial responsibility … in writing." Jackson looked pleased with himself.

"Super!" Moria got up from the swing. "I've got to call Maxine."

"I think she knows by now. Jeremy asked me if we could stay gone all summer. I think he's expecting fireworks and wants to take cover. Hmm … not a bad idea." Jackson winked at her. "Have I got you revved up so we can go to bed? I'm hanker'n for some rodeo'n."

Dixie and Hero stretched out on the porch for the night, exhausted by the human mouth noises. Dixie wagged her tail and licked Hero's face, *I'm glad we're not people.*

Moria spent a restless night dreaming about rodeos, thunderstorms, escaped horses, angry voices, and above all, Sassy's triumphant voice, *Mousey and I are gonna manage the ride.*

"No," Moria shrieked, thrashing about and pulling the covers from Jackson.

He sat up and took her by the arm. "What's the matter?"

"Mousey and Sassy are going to manage the ride."

"Huh? Maybe Jeremy's right. We need to take cover, sooner than later. Don't worry, Missy." With those words, he rolled over and curled the distraught cowgirl into his arms. All seemed well on the farm, till morning.

Chapter Five

Predawn light crept through the blinds, encouraging Moria to meet the day with courage, as the phone rang at Peace in the Valley Farm.

Jackson answered, "Hold on," and handed the phone to Moria. "It's your new best friend," and headed to the coffee pot.

Moria sat up, struggling to clear her head from the night's ravage of her dream. Squinting to see the display number she answered, "What?"

"And good morning to you," Jada's cheerful voice responded.

"Good news. We've gotta ride date."

Moria sat up and swung her feet to the floor. "When?"

"September 25. Somebody's ride was cancelled. I need to come over, right now. Maxine's on her way."

Moria fell back on the bed and closed her eyes. "Give me about an hour. Okay?"

"I'm halfway there," Jada answered.

"Well, bless your heart. When you get here, go in the kitchen and have some coffee while I get dressed."

Maxine beeped in on the line. "Just wanted to give you a heads up …"

"I know, I'm getting dressed. Coffee's on."

Jackson came in the bedroom to say goodbye as Moria gathered up her clothes and trudged to the shower. "Jeremy and I will grab lunch in town so we won't interrupt your exciting day," he teased, ruffling her hair.

Moria gave Jackson a hug. "Don't worry if I'm not here when you come home. I'll meet you in south Georgia. Maybe I'll join the rodeo circuit. Have a good day." She dressed and could find no excuse to avoid the kitchen. Maxine and Jada faced each other across the table, seeming to have a normal conversation about the weather. *Where to sit? Between them? Closer to Maxine? Where's my coffee?*

"Here's your coffee," Maxine said, pointing to the end of the table.

Moria gave her a grateful smile, then turned to Jada, who had a sheaf of papers spread out before her. "Well, what have you brought us? Looks like you and Richard have been busy."

Jada gathered the papers, stacked, and fanned them out, handing the two women each a sheet. She paused to let them take a look at the outline. "Richard and I have been hard at work since you all left. I think we're about done."

Moria and Maxine gave each other a *hell no, you're not* look.

Maxine said, "Tell us what you've got."

"We called a couple of ride managers and got some guesstimates on expenses." She frowned. "This is going to cost a few thousand dollars."

"You better hope the ride pays for itself," Maxine answered.

"We could save some money if we didn't have to pay a camping fee to you," Jada complained, looking at Moria.

Moria opened her mouth to blast Jada's delusional request. Feeling a kick under the table, she smiled, saying, "Did you get a *guesstimate* on what it'll cost to repair and reseed our pasture?"

Jada smiled back, "We thought that'd be your donation."

"Well, it's not. End of discussion. We're charging fifteen dollars per day per rig. That's a bargain. We could charge per horse."

Jada threw the papers on the table and shoved her chair back. "Whatever. You do the damn ride."

Maxine grabbed Jada's arm. "Sit down. You started this, and you're going to finish it if we have to kick your butt all the way to the awards meeting."

Surprise and doubt shadowed Jada's face. "What if I don't?"

Moria summoned up her best schoolteacher face. "Look at me. You *will* because if you don't, you'll wish you'd never moved to Cherry Valley. What do you think the other endurance riders in our neighborhood, and even farther away, are going to think? Just because you're cute, you think you can make promises and not keep them? Offering to put on a ride is serious business to us."

Jada sat. Her eyes narrowed, seeming to say, *you've won this round.* "Okay."

Maxine picked up the stack of papers as if nothing had happened and flipped through them. "I don't see where you've checked the price on Porta Pottys, or generators to pump water from the creek. We're not using Moria's bathroom or their well water." Maxine added these items to the list.

Jada snatched the papers back, saying "It was just yesterday when all this came about."

Moria smiled at Jada, " You can get back to us on what you want us to do."

"All of it," Jada snapped, slapping the papers onto the table.

"So *we're* going to be the ride managers, not you?"

Jada laid her head on the table, muttering to herself. Maxine took hold of Jada's shoulder. "Sit up, woman. You're not in fourth grade. Be a grown up." Moria brought her a glass of water and sat down to look through the papers again.

Jada sat up, drank and gathered her thoughts. "I'll be the ride manager." She gave the two women a sly look as she took her copy of the papers. Moria handed one to Maxine and placed hers on the table.

"So, I'll be going," Jada announced. "By the way, I've ordered a tent and tables and chairs. Where should we put them?"

Moria opened the door and ushered her out. "That's a pretty big expense. Besides, we won't need them until September."

Jada dug in her pocket and waved a credit card at them. "Not to worry."

Moria closed the door and sank to the floor. "Let's saddle up and go for a ride."

"After lunch," Maxine answered.

Just then, the phone rang. Moria answered, saying, "Sure, cowboy, y'all come on. We'll make some sandwiches and entertain you with the story of our morning." As she hung up, Moria gave Maxine a dazed look.

"What just happened here? We're going to manage this ride? How'd she do this?"

Setting out some paper plates and napkins, Maxine frowned, "Beats me. At least we didn't lose the farm … yet. I'm sure the guys are going to want all the details."

Moria searched in the refrigerator and handed Maxine the tomatoes. "BLT's, chips and apple pie."

"Sounds good to me," Maxine said, as she began to prepare the sandwiches. "I hate to tell you these tomatoes are a little soft and the bread's got about one more day. What about lettuce?"

Moria checked in the vegetable bin. "Lettuce? We can't even stretch a few hours out of it." She tossed the withered leaves in the trash. "Slice the tomatoes thick. These sandwiches are going to be messy, anyway."

Moria reached into the fridge for the bacon and sniffed. "About one more day on this, too. We can toast the bread. That'll help." Then she began to fry the strips of iffy bacon.

The dogs, set in motion by the bacon scent, stared through the screen with soulful eyes.

Jackson's truck turned into the driveway and the dogs sprang off the porch to greet their favorite ear scratchers. Jeremy and Jackson obliged, and soon entered the house, leaving the dogs with twitching noses and wagging tails.

The two guys hung their hats on the deer rack inside the hallway and headed to the sink to wash up. "Smells good," Jeremy said. "Maybe you girls can work at The Diner in your spare time."

Moria laughed, "We have no spare time. We're employed by Jada to manage the ride so she can take credit as the ride manager."

Jeremy gave Maxine a hug. "Sounds like a page turner. That includes you, too?"

Maxine leaned into him, "Yeah, me too."

Jackson reached for Moria, who gave him a welcome home kiss and said, "You won't believe this …"

The cats leapt off the back of the couch and crept into the kitchen. *Here's our chance* exclaimed Pounce. *Quick, jump on the counter and grab the bacon.*

Pandora's nose wrinkled. *What about you?*

Throw down what you can. Be quick and we'll scurry away.

Pandora lashed her tail. *Why do I always have to do the dangerous work? What kind of a word is scurry?*

Pounce growled, *it means get your ass up there and get the bacon, pronto. Pronto means scurry, too.*

Pandora obeyed. Just then Jackson saw the impending event. Letting go of Moria, he snatched the saltshaker and threw it toward the cat.

Pounce made a speedy exit and Pandora followed, yowling at the departing gray cat's back.

Moria grabbed the counter saying, "Well, there's Southern hospitality for you. Someday, those cats are going to put me in the hospital with their antics. Now that we've had our entertainment for the day, let's eat."

Food was served and Moria began to tell a tale of the day's events. With vigor, Maxine added her thoughts about the morning, concluding with, "Somehow Jada's tricked us into managing the ride, in her name. How did this happen?"

"In my opinion, she's crazy like a fox," Jackson commented, slicing into the pie. "Jeremy and I are leaving this afternoon. We're taking my trailer, so we won't interrupt your adventures when you get out and about."

Moria's fork clattered to the table, "So you're leaving us with this mess?"

Jackson grinned at her as he pushed back from the table, "Yeah, I guess so. Keep in touch." He reached for his hat and the cowboys left.

Later in the afternoon Jackson returned to pack. Moria sat on the bed watching him and realized his heart and mind were already at the rodeo. *He loves the rough life of the rodeo. It's in his blood, as endurance is in mine. I'm being selfish to want him to live my life. Sure, he likes endurance, but he loves the rodeo circuit. I need to follow the ribbons before I get off trail.*

"Jackson, if you want to keep the horses and do some rodeos around here or wherever, I'm good with that. It's not all about me."

He turned from folding his shirt and looked into Moria's eyes. "What's this about? You think I'm not coming back?" He sat down on the bed, taking Moria in his arms. "I love you or I wouldn't be here. Being married is our choice. We're lucky, we can do the things we want to and trust each other to always to return."

She buried her face on his shoulder and answered in a muffled voice, "I know, but this is the first time we've been separated when you are going off to have fun." She sniffed and reached for the sheet to wipe her face then smiled. "Hey, some of your clothes are still in the dryer. I'll get them." Moria tipped Jackson's face to hers and kissed him. "By the way, is your insurance paid up?"

"Get outta here," he laughed, reaching for another pair of boots.

A cloud of dust blew across the driveway as Jackson's truck left the farm. Moria watched the dust settle on the cedars, remembering dust in her face on the rides, the rides where she would drop back behind the front runners in the last mile … afraid to race. *Does it really matter? Who cares?*

~ ~ ~

Early the next morning she called Maxine. "Time to saddle up. We always think better in the woods with the horses. Don't forget the bug spray."

"Need I ask what we're going think about," Maxine answered. "I'll be there in about an hour."

Later, as they trotted side by side toward the forest, Moria said, "With the ride starting on our road, it'll give people time to spread out before they get to the trail."

"Good idea. We need to sketch out a map of sorts and get over to Rodney's. According to our ride manager, Rodney's in charge of the trails. He didn't seem too happy about his assignment. If the saddle club people will take care of the stretch along the river, that would be a huge help."

Soon the riders were in their favorite world, the pine scented woods. July sun filtered through a canopy of leaves dappling the trail with splashes of light, as if to lead the riders higher onto the mountain. Travelling on an overgrown logging road, the horses scrambled over rocks as the riders pushed strands of kudzu away from their faces. The snaky, green vines seemed possessed, catching on saddles and riders as if to claim this prey for their own.

An unforeseen vine caught Rainbow under his neck. The frightened horse threw his head upward, just as Moria leaned over to release the vine. Rainbow's head collided with his rider's face knocking her sideways. She grabbed his mane. The horse lost his balance and fell. Moria tumbled off, slid down the mountainside and disappeared into a dense wall of greenery. Then the noise of ripping vines stopped and from deep in the kudzu she called, "I'm okay. Get the horse," and climbed up the hillside. "Where is Rainbow? Is he hurt?"

Moria reached the trail as blood streamed from her nose. Maxine handed her a bandanna, "Jeez. What about you? Looks like you got the worst of this drama. Your buddy's knees and his nose are banged up but they'll heal."

Moria felt her face and checked her teeth. "The bleeding's almost stopped. I think I can ride. Nothing's broken, it was pretty soft down there. My head's a little jumbled, but let's keep going," Moria mumbled. "Do you have some tissues? I need to pack my nose."

Maxine searched in her pack for tissues and the two riders continued their mission. At the creek, they paused to let the horses' drink. Moria rinsed her face in the stream and sponged Rainbow's neck and head.

The horse pawed the water to cool his legs and glistening drops caught the sun's rays, casting a rainbow above the stream. Moria smiled as she watched the colors fall back into the water. "Guess that's a sign from two rainbows," she joked. "We need to go ahead and check out this logging road while we're up here. I think it might be a connector back to the main trail."

"You think?" Maxine laughed.

The riders continued for about thirty minutes, climbing over deadfall and fighting the kudzu. The red clay trail suddenly made an unexpected turn into the undergrowth and stopped at a drop off to a jeep trail below.

"Hey, I think I know where we are." Moria peered down through the brush. "Remember the cabin off the power line? We cut through that way." She turned Rainbow into the undergrowth. The chestnut sat back on his haunches and slid down the bank.

Maxine and Catch On Fire followed. "Okay, Missy, lead on. I hope you're right 'cause turning around is a long way back."

The riders urged their horses to trot. "I think this is the road that will bring us to the powerline," Moria answered. The footing on the jeep trail encouraged the chestnut and the bay to move into a canter. Around a bend the horses broke their pace and skidded to a stop where a gated chain link fence blocked the way.

The women looked at each other and then at the outside of the fence line. Waist high blackberry vines stretched in both directions and un-tended pines huddled together as if to say, *be gone.*

"Well, this is a fine kettle of fish. Reckon the owner will let us cross the property?" Maxine asked. As she spoke, two German Shepherds raced out from a nearby shed, rushed to the fence, and threw their weight against it. The rusted chain link tilted toward the riders and the dogs scrambled toward the top then fell back to the ground. Rainbow and Catch On Fire whirled around as the women struggled to stay in control.

Someone near the house called, "Hey, dogs, off. Come."

Moria and Maxine stared as the dogs wagged their tails and ran to their owner. The horses settled and Maxine took a deep breath. "What now? He's coming this way. Let's wait and see if he's going to let us cross."

"Yeah," Moria whispered, watching the guy approach. *What to say?*

"Kin I hep yuh?" His dirty jeans and torn shirt gave the appearance of a farm hand. A ragged baseball cap shaded his eyes, and his voice was not friendly.

Moria scanned the enclosure as the man approached and waved to them. A small cedar-sided cabin crouched beneath a stand of oak trees. Tall azalea bushes hugged the house and Carolina jasmine draped over the chain link fence which bounded the property. Several chicken houses stretched along the opposite side of the fence. The chickens, disturbed by the ruckus, came scurrying out from a nearby shed.

Maxine flashed him her best country girl smile, saying, "Well, this is embarrassing … Uh, we're lost. Rode over from Cherry Valley and now we're all turned around and it's getting late." She glanced into the deepening shadows and then across the property. "I think if we can cross your yard and get to the powerline, we'll make it home before dark." She slumped in her saddle with a worried look.

The guy pushed his hat back to get a better look at these unexpected visitors. "So, wha'daya want me tu do?"

Maxine looked at the ground for a moment as if deciding what to say next then looked back at the guy. "Will you open the gate and let us pass?" Biting her lip, she waited.

The guy looked at them in disbelief. "What a couple of cowgirl drama queens. I wer'nt born yesterday. I seen y'all at The Juniper Tree dancin' with yo're fancy cowboys. I heerd y'all go on long trail rides. Lost? What a crock'a shit."

An *uh oh* look passed between the two women. Maxine shrugged, nodded to Moria and said under her breath, "Give it your best shot, Missy."

We can always turn around and run. Moria gave the guy a wink and said, "Please?"

The guy scratched his stomach and grinned, "What's it worth to ya?"

"If you open the gate, we can talk about it."

The farmer puzzled for a second, facing the reality of his visitors. "Wal, I guess y'all kin cross this time."

"Thanks, we really appreciate it. One more thing, can you put the dogs up before we come in?"

"This ain't no resort, woman," he answered. "What ya see is what ya git." With those words, he opened the gate. The dogs took an alert stance, ears up, waiting for the chase. But the owner waved his hand with a quick gesture and the dogs departed, slinking away to the shed.

To break the awkward silence as the guy and the two riders crossed the property, Moria asked, "Have you live here a long time?"

"None ar' y're beeswax," he snarled.

They reached the gate and the riders could see the powerline just across the dirt road. "Thank you, Jesus." Moria whispered.

Maxine smiled at the guy as they passed through the gate, "Hope to see you again soon," she lied.

The banging gate was his only answer as he whistled for the dogs and turned toward the house.

The sun's rays lit the power line and the road with a wavering light. "Okay, let's roll before we're doing a night ride. We'll stay on the road as far as we can," Maxine said.

Moria was unusually quiet as they moved along. "So, what do you think?"

"This escapade could have had an unhappy ending. We might have been shot, since he obviously didn't want us on his property. Wonder what he's up to? Being up here by himself, you'd think he might want some company," Maxine answered.

Moria gazed out into the darkening forest. "He could bury us in the back of beyond and no one would be the wiser." She twisted Rainbow's mane around her fingers. "Or, even worse, he might have kept us for sex slaves since we teased him."

Maxine laughed and picked up the story. "What about the horses? He couldn't sell them around here."

Moria thought for a moment. "Well, he could make us ride around his yard like Lady Godiva, or he could take the horses to slaughter somewhere far away where nobody knows them."

Maxine was getting into the drama. "What would he do with us?"

"Maybe he has a friend. Enough already. Let this be our last visit to his little patch of dirt."

Maxine said, "Yeah, but here's the thing. We really need to use the logging road. We can't bring a hundred horses across his property. I think he was grandfathered in for a certain amount of acres when the National Forest was created. Maybe we could cut a single- track trail to the power line from the jeep road. Don't forget the creek and the water running though there to the valley is too deep, not a good crossing. We'll have to see if the Ranger can help us."

Moria laughed, "Just in case we have to get his permission, since we don't know his property lines, here's a job for Jada and her enticing ways."

As the two riders continued the journey home, the day's events morphed into a wild story to tell the guys.

"You know, we should write a book. Seriously, the first chapter could be Fourth of July," Moria said, lost in her world of getting on Oprah's Book Club.

Maxine had other thoughts. "Why don't we see Rodney before he gives up his job of planning the trails? Seriously, he just needs a little encouragement. We've got plenty to do, but we can help him. I'd rather be on the trail, anyway, instead of on the phone."

As the riders parted, Maxine stopped her horse at the mailbox and leaned over to retrieve the offerings. "I'll give Rodney a call and see what they're doing." She laughed, "And I guess those little yahoos are deep in the books."

Chapter Six

The next morning Maxine called Moria. "Rodney said he would appreciate it if we could get some maps and give him an idea of where we think the trail should go. I assured him we only need twenty-five miles. He was relieved and said he would contact the saddle club and let them know we're going to give it a try, in spite of Jada's antics. He's busy this afternoon waiting for a load of hay to arrive. So, let's head to the Forest Service office."

Moria said, "Maybe we can get some updated maps and meet the new Ranger. Anyway, it never hurts to have him on our side while we're on this project. Now we'll have to start all over making friends. Too bad Ranger Kam's not still here. I looked him up. He's in California and it appears he has a ranger's job. I bet he was glad to leave Georgia. At least our devious ways got us money to repair the covered bridge."

The two looked at each other and began to laugh, remembering their seductive swim in the river and later holding the ranger's phone, and memory card from the camera, hostage until they got a promise of money for the bridge. Maxine grinned. "No wonder he moved."

"Wonder how much Kam told the new ranger about us?"

"We'll know pretty soon. The Forest Service truck is here."

The two women climbed the steps to the porch as the weathered boards creaked and pine needles littered the floor. "Some things never change. Let's hope the priorities are being tended to inside."

The small office was managed by their neighbor, Fran. She smiled as they entered. "Oh no. The Bad News Bears have returned. Wha'cha need?"

Maxine laughed and said, "That's us, prowling around again. We need some maps and maybe meet the new ranger if he's here."

Fran got up from her desk. "I'll see if *she's* busy," smiling at their startled faces.

Maxine looked at Moria, saying under her breath, "Good thing we didn't send the guys. Maybe she's old."

The ranger's office door opened and there she stood, a sturdy presence with short curly blond hair and a wide smile. She extended her hand, "Hi, I'm Cassie Levant. May I help you?"

Moria smiled in response and shook Cassie's hand. "Hi, I'm Moria Durant and this is Maxine Harris. Welcome to Cherry Valley. If you have time, we're doing some work on the horse trails and need to see any updated maps you might have."

Cassie ushered the two women in and motioned them to a couple of vintage leather chairs facing her desk. "Haven't been here long. So far, the town's treating me pretty well as long as I stay out of their business."

Always curious about matters affecting the forest, Moria wanted to know more. "We ride the trails around here pretty often. Let us know if we can help."

Cassie rocked back in her chair, appeared to size them up, and decided they weren't fazed by much. Ranger Kam had filled her in on people he knew who rode in the forest.

"Well, I shouldn't even be telling you this, but I could use some more eyes in the forest to be on the lookout for anything unusual. To be honest, I haven't been in the forest, yet. I've had the maps out trying to decide where I need to start exploring. Maps are useful but being out there is better."

Maxine said, "Over the years we've met some of the people who homestead inside the forest. Do you ride?"

Cassie reached in her desk drawer and pulled out a picture, turning it toward them. "Yes, I've done a little riding."

Moria and Maxine stared in disbelief to see the iconic photo of Cougar Rock at the Tevis Cup 100 Mile Ride in California. And yes, there was Cassie, aboard a stunning grey Arabian.

Maxine recovered enough to say, "Well, damn! I guess you *do* ride."

Amazed by the ranger's accomplishment, Moria dared to ask, "Did you finish?"

Cassie stood, patted her waist and revealed the coveted silver buckle.

Moria gave a wistful smile. "Someday I hope to do that ride. We'd love to hear about your adventures. Congratulations."

"As I started to say," Moria grinned, "before your big reveal, our neighbor has several horses and would lend you one if you want to go with us. Some of the trails are single track and you couldn't get through on an ATV."

"I need to get out there. Going out in the forest with you would be a huge help. Kam and I traded jobs so that's how I got here. Now, let's get back to the task at hand."

Maxine looked at Moria, gave a slight shrug as if to say, *Kam must not have shared his experiences with us to Cassie since she didn't show us the door.*

Moria answered her with a smile.

Cassie searched in the drawer and returned with an armful of maps. "Come over here to the table and let's take a look and show me where you usually ride." She sorted through the papers and smoothed one out.

The three women studied the map and the two riders oriented themselves to the locations of their farms. Moria said, "Here's where we go up to the trails. Then we ride wherever, nobody seems to care. Kam appreciated us to keep an eye out."

Maxine kicked Moria's foot. *Shut up.*

Cassie chuckled. "Your reputation has preceded you. I know where you live."

Moria back-peddled quickly. "Uh, yeah. Well, sometimes we didn't agree on things. Kam could be pretty adamant about rules. And we would forget that he was the boss of the forest."

Maxine interrupted. "Did he tell you about the grant to repair the covered bridge?"

Cassie nodded toward her desk. "I have the paperwork. I understand this is to be done by volunteers qualified to do the work." She smiled, appearing to know the back story of acquiring the grant.

"Thanks," Maxine said. "We'll get on it soon. Okay about the maps. Some of us Cherry Valley riders condition horses in the forest for endurance riding competitions. We need to measure the trails so we'll be able to improve our conditioning plans."

Cassie looked hard at Maxine, saying, "So you can put on an endurance ride in the forest?"

Maxine gave a sheepish grin, "Well, yeah. How'd you know?"

"Word gets around."

"Okay. So, can we?"

Moria interrupted, "This isn't exactly how we planned to present the idea." *What to say next?*

Cassie turned back to the maps. "Let's do one thing at a time. Get your trail design together and we'll talk about it."

She picked up a pen and circled a parcel of land within the forest. "Be on the look out here. This property was grandfathered in for homesteading when the acreage was taken by eminent domain for the National Forest. It cannot be sold. If no family member lives on it, the land must be returned to the National Forest. There's a resident living there now. You have to get permission from the owner to cross his land."

"Who lives there now? Do you know him?" Moria asked in what she hoped was just a curious tone.

Cassie folded the maps and handed them to Moria. "No, haven't met him. Keep in touch. Maybe I'll go out with y'all one day if I can borrow your friend's horse."

Moria took the maps, handling them as if they were ancient scrolls. "Thanks for your time and the maps. We'll look forward to you riding with us. Oh, one more thing. We're not actually the ride managers. Do you know Jada Deavers?"

Cassie raised her eyebrows. "Uh, yes. I do. She's the manager? Good luck!"

On the way home, the women discussed the events of the past three days, concluding that Jada would be the ride manager and they would be her minions ... at least for now. What to do about the grump up on the mountain? They need to cross his land.

Moria waved goodbye to Maxine and walked onto the porch to be greeted by hungry dogs and cats. "'Scuse me? Am I late with your dinners? Hold on. I need to put the scrolls in a safe place." The dogs jumped up and down, twirling in circles, with drooling tongues dripping on the already spotted floor. The cats leapt onto the counter to observe preparations. "Furballs, off with you." she laughed, setting the food bowls in the appointed places. "Now the horses."

The phone rang just as she settled down for the evening. "Hey, cowboy, how was your day?"

"Horses are doing great, not sure if I want to sell them. We've more than paid expenses from our events today."

Moria heard the pride in his voice and responded, "You know, you don't have to sell them on my account. I'd just like to see them being used. They're quality stock and deserve a chance to rodeo their way to the top." *What am I saying? I'll probably never get Jackson on the trail again. And, what about Silver Dollar? He's such a good horse ...*

Her thoughts rambled away into the future, interrupted by Jackson's repeated words, "Hey, are you still there?"

"Sorry, I think we have a bad connection. What did you say?"

"Jeremy and I are going to stay over. There's an event in Waycross next weekend. We're on a roll, just can't walk away from this."

The thrill of success has captured your heart. I get it. By now Moria was pacing the floor. "No problem. All is well here, take care and good luck," putting a smile in her voice.

Should I tell him about our stressful encounter with the farmer guy? Probably not. He needs to stay focused and not worry about me.

"Thanks, Missy, for letting me run to the end of my leash. You know I'll be back. Get ready for your R-rated bedtime story. Love ya."

Moria replaced the phone and stared off into nothingness for a moment. "Come on, cats. We'd better get to bed. We've got a ride to put on. Time's a wasting." Pounce and Pandora soon gave up sleeping on the bed as their girl tossed and turned, mumbling into the night, *Rainbow, where are the ribbons? I know I hung them high. Were they stolen by the rodeo horses?*

Her trusted horse answered, *only if you let them.*

Chapter Seven

The following day, Maxine met Moria at her barn. "You talked to Jackson last night? Sounds like they're not heading home soon. Guess that's a perk of owning your own business and your buddy works with you."

Moria closed the feed room door, took the rake from the wall and began to clean up loose hay and shavings. "It's just as well they're gone for a while. We've got a lot of work to do. Guess we'd better get Rodney and Jada on board about the trail and get a good look at the maps."

Maxine sat down on a hay bale, looking toward the nearby foothills. "You know, we gotta long way to go and a short time to get there. The ride will be here before we know it … and school."

"Well, let's get busy." Moria replaced the rake. "Just askin,' do you think the guys will get mixed up with the cowgirls at the rodeo?"

Maxine stopped at the gate and turned toward Moria. "Where'd that come from? We're not in middle school. You've been watching too much TV. If you're so worried, why don't you pack up and go to Valdosta or Waycross?"

"Uh, no. Thanks for the kick in the butt. As Miss Scarlett says, 'I'll think about that tomorrow. Tomorrow is another day.' Do you still have that trail measuring thing you bought?"

"Yeah, but I'm not sure how to use it yet."

"How hard can it be?" Moria laughed, as they reached the house.

"I'm going to see if Cassie can get me started with it," Maxine said. "We need to remind Jada to apply for the Forest Service permit since she's already got a ride date. We can draw up a trail map soon for her to take to Cassie for approval. Do you think we should let her go by herself?"

"Well, we can't do everything. I think Cassie has Jada's number. Let's let her run with it and see what happens."

They settled at the kitchen table with the lists, coffee and the maps. The two riders studied the intricate patterns on the pages and soon the forest trails became their world. Hours passed as they routed and rerouted possible trail designs.

Maxine said, "Here's a list for Jada. She can check with the church people and see if they will consider doing the food. Whatever money they make can be a donation to the church. Then we don't have to worry about food. Worth every penny. The Over the Mountain Saddle Club people probably need a heads-up that we're going ahead with the ride."

As Maxine left, she said, "I think the saddle club folks were a little spooked by Jada's aggressive approach about the ride, but they shouldn't have any trouble cleaning up some of the trail. Maybe the 4-H Club will take a section and do some of the harder work. We could provide tools and one of their leaders is a retired forest ranger. We'll need to watch Sassy and Mousey so they don't mix it up with these kids. I'll call Rodney when I get home and see if we can meet at Jada's in the morning."

Later in the evening Moria sat in the porch swing surrounded by her loyal fur tribe and thinking about the days to come *We've got to get the trail design together, which we don't have approved by Cassie ... yet. Be sure AERC has all their paperwork and get the word out about the ride. At least Jada's got a ride date for us, she says. We better check on that. Jackson didn't seem too worried about the riders camping in our pasture. What if it rains? Some people will opt out and expect a refund. I don't think there's a rule about this. Well, that'll be Richard and Jada's problem.*

~ ~ ~

The next morning Maxine, Rodney and Moria were on their way to Jada's. Moria held the maps in her arms and took a deep breath, *Jackson, hope you're having a good time. Could really use you here.*

Maxine broke the silence. "Well, let's hope Richard's talked some sense into Jada about how we should proceed with the plan. At least he received the ride manager's packet and has been in touch with some Southeast managers."

Jada met them at the door.

Rodney removed his hat and stood behind Maxine. Jada glanced his way. "What are you doing here?"

Moria looked at Jada and frowned, saying, "I believe you designated him to be the trail master. We invited him today." She waited.

"Uh? Oh, yeah. The trails."

"Isn't that why we're here?"

"Why don't we talk about the awards? We can handle the trails later," as if to dismiss Rodney's involvement.

He turned to go but Maxine caught his arm.

"No, Jada. The trails. No trails, no ride."

Jada threw her hands in the air, whirled away, her back to them, "Who's in charge of this ride?"

"Guess you are," Moria answered, motioning the others toward the door.

Jada looked over her shoulder just in time to see them leaving. "Wait. Let's talk about this."

Moria turned around, crossed her arms and took a deep breath. "This is going to be a long, hot summer if you don't get your shit together. We don't care whose name is down as ride manager. We care if the Cherry Valley riders make a good showing with this production. Pretend we're making a movie and we want to get an Academy Award."

Jada's eyes sparkled as she smiled and ushered them into the sunroom. Well then, welcome to the studio. Let's get started."

Moria and Maxine gave each other a worried look and sat down on the sofa. Rodney took a nearby chair and twisted the brim of his hat, looking wistfully toward the door.

Jada began to pace back and forth, saying, "I've got an excellent camera. We can make a movie about putting on the ride, have all sort of disasters happen and have a race at the end. Who would win the ride?"

Jada was off in her make-believe world of stardom. Rodney muttered, "What's the matter with her?"

Maxine waved her arms to get Jada's attention. "Wait a minute. Sit down so we can talk."

Heedless of Maxine's voice, Jada continued, "We can start with fire-works. What a great opening shot. I'm sure lots of people took pictures that night."

"Hey, girlfriend, take it down a notch." Maxine stood in Jada's path, interrupting her back and forth strides.

Jada snapped back, "What? You don't think we should make a movie?"

"No, I don't," Maxine answered.

"Me either," Moria echoed in her best teacher voice.

Rodney slapped his hat on his head, growling, "Wal, gol dang, you crazy woman. I'm outta here." With those words he jumped up from his chair and headed for the door.

"Wait." Moria called, "You're our ride home."

Rodney hesitated. "I'll be waitin' outside," and slammed the door.

Maxine waved her hand in Jada's face and pointed to the nearest chair. "Sit." she commanded in her best dog obedience voice.

Startled, Jada sat. Silence hung in the room. She smiled, "Okay, let's make a plan. What about if *I* make the movie and *y'all* manage the ride?"

The two women looked at her in disbelief and then at each other. "Where's Richard?" Moria asked at last.

"He's away."

"Why don't you run the movie idea by him?" Moria continued, glancing at Maxine, who nodded an okay and looked toward the door. "Call us after you talk to Richard." With those final words, Moria picked up the maps and she and Maxine walked out.

Jada stood in the doorway, smiling. "I'm going to make a movie. Where's my camera?" she said aloud.

Rodney cranked the truck when he saw his passengers approaching. As they drove away, their laughter echoed across the fields. Maxine told Rodney about how things ended and the need to get Richard back in the loop before anything worse happened.

"Well dang, guess we're gonna have a ride after all and a movie, too," Rodney commented as they travelled home.

Moria fell back against the seat and closed her eyes. "Tell me this is a bad dream. So, what happens now?"

Maxine said, "Let's go to my house and study the maps to see if we've got enough established trails for this ride. "Then," she added, "we'll put on the best damn ride in the Southeast and it will be preserved forever in a movie!"

Chapter Eight

E arly the next morning, the phone rang at Peace in the Valley Farm. Moria reached for it, knocking the lamp off the nightstand. She could see Jackson's name on the readout. "Uh oh, something's happened," she announced to the cats, who crouched at the foot of the bed, knowing all was not right in their world.

"Hello? Jackson, are you alright?" A glimmer of light seeped through the blinds washing over her troubled face.

"Yeah, we're okay, but the horses have had enough. Patches is having a tendon problem and Ringo stepped on his shoe and pulled a chunk off his hoof. Star is in season and not worth shit. Actually, I'm leaving her here to be bred. I met a guy with an exceptional Quarter horse stallion. I will go get her when she's ready. We're stopping at Cracker Barrel then heading home. I've really missed you, sweetie. Rest up."

Moria took a deep breath. *Just what we need. A pregnant horse.* "Sorry about the horses. Looks like a job for the vet and the shoer. We're doing fine, *with the exception of Jada's laid back ears.* Steaks on the grill tonight?"

"Great. We'll be home late this evening."

"Drive safe," Moria answered as she headed for the coffee pot.

"This might be a two cup morning. I've got a lot to do," she announced to Pounce and Pandora as they trotted down the hall behind her. "I need to call Maxine."

"Guess you've heard from Jeremy. I was hoping we could go back to the Rangers Station today, meet with Cassie, and see if we can go ahead and get a ride permit to send AERC. She can always revoke it if things don't work out. Right now, I need to clean the house, the barn, and get some food in the pantry." She paused for a breath.

"Yeah, and don't wear yourself out. Bet there's an interesting night ahead of you."

"Same to you," Moria laughed. "We'd better get busy. Maybe we can go to the Ranger Station tomorrow."

Maxine thought a minute, saying, "Why don't we get Rodney over in the morning and work on a trail plan some more before we go to Cassie's?"

"Good idea. Enjoy your evening, too. By the way, do you think we should tell the guys about our visit to the grouchy country bumpkin?"

"Might as well. They're going to find out before long anyway. Maybe they can help us get access to that property."

Moria headed outside, second cup of coffee in hand, followed by her entourage of animals. The dogs rambled in the bushes hunting for unsuspecting chipmunks and the cats raced ahead in case mice were on the menu at the barn. The horses galloped up as she opened the gate and headed to their stalls.

The soft air from the early summer morning gave her pause to question, *am I lucky or am I blessed?* Looking up at the cirrus clouds streaming across the sky she answered her own question. "Maybe a little of both. I'll ask Jackson." With those thoughts tucked away, she fed the horses, cleaned the water trough, then opened the stall doors and shooed Rainbow and Silver out to pasture.

"Time for cardio work and clearing my sinuses," she said aloud, taking a pitchfork and going to work on the stalls. Shavings flew into the wheelbarrow like dirty snow and new shavings replaced them. "I love the smell of fresh shavings. Wish cleaning the house was as rewarding as cleaning the barn. I have some Pinesol. I'll clean with that. It'll give the house a woodsy smell. Ah, the last task," and began raking the aisle way.

Returning to the house, Moria sat a moment, deciding what to do next. Looking at the clock, she frowned, "How did early get to be so late?" With those words, she hurried through the house, sweeping, moving clutter out of sight, wiping counter tops, cleaning the bathroom and changing the cat litter. *It's about time*, Pandora meowed, jumping into the box immediately to check it out. Moria headed to the truck and sped away to Piggly Wiggly.

At last, she collapsed in the porch swing. "What a day." Pounce curled up in her lap, purring softly. *I am a comfort cat*, he thought. Just then he heard Jackson's truck coming up the driveway. *Well damn, buddy, we were just getting settled. Guess I'm out of the picture now*, he growled.

Moria ran to the edge of the driveway as Jackson stopped the trailer. "Hey, cowboy, welcome home," joy and relief in her voice.

Jackson bolted out of the truck, enveloping his girl in a heart-stopping hug and slow-motion kiss. One of the weary horses kicked the trailer and whinnied, *Y'all get a room.*

"Yeah, we hear you," Jackson answered. "I'm going to keep these guys here a few days so I can tend to them. Come down to the barn and give me a hand. Then, I'll show you some rodeo tricks," he grinned.

Moria hosed Patches and Ringo to cool them from the heat of the trip while Jackson got their feed ready, saying, "Guess they could use some beet pulp tonight. I don't want to come down here in the middle of the night to treat them for colic. Enough of that." The thunder of hooves brought the rodeo horses to attention as Rainbow and Silver cantered to the barn. They skidded to a stop, whinnied at the new arrivals, and looked hopefully at the open feed door. Jackson stepped out with his horses' feed. "Let's put them in the stalls while they eat."

Moria looked at her freshly cleaned stalls. "Sure. Otherwise, we'll have a food fight and a mess to clean up." She winked at Jackson, "I've got other plans for you." Soon the couple walked to the house carrying items from the trailer. She pushed back sweaty hair from her face and glanced at her grimy clothes. *Good excuse for a friendly shower*, she smiled to herself.

"I really need a shower," Jackson said, as if reading her thoughts.

"Race you," Moria answered, running toward the house.

The cats and dogs ran with them. Pounce yowled to his friends. *I know this pace. It'll end with us sleeping on the porch.*

Dixie said, *We like the porch. You all can have the swing.*

Sure enough, the critters camped out that night.

~ ~ ~

The next morning at breakfast Jackson said, "I told Jeremy not to come in till noon. We don't have any pressing cases right now. Both of us need to regroup and get back to real life. That rodeo business is pretty intense." He reached for the coffee pot and poured each of them another cup. "So, what's been going on in the neighborhood? Seems like I've been gone a month."

Where to begin? "Well, Jada's going to make a movie about putting on the ride."

"Huh? You're kidding." Then, Jackson reached for a donut, saying, "Let's move to the couch so I can prop my feet up." Then settled down for what was bound to be a barely believable tale, knowing the characters.

Moria related their visit to Jada's, and Rodney's reluctance to be a part of the event with 'crazy' Jada. Concluding her account with the decision that she and Maxine agreed to move on with the ride plan, since it looked like they were going to manage it anyway.

Jackson laughed, saying, "Would'a loved to be a fly on the wall for that scene."

Moria, frowned, "It's not funny. We don't know what Richard will say."

"He'll probably be glad to turn her loose with just the camera and grateful it's not his credit card. Richard's on the same page with us. He wants to have a decent ride and is willing to foot the bill. We should get some sponsors to encourage him." Looking at Moria's anxious expression he sensed there were more stories to be told. "The horses look good. So, what else is going on?"

"Well, Maxine and I were riding the other day, looking for some trail connections, and we came upon a farm where we needed to cross the property to get home before dark."

Jackson looked at Moria's tense face and knew there was more. "And …"

"The owner let us cross the property, but he had some really bad dogs."

"Come on, Missy. There's more to this story. You've got my attention."

"Okay. We need to put a trail around the edge of his property and he's not very … friendly."

"Because?"

"I don't know. He's just a grouchy old bastard. You'd think he'd be glad to have some company. The Ranger said he's on dedicated land from eminent domain in the forest. He can pretty much do what he wants to as long as he doesn't break any laws."

Jackson put his cup in the sink, saying, "Let's put your problem on the back burner for now. I've got to check on the horses, and I can feed them while I'm down there. I also need to call Dr. Barr."

~ ~ ~

Maxine and Rodney were grouped around the kitchen table while Moria made a fresh pot of coffee. Then they spread the maps out and got down to business.

Rodney started the conversation with, "How'er we gonna measure the trails when we figure out where we're going? I know them ride people are pretty particular about distance. If the trail's too short, nobody will probably say a thing except the sorehead losers." He chuckled, "But if it's too long, all hell'll break loose."

"Been there," Maxine laughed. "Short or long. We know our Arabs can walk about four miles an hour. We could clock them on the road to be sure."

"We can't measure at the trot because of the terrain," Moria added. "The Over the Mountain Saddle Club might be willing to help us. I've heard they measured that stretch on the way to the water crossing. We probably need to check it ourselves. At least it's on public land so we should be okay with that. Then there's the surveyor's wheel." The three people groaned in unison. "What about the hiking club? They're always looking for a project and they use these trails." Rodney and Maxine looked relieved, not wanting to go on a hike in July.

Maxine said, "Add the hikers to the list. Do you all think we can trust Jada to approach them? It wouldn't take much for her to screw up. Let's work on laying out the trail, get some idea of the mileage, and run it by Cassie before we get too far."

They studied the Forest Service maps for a few minutes, orienting themselves to roads and trails they knew. Moria said, "See how this might work. When we leave camp, let's take them past Rodney's to where the road dead ends at the gate to the forest trail. The road should give the riders time to spread out before getting into the woods."

Rodney nodded in agreement, then asked, "Ford the creek at the bridge? Yu know about the bear?"

"Yeah," Maxine laughed, "we met her and her cub there one night when we were riding. I can't imagine she'd hang around with us back and forth working on the trail. It is a little risky, something to be considered. Guess we could find another crossing that would be acceptable to the Forest Service."

Moria put a question mark by the bridge. "Thank goodness this is our copy of the map so we can mark on it."

"Okay, let's assume we're going to cross the creek," Maxine said, picking up the red pencil and continuing the line. "It's an easy stretch past the saddle club. We need to stop here and decide if this is going to be the short loop. I'm guessing it's about ten miles if we cross the creek again and head back toward camp. That terrain is mostly rough with some wash outs, if I remember."

Rodney raised his head from studying the map. "We call it th 'ups and downs.' It'll need more clearing, for sure. I'm gonna take another look around there."

The phone rang, bringing the trail planners out of the forest and back to reality. Moria answered and turned toward the others. "How about some pizza? Hand delivered by the Downtown Cowboys?"

Rodney wrinkled his forehead in puzzlement. "Is that a new pizza place?"

"You'll see," Moria grinned. "Let's leave our stuff on the table and eat outside. You all can go ahead and wash up," she continued, reaching for paper plates and napkins, a staple in her house.

They sat on the porch, waiting for the Downtown Cowboys Pizza to arrive. Dixie and Hero gazed up the road, sensing there would be an event. The sound of Jackson's truck sent the dogs bounding off the porch and racing to meet their favorite ear scratcher.

Rodney did a double take as Jackson and Jeremy lifted boxes of pizza from the back seat. "Wal, I'll be danged. Them's the Cowboy Pizzas, I reckon."

Seated around the picnic table out back under a maple tree, the friends were not shy about devouring their lunch. The trail designers shared their tentative efforts for the ride and waited for a reaction.

Jeremy wiped his hands, placed his napkins in his plate, empty except for crusts, took a drink of Coke, smiled and said, "Keep up the good work. Sounds like a plan. Has the ranger seen it yet?"

Moria brought a trash bag out to collect the remains of their feast. "No, we want to get both loops ready. I think we can finish this afternoon. Maybe we can go see her tomorrow. We're in a time crunch to get all the information to AERC in time to have the ride approved. Damn Jada. How can she be so dumb and so smart at the same time?"

Jackson grinned, "You're the teacher, Missy. Consider her your most disruptive kid. Figure it out. You've got another teacher, Maxine. And Rodney, he's dealing with Sassy and Mousey. Get Rita on board, I think she'd give Jada a run for her money."

"Save the crusts for dog snacks," Moria said placing her plate in the middle of the table and handing Maxine a zip lock bag. "Take some for your fur babies, too."

As the two men picked up their hats to leave, Rodney said, "Thank ye for lunch. What 'da I owe ya?"

Jackson winked at Moria, "The cowgirls are picking up the tab. Right, girls?"

Maxine laughed, "Yeah. Good thing we're not riding all over the countryside wearing ourselves out so we can pay for lunch."

Rodney's head swiveled back and forth following the conversation, grinned and said, "Thank ye, ladies, let's get back to work."

Moria picked up a pencil and studied what they had done so far, running the pencil lightly over loop one. "Okay, let's move on to loop two. It needs to be longer, at least fifteen miles. We're going to have to use the power line and cross the mountain guy's land, going or coming. Here are his property lines." She outlined his farm in purple. "I guess we'll call this a hazard."

Rodney looked at the purple enclosure. "I know that ole guy. He shows up at the pool hall sometimes. Name's Pete."

Moria's eyes brightened. "How well do you know him?"

Rodney hesitated, shifted his gaze back to the map and said, "Let me get a closer look at the map." He studied it for a minute, then said, "I don't think he's gonna let nobody on his land."

"Because?" Moria asked, studying his face.

"Well, I don't know for sure, but word's out that he has a little farming project going on."

"We saw his chickens," Moria answered, puzzlement clouding her face.

Maxine slapped her forehead, "Damn! He's growing pot."

Rodney nodded, "Well, I ain't actually seen it ..."

"Okay, let's move on for now," Maxine said. "We need a plan for the hazard. Rodney, put some thought on this. In the meantime, let's count his property as part of the ride. The rest of this is easy. We need to decide which way to run the loops so the twenty-five milers and the fifties won't get in each other's way, especially at the finish line."

Moria brought out a pitcher of special sweet tea. "Maybe this'll get us through the rest of the afternoon."

"Oh, yeah." Maxine and Rodney agreed, as they toasted to the potent Long Island sweet tea and settled down to work.

Maxine said, "I'd like for us to have a possible route finished to show Cassie tomorrow. I'll take the GPS and see if she has time to help me get started with it. Back to the map, we can use the Rutherford's Road, the power line, cross Pete's to the old logging road and the kudzu trail. That would put us at the water crossing and home over the woods trail. They'd still have almost a mile of flat road to the finish line."

Moria poured another round of sweet tea. "We'll have to do some measuring before we set the trails and start clearing. The map does have a key. Maybe we can use a piece of string. Leave the map here tonight and I'll try to do some estimates. Rodney, do you want to go with us in the morning?"

"Naw, guess not. I promised Rita and the little cowgirlies we'd go for a ride. Any place special you want us to go?"

Folding the map and clearing the table, she answered, "Try what we're calling the Red Loop, if it won't be too far for the girls to ride. Just get some idea of how much clearing needs to be done."

Rodney picked up his hat to leave. At the door he turned with a smile, saying, "Them young'uns is planning to be a part of the ride and not work at the vet check. They've studied a lot about conditioning and think they're gonna win the ride."

Moria filled two Mason jars with the sweet tea to go and handed them to her friends, "Enjoy your evening. Okay, buddy, I want to see the cowgirlies and their ponies well-conditioned by ride time," laughing as she opened the door.

"Depends on when they have to show up back in Atlanta for the trial. Guess we'll see. Let me know about the meeting at the Ranger Station."

"Will do."

As Rodney drove away Maxine said, "Let's try to get to Cassie's early if she's available. See you tomorrow and thanks," Maxine grinned, lifting the Mason jar in salute.

~ ~ ~

Evening shadows lengthened as the sun cast farewell beams over the valley. At Peace in the Valley Farm, lights shone from the barn as Moria and Jackson went about their nightly chores. Rainbow and Silver watched with interest as Jackson brought Patches and Ringo from their stalls to fasten them in the cross ties.

Silver cocked his head at Rainbow, *What'a you think? New endurance horses?*

Not a chance, Rainbow mumbled with a mouthful of hay.

Patches switched his tail in Silver's face, *Not on your cowhide, buddy. Jackson's my guy.*

Silver reached out and bit Patches on the hindquarters. The Paint horse kicked the stall door in answer.

Jackson came out of the tack room and closed Silver's top door. "Stop being a baby." Glancing at Rainbow and seeing that the gelding had backed up to his door, he said, "Mind your manners, dude." Then, to Moria, "Let's groom these guys. Dr. Barr is going to stop by on his way home and check out the injuries."

When the vet's truck arrived, Moria went to open the gate. "I'm going on up to the house. Hope everything is fine."

"Good evening, Dr. Barr. At least it's not the endurance horses this time. Thanks for coming by so late."

Moria returned to the house, spread the maps out on the table and dug in the kitchen drawer for a piece of string. It didn't take long for her to see that this measuring tool wasn't going to work. The string took on a life of it's on as she tried to lay it out on their Red and Blue Trails. Pounce jumped on the table and watched the string wander over the map, grabbed his new toy and ran to the loft.

Moria sat, staring at the map, looking at the key, knowing they had to get the trail measurements right. *Nobody wants to walk behind the surveyor's wheel to get this done, except where we have to. Maybe Maxine will learn how to use the GPS thing.*

Jackson's boots sounded on the steps, a welcome distraction from her unsuccessful task. "What did the vet say?"

"The tendon is going to need rest, daily wrapping with medication, and limited turn out. Guess he can stay in the paddock. Will you have time to tend to him in the mornings?"

What can I say? "Of course. Is everything I need at hand?" *He would do this for me if it was school time. .I'll just have to get up earlier. Trail clearing's going to be at dawn, anyway.*

Jackson sat down at the table and looked at the map. "Looks like you all have been busy today."

"Well, we've got a start. Cassie needs to check it out. She hasn't even been in the forest yet. Guess the most important things are the water crossings and if there are any endangered plants or whatever where we want to go. We're kind'a limited by the terrain, too."

Jackson looked up from the map. "Cassie? That's the ranger?"

"Yep, she seems to be on board about the ride, as long as we don't cause any trouble. We're going to her office tomorrow with what you see there. You've ridden these trails enough to know if there are any apparent issues, being that you're environmental lawyer."

Jackson took another look at the map and the proposed trails. "Actually, when I get out in the forest with you, my job is to stay topside on the horse and manage Silver's pace. I am interested the ranger's evaluation of this area. This environment is not like Wyoming, for sure." He moved Moria's copy of the maps aside and smiled as she dished up their meal.

Moria brought their plates to the table, her concoction from the crock pot. *Thank goodness Jackson isn't choosy about his food.*

"Well, nothing stood out. We'll see what the Ranger says."

Later, as the couple sat on the porch swing, the nightly ending to their day, Moria said, "I've got a surprise for you."

Jackson laughed, "On the porch? Seems like we tried that once. If I remember, it didn't end well."

She smiled, "This will end well, I promise."

"Surprise." Moria grinned, handing Jackson a glass of Long Island tea. He sighed as he took a sip. "What do you want, Missy? I'm all yours."

"Just you," she whispered and leaned against his shoulder as Jackson pushed the swing and rocked her to sleep.

Sometime later he gave Moria a little shake. "Hey, Missy. You're asleep and so is my arm. "Reckon we can make it to bed? We've both had a long day."

She awoke with a start and groaned. "Too much sweet tea."

Chapter Nine

M oria reached for her sunglasses as she drove to the Forest Service Office the next afternoon. "Man, the sun seems extra bright."

Just then, her cell phone rang. "What?" she asked, hearing Maxine's voice.

"We've got company at Cassie's office. Jada called. Wanted to know what we were doing and if it was something she could film. Stupid me. I told her we were going to the Ranger Station. So, we're going to be movie stars today. I don't know how this will sit with Cassie. I'll give her a call."

Moria clicked the phone off and threw it on the seat. "Just what we need," she growled, pulling down the visor to check her lipstick. "I should'a done a better job on my face." Then, she grazed her hand over the maps on the passenger seat. "Never mind. It's all about you."

As she went up the steps to the Forest Service building, she could hear Jada's strident voice through the open window. "Now y'all sit here and look busy … no, wait. Go to the door and greet each other. Smile and look friendly. No, look uncertain."

At the reception desk Fran rolled her eyes, nodded toward Cassie's office and said, "Rescue nine-one-one."

Moria opened the door to a chaotic scene. Maxine had planted herself in the middle of the room, hands on hips and a frown to match her stance. Cassie sat behind her desk with annoyance mirrored on her face. Jada stood on the coffee table, camera in one hand, the other hand pointing to the window blinds.

"Open the blinds. We need more light." Jada instructed Moria as she entered the room.

Dear Jesus, don't let me hurt this woman. "Jada, get down. Stop this nonsense."

Jada froze at Moria's orders. "Who's in charge here?"

"Not you. Sit." Turning to Cassie, she said, "Sorry for the distraction."

Maxine glared at Jada. "You need to leave."

Cassie stood up from behind her desk. *So, this is what it's like living the South? No wonder Kam left.* "Okay, folks, let's not waste our time." Ignoring Jada, Cassie continued, "Moria, Maxine, what do you need? Jada got here first and said she is making a film about putting on an endurance ride. Maxine came in, Jada started bossing us around and you arrived." She frowned. "I don't need this. If she," nodding toward Jada, "comes with the package, we're done."

Chastened by her failure, Jada displayed a puppy dog face and gazed up at Cassie, saying, "I'm so sorry. Please forgive me. I'm just so excited about the ride."

Cassie's stern voice got Jada's attention. "There's not a ride, yet." Then looking at Moria, who held the maps, she continued, "Let's see what you've got."

In a meek voice, Moria had never heard before, Jada asked, "Can I stand in the corner and film?"

Cassie said, "Fine with me. I need to review your film before you leave. Okay with you, girls?"

"It's up to you," Moria replied, ignoring Jada's presence.

Cassie cleared a long table and Moria spread out the maps. "Thank goodness you know something about endurance riding. You'll probably have some suggestions we haven't thought about."

The ranger began to study the map and the red and blue lines. "What are your biggest concerns? At least you have a camping place and no away vet checks." She continued to trace the lines on the map and study them intently as silence filed the room.

Jada blurted out, "Say something."

Cassie walked to the door, opened it and stood aside. She motioned for Jada to leave. "Thanks for your dedication to this endeavor. Wait in the lobby. I want to see your film before you leave." Speechless, Jada marched out the door.

Then, as if nothing had happened, Cassie said, "Your concerns?"

Taken aback, Maxine grinned, "Maybe you should manage the ride."

"Not on your life," Cassie replied with vigor.

"Okay, our concerns," Maxine continued, "we don't want to trample over or cut any endangered plants and we have two water crossings. We want to know pretty soon about these possible issues."

Moria added, "We need to get as close as we can on the trail's distance measurements. Maxine has a GPS but needs some help with it."

Cassie reached on the shelf behind her, retrieved the official manual regarding endangered or threatened plants and animals and began to flip through it.

"Looks like this information is up-to-date, as far as I can tell." She continued to scan the pages. "I need to study your maps some more to be sure we don't miss anything. About the GPS. I have one too, just haven't needed to use it. Maybe we can learn together," and smiled at Maxine. "Leave the maps with me and I'll get on this right away. I'll call you in a day or two. If we're done here, I need to get to my Jada task. God bless you. I need to borrow your friend's horse and ride with you all soon."

"Looking forward to it," Maxine said as she and Moria walked quickly through the lobby.

"Talk to you later." Moria waved goodbye to Jada as if nothing had happened.

The two women walked to their trucks and looked at each other in shock. Moria threw her hands up saying, "Well, what now?" They perched on the tail gates of their trucks to rethink the ride situation amidst the swirling uncertainty of Jada's constant interference. Heat and humidity pressed down on them, a blanket of discouragement.

Maxine wiped her sweaty face on her sleeve. "We're at the last ditch to abandon the cause. Once Cassie agrees about the trail and we already know Jada has a ride date, there's no turning back. Maybe Cassie will nix the filming. She knows it will be a problem."

Jada opened the office door and came down the steps toward them. "I see y'all are lying in wait for me. Cassie said the film from today would do. Just needed some editing to make it more professional. I know that. She needs to see all filming done on Forest Service property before it's approved for use. So, what's next?" She flashed the women a faux smile and waited for an answer.

What's next? Run away, run away. Gathering her teacher wits, Moria said, "We need to have the volunteers meet at your house as soon as we hear from Cassie. I think it's going to be approved."

As Jada drove away, Maxine squinted up at the cloudless sky. "Hey, Up There, we could really use some help. We'll take good care of your property because we cherish what you provide for us. Just sayin'. Amen."

Moria gave Maxine a startled look. "Was that a real prayer or were you being a smart ass?"

"Missy, I'm betting we're all going to be on our knees before this is done. You might want to put in your two-cent's worth."

"Now?"

Maxine smiled. "No, just when it comes to you. Think about it."

Not knowing if her friend was serious or not, Moria took Maxine's words to heart.

~ ~ ~

When Moria turned into Peace in the Valley Farm she noticed Jackson's truck was already there. Running a mental short list of what food was available for the evening meal, she thought, *sometimes we have breakfast at dinnertime. Maybe that would work.* "Hey, you're home early."

Jackson looked at his watch. "No, Missy, You're late. What's for dinner?"

"Bacon and eggs?"

"No, I was hungry for some barbecue and all the fixin's from The Diner. It's all here. Horses are fed and I tended to Patches and Ringo. We can have a late lunch or an early dinner."

Dear God, Thank you for sharing this human with me. He is a blessing, or am I just lucky? I will treasure him forever. Amen.

At the table Moria relayed the day's happenings with Jada and watched Jackson's face as she unraveled the latest events. By now, he had stopped eating, caught up in the drama.

Moria stopped for breath and Jackson winked at her saying, "Well, bless her heart. What's your plan, Missy?"

Moria pushed the food around on her plate making a question mark in the barbecue sauce. "We're waiting to hear from Cassie if the trail layout is okay. She wants to ride out with us soon. Do you think she could ride Silver?"

"I don't want her to get hurt. Do you know her riding background?"

Moria said. "She rode Tevis last year. I think she can handle Silver, although he can get scrappy at times." She watched Jackson's face change from unsure to surprise. "Or she could ride one of Rodney's horses."

Jackson frowned and said, "What would I ride? You seem to be the wrangler, here."

Realizing she was in deep water, she answered, "I meant if you were at work," and paused.

"Get her set up to ride with Rodney first. She's going to need to be observant about her new workplace, the forest, especially if she hasn't been out there, yet. Riding Silver would take all her attention."

"You've got a good point."

"What? You're not going to argue with me? Saints preserve us. What do you want?"

"Some ice cream from Merry's." Moria said, dangling the truck keys in front of his face.

"We're going to town?"

Before long, the couple occupied a bench outside the ice cream shop. Moria licked her strawberry cone and held it up to Jackson's orange sherbet. Laughing, she said, "To quote Jada, 'a toast to the Cherry Valley Ride.' And to quote Maxine, 'may we all finish and one of us wins.'"

And to quote Jackson, he said, touching his cone to hers, "Don't let this cost us anything but time."

"Hey, here comes Cassie. You'll get to meet her." Moria waved the Ranger over. Jackson stood as she introduced them. "Cassie, I'd like you to meet my husband, Jackson Durant. Jackson, meet Cassie …" Stricken, Moria said, "Oh, I don't even remember your last name. My mom would kill me."

Cassie smiled as if nothing were amiss and shook hands with Jackson. "Cassie Levant. Glad to meet you, Jackson. Looks like we all had the same idea," she said, opening the door to the ice cream shop. "Be back in a minute."

When Cassie returned, the couple moved over on the bench and she sat beside Moria, beginning to lick her mint chocolate cone. "I'm really liking this town, so far. Have you all lived here long?"

Jackson looked at Moria with a *you tell her look*. So, she gave the short version: Growing up in Cherry Valley and living on one of the few original land grants left in the state, Jackson's arrival from Wyoming to open an office as an environmental attorney, and concluded, "Last year we were married." She smiled, "And you know where we live."

Jackson added, "I hear you're from California and lay claim to riding the famous Tevis trail."

"Yeah, that's probably what'll be on my gravestone," she laughed.

Cassie had licked her ice cream down to a safe level. "Moria, I was going to call you in the morning with the good news, so far. I signed the permit for the quadrants of the forest you all want to use. After you left, I called Kam and he said he didn't have any issues in those areas, to speak of." She paused, then added with a grin, "He did say those endurance riders bear watching."

Moria flinched at Kam's warning. *Never mind, you were a bunch of trouble yourself.* "Don't worry, we want the ride to be a success. We'll keep you posted on our progress and if we see anything unusual."

Jackson turned to Cassie, "You and Kam know each other?"

"Yeah, we traded jobs. We used to work together in California. He wanted a change and moved here, but the South turned out to be a little too much for him. The Forest Service didn't mind if he went back to his old job and I came here, but we had to pay for our moves since it was our idea."

Dusk settled over the town as lights came on in some of the shops. Streetlights through the trees cast shadows on people walking around, enjoying the cool evening and letting children play in the park.

The three became silent, each with their own thoughts for a moment, then Cassie said, "I'd better get some sleep. Looks like I'm going to have some work to do," and smiled at Moria.

Jackson stood and said, "Nice to meet you, Cassie. No doubt our paths will cross again. Thanks for your support concerning the ride."

Cassie grinned, "Nice to meet you, too. Just remember, it ain't over till it's over."

On the way home Jackson commented, "Cassie seems pretty easy to get along with, so far."

"Easier than Kam, for sure. He was so bossy."

"Yeah, well, I'm thinking about being bossy in bed. Let's see how that works."

Jackson closed the door in Pounce's face. "Goodnight to you, Mister."

Chapter Ten

A pink and gold sunrise ushered in the day, but made no promise about events to follow. Moria sat on the porch with her coffee, and the furry tribe waited for breakfast, as she relayed the good news about the trails to Maxine.

In response, Maxine said, "Guess we'd better get Jada in the loop and have her start contacting some volunteers. Maybe they'll think it's worth putting up with her imaginative life in order to have the ride. Why don't we check out the trails this morning? We know life always looks better from the back of a horse. I'll call Jada with the news. Maybe Rodney's crew would like to go out with us. Do you think we can depend on Jada to round up some people?" Then, answered her own question. "She can be pretty persuasive when it's going to benefit her."

"Okay, you deal with Jada and I'll call Rodney. I need to take care of the horses and doctor Patches. Why don't we meet at Rodney's house about ten if they're going with us?"

"Pack your patience, Missy. Later."

As Moria approached Rodney's farm she could see Maxine had already arrived and was at work holding Mousey's pony while the youngster mounted. The child's face, one of concentration, biting her lip, grabbing the mane and reins in one hand and back of the saddle with the other, then settling into the saddle with a sigh of relief. "You can let go," she announced to Maxine. "I'm good." She gave a bright smile, gathered the reins and slid her feet into the stirrups.

Moria welcomed the child's air of confidence once she was mounted. *Guess life does look better from the back of a horse.*

Sassy, already astride her Mustang, waved, tightened her helmet strap and called to Moria, "To finish is to win."

"Sounds like you all have been studying up on your adventure."

"Miss Rita found a lot of information about endurance riding on the internet and Rodney has some books. We're going to win the ride."

Okay, here we go. "Have you all been conditioning?"

"Well, today we're off restriction for the incident with Mr. Jackson. Miss Rita and Mr. Rodney said they would help us." Her hopeful look washed away the usual know it all attitude as she announced, "Let's hit the trail," and turned her pony toward the hills.

Moria and Maxine looked at each other with *you gotta be kidding looks* and then at Rita, mounted on a Buckskin Quarter horse.

She shrugged, "Kids! Come on, Dillon, let's go," and turned to Rodney for instructions.

Maxine returned to Catch On Fire and Rodney brought his Appaloosa mare from the barn, asking, "Where to, ladies?"

"Why don't we do the red loop? It's the shortest, and a good conditioning ride for starters," Moria suggested.

Calling Sassy back, Rodney gave the girls a no-nonsense look. "Pay attention to these ladies," nodding toward Moria and Maxine. "They'll help you with conditioning and whatever else you need to know."

"Yes sir," the girls answered in unison, and waited for further instructions.

The group headed out Rodney's driveway and turned left on the road toward the trail. Maxine led, Rodney next, then Rita and the girls just ahead of Moria. The horses' hoof beats on the road, bird cries and wind through the trees seemed to be the only sounds in the forest.

This is weird. "Hey, it's alright to talk," Moria called out.

Rodney motioned Rita and the girls to come near him. "Once upon a time …," he began, "Indians lived all around here. Just Indians." The girls inched their ponies closer.

Sassy looked into the forest. "Where are they now?" she asked, as if expecting an Indian brave to step out of the bushes around the next corner.

Rodney replied, "Wal, I guess you haven't gotten to that part in your studies. Anyway, all I know is that they were here. They came from somewhere. Look it up. Mostly, they lived peaceful-like. Sometimes they fought over hunting grounds but that was about it."

"So, where are they now?" Sassy repeated.

Wal, all good things must come to an end. The settlers arrived and began to take over the Indians' lands. There was terrible battles and finally …," he paused. "They was sent out West to live on Reservations."

"Like at the zoo?"

"Yeah, sorta. Miss Rita, here's some lessons for your kids."

By now, Mousey had tears on her cheeks. "I hate the settlers."

"Wal, cowgirlie, them settlers was our people."

Mousey sniffed and rubbed her eyes, leaving dirty streaks across her face and did not answer.

Moria called to Maxine, "Let's stop at the end of the road by the gate."
What to say? It is true, but we need to put a different spin on this.

The wind blew through the pines as if to say, *there is no other spin.*

The riders stopped at the gate and Moria said, "Okay girls, yes, Mr. Rodney told the story straight. In today's world we wish it had been different. We can only learn and try not to make the same mistakes again. Life's lessons can be hard. This is one of them. Just try to do some good in the world as you grow up."

Sassy, grinned, "You sound like a teacher, just saying."

"We're Girl Scouts. Sometimes we help people," Mousey added.

Moria gave Mousey a thumbs up and said, "There you go. Keep up the good work. Let's ride. Time to trot."

Maxine dropped back beside Rodney and said under her breath, "Enough lessons for today and you might want to skip the part about plantations. Maybe let Rita handle that."

Rodney laughed, "You don't like my stories? I say tell it like it is, and you should, too."

Maxine picked up the pace, saying, "When I come to that page with my fourth graders, I'll invite you to be the guest speaker."

"Does it pay well?" he asked in a serious tone.

Maxine laughed, "You better stick to summer visitors."

The riders had reached the first climb. Moria called a halt. "Okay, when you climb you need to help your horse so he won't get sore. Get up out of your saddle, off his back. You can hold on to the mane if you need to, be sure your heels are down, tighten your legs, give your horse enough rein to work, just steady him. Questions?"

No one spoke. Moria called to Maxine, "Lead on." She watched the two youngsters do as they were told and with excellent balance. *Must have had good instructors. They've done this before. Maybe learning to jump?*

"Looking good, girls. Glad you've had some riding experience," Moria called to Sassy and Mousey.

Single file, the riders wove back and forth, up the steep switchbacks to the ridge. At the top they paused to let the horses recover for a moment and Moria said, "Let's walk a couple of minutes before we trot again. Next time, you can learn to check pulses. Remember, if your horse's pulse doesn't come down in the allowed time at the vet check, you're done for that day."

"So, we can't finish the ride on our own?" Sassy asked.

"Absolutely not," Maxine chimed in. "Even if you're at an away vet check, you're trailered back to camp. Not an option. Tend to your horse and save him for another day." Several minutes passed during the resting walk as Maxine continued, "The footing's good on this ridge for an extended trot. Don't push your horse into a canter right now. We're working for a steady pace. There's a couple of sayings to remember, 'trot when you can; walk when you have to,' and 'trot in the sun; walk in the shade.'" She waved to Moria, "Let's trade. You lead a while." Then turned to the others, "It's good for the horses, and riders to take turns leading."

The two riders swapped places and the group moved across the ridge at a trot. A summer breeze blew through the pines and hardwoods. Moria looked across the valley as cloud shadows travelled over the land. The beauty of this familiar world would always be a part of her heart. "Oh, beautiful for spacious skies, for amber waves of grain," she began to sing. As if on cue, the others joined in, "For purple mountains majesty above the fruited plain."

They reached the creek by the old covered bridge and Moria instructed, "Okay, guys, spread out and let your horses drink. I see Rodney had provided you all with sponges. Be sure and drop your sponge to the side of the horse where the water is flowing away from you, so you don't get the string wrapped around your horse's leg." Moria laughed as she dropped her sponge in the water, "That's called a creek wreck."

Rita caught on right away, able to take care of her horse, Dillon with no trouble. "Man, there's a lot more to endurance riding than I thought. Glad we're doing this ride today. We've just been cruising around different places letting the girls get used to their ponies."

Moria tied her sponge back to the saddle saying, "Lucky for you, you're going to be doing most of your training on the actual trail for the ride, unless Rodney trailers you all off somewhere else for practice."

Rita shook her head, "No, we're staying close to home. Besides, the girls are in a summer reading program, we have chores to do for Rodney and they have the full care of their ponies."

Mousey had wandered a distance downstream looking around, off in her own world. "Hey, Mr. Rodney, come look at these animal tracks. What kind are they?"

Rodney, Moria and Maxine looked at each other. Somehow, they already knew, the bear had not left the premises.

The grizzled cowboy splashed his horse toward Mousey and stopped beside her, looking at the muddy bank.

"Wal, them's bear tracks."

Mousey wheeled her pony around as fast as she could, impeded by the water. She shrieked, "Is there going to be a bear in the ride?"

"Calm down, young'un." Rodney reached down and grabbed one of her reins. Mousey flew forward, clinging to the pony's neck. "You need to straighten up here and be a real cowgirl," he said, looking to the others for help. They smiled and waved.

Mousey's voice quivered as she asked," I have to ride with bears to be a real cowgirl?"

Rodney laughed, letting her rein go, "Yeah, yeah you do, sometimes. Don't worry, we'll give you some bear training before the ride."

Mousey and Rodney splashed back up stream. The youngster called to the group as they approached, "Mr. Rodney's giving us bear lessons before the ride." She looked over her shoulder at Rodney, "Will there be a test?"

In his most serious tone, he answered, "Only if the bear shows up."

The adults tried to keep straight faces as the two returned. Sassy, taking her cue from the others, said, "We'll cross that bridge when we come to it. Let's ride," then turned her pony out of the creek.

"Sassy, why don't you lead for a while? We've got one more climb and then we'll come out on a straight-a-way past the saddle club. It is a two-lane dirt road. Let's see what you've learned.

The young rider saluted and said, "Heels down. We're moving on."

Rodney followed, next Rita and Mousey, then Moria and Maxine. As they scrambled up the single track, Moria turned to Maxine, "Are your heels down? I think we've unleashed a couple of mini endurance riders. I hope we can keep up with them."

As the riders reached the dirt road, Maxine answered, "Here's the test. Let's see if she can keep the pace."

Sassy never looked back and trotted down the road for a couple of miles. She stopped, turned to face the arriving riders and said, "Good job. Y'all, keeping the pace. What now?"

Moria scrambled to keep ahead of Sassy's take charge attitude. *Could be worse. She could be whining and wanting to go home.* "Just shortly, we're going to reach another creek. The water is swift there, so pay attention. We need to cool the horses again. Remember about your sponge string. Well done, Sassy."

The young rider wiped sweat from her forehead. "Can we tie the horses up and get in the creek?"

"Not now," Moria answered, as if this was not an unexpected question. "There will be times and places when you ride in the heat that you might do that. Not today. If you got in the creek during a ride, guess what? You'd be left behind. Believe me, no one would wait on you."

Maxine volunteered to lead again, saying, "This next part of the trail is tricky. Some parts are washed out. There are places where we can trot but walk in the rough spots. This could be a make or break stretch on your ride. Lucky for you guys, you can come out here and practice."

Rita checked her watch. "We've only been out here a couple of hours, seems longer. Maybe it's just the heat," she said, reaching for her water bottle. "Guess we're gonna have to get used to it. Maybe we can do our rides earlier in the day. At least we know one of the trails."

"The hard part is going to be the fifteen-mile loop. At least, we think that's the mileage. The powerline will be okay," Maxine answered. "There's an overgrown kudzu trail and some rough terrain to work on. Then, there's the old grouchy farm guy who won't let us use his property."

Rodney laughed, "Yeah, ole Pete. Better leave him alone."

Moria said, "Okay, we'll work something out." As the riders traversed the gullies, Moria thought out loud about possibilities to improve this section of the trail. "You know somebody with the right machine could fix this but if they didn't know what they were doing, it could end up worse. We can ask Cassie, but I don't think there's any money set aside for this area since it's not a designated horse trail."

"I agree," Maxine said, looking at the steep banks above them and the drop off below. "We couldn't tie the Red Trail into the Blue Trail because it would put too many twenty-five milers and fifty milers, coming and going. Well, this section and the old logging road are the only hard parts." She laughed, "Besides we want this to be a ride to remember."

The riders reached the Rutherford's Road and continued to the intersection where the trail turned right to Rodney's or left to Moria's. "Thanks for the ride today," Rita said with a tired smile. "Rodney said there are some other places we can ride, too, not connected to your trails."

"Keep up the good work," Moria answered. "You all did great today. We'll go out again soon to do some more planning."

The two endurance riders continued on and Maxine said, "Come in for lunch and we can figure what to do next."

"Sounds good. You probably have something better than wilted lettuce and soft tomatoes. Thanks."

The cool aisle of the barn welcomed the riders as they untacked, hosed the horses and turned them out to graze. "Glad our critters know each other," Moria commented as Rainbow Chaser and Arctic Cat did a little dance around each other, huffed, pawed and then raced away after Catch On Fire.

Settled at the table with chicken sandwiches, chips, watermelon and Cokes, Maxine said, "Well, what do you think?"

"I think we should have gone on a cruise this summer," Moria answered in all seriousness.

Startled, Maxine said, "Huh?"

Moria laughed, "Or else we should have sent Jada on the cruise and we could be having peace in the valley. Where was she this morning?"

"I hope rounding up volunteers." Maxine picked up the phone and dialed Jada's number. After the short conversation she got the answer. "Actually, she got in touch with a few people and they'll be at her house in the morning. That's a miracle. Let's hope she doesn't run them off again. Why don't we take our map and see if we can get some commitments for sections of trail work?"

"Good idea," Moria answered, setting her glass in the sink. "What we really need are individual maps for the workers. Let's take a few minutes and sketch a rough draft with landmarks so each person can keep up with what they're doing?" The two women got into teacher mode and within an hour accomplished their task. "Next time out, let's you and me go back to the Logging Road and take another look. We've just got to find a way to connect this part of the trail. Pete's farm is at the bottom of a bluff on one side and bordered by a ravine and creek on the other. There's only a small place to put our trail. We need to keep looking."

Moria brought Rainbow in from the pasture saying to him, "You are a mess, at least the dirt's dried on you."

"Maxine, I need to borrow a brush before I can saddle this joker."

Moria headed home, waving to Maxine, "See you tomorrow. Don't forget the maps."

Hero and Dixie met the horse and rider in the driveway with joyful barks and leaps. Rainbow lifted his hind leg and gave warning kick. Pounce and Pandora sat on the porch swing watching the antics. *What a waste of energy, dingbat dogs,* Pounce growled.

At least she came home. It's dinner time Pandora meowed and headed for the back door.

By the time Jackson arrived, Moria had finished the barn work, taken care of the horses and dinner was on the table.

Jackson did a double take as he looked at the table holding a pot roast, green bean casserole, corn and potatoes. Moria poured tea as if this were an everyday offering.

"Well, Missy, what do you want?" Jackson grinned, taking her in his arms.

"I've always heard, the way to a man's heart … she smiled, melting into his closeness. "Let's eat. I've got a lot to tell you."

After hearing the events of the day, Jackson moved over to the couch. "Come on, never mind the dishes," and beckoned to her, propping his feet on the coffee table.

Pounce purred, jumped up and stretched out on the back of the couch behind Jackson's neck.

Pandora took her place in Moria's lap and the cats settled down for the mouth noises.

Her tale of the day held Jackson's attention. His only comment, "I don't see how this business is going to come together by September unless you get some more help. Jeremy and I have some weekend time to do some of the heavy work, and we're planning to take off the week of the ride. What about you and Maxine? You all will be back in school before you know it."

Moria leaned back in the crook of Jackson's arm. "We're going back to Jada's in the morning. Sounds like she's rounded up her minions again. Also, I'm thinking that the bridge needs to be repaired before the ride. If the creek gets too high there'll be no way to do that loop."

Jackson tensed and sat forward, disturbing Moria, and Pounce jumped to the floor.

"Look here, Missy, the bridge repair is going to take some manpower. Jeremy and I took a look at it the other day. You need qualified people to do the work. Then it will be inspected by the grant donors, which, I believe is the State. You need to be thinking about an alternate crossing."

"Or maybe some of the volunteers would rather work on the bridge. If we can get the floor done and secure the roof for the time being, would that work? You and Jeremy could oversee and order supplies."

Jackson frowned, "We'll see."

Moria put her face in her hands, "I wish we'd never started this. It's all Jada's fault." Pandora slid from Moria's lap to the floor and whined, *get over yourself, Missy.*

Jackson took Moria's hands and brought her to her feet saying "Remember you need to know when to hold, know when to fold and... know when to walk away. Your choice." He held her hands as she faced him. "I know you better than this. You're not walking away. You better put your boots on." With those words he took his cowgirl in his arms and held her close.

"Thanks, mister, I love you." *but I'm going to check this out with Cassie and get her thoughts* "Follow me, I've saved the best for last."

The bedroom door closed and the gray and yellow flashes of fur headed to the kitchen and leapt onto the counter. *She forgot to do the dishes.* Pounce's elated yowl echoed through the house, but only the yellow one heard as they settled down to a fine plate lickin'.

Chapter Eleven

ada stood at her front door welcoming everyone and ushering them into the family room. When Moria and Maxine came up the steps, she smiled, saying, "Glad you all could make it," as if no sparks had flown and she had ripped the unpleasant pages out of the story. "Looks like it might rain so I've set up inside."

The comfortable family room seemed to put people at ease. Couches and chairs were occupied by some, and a few people sat on the floor. Richard leaned on his desk in the corner, unobtrusive, but ever watchful.

Moria whispered to Maxine, "Let's be quiet and see how this goes." Maxine nodded in agreement as they, too, settled on the floor.

Jada stood in front of the fireplace, facing the group. "Thank you all for having the courage to return so we can move forward with plans for the Cherry Valley Ride." A few chuckles drifted across the room. "Some of you know, I'm planning to make a movie about our journey in this exciting adventure. I have release forms for each of you to sign saying that you agree to be filmed and will not receive any compensation from this project. Also, the Forest Service requires a release. Questions?"

One of the riders from the saddle club raised her hand. "Are you planning to sell the movie? Who would buy it?"

Apparently expecting this question, Jada waved a piece of paper that appeared to be a list. "We've," nodding toward Richard, "approached some ride managers and endurance clubs who are interested but want to see the finished product. They can possibly use it for their own purposes when putting on rides and clinics." The lady nodded her head as if she agreed.

Richard handed Jada a small pack of papers that appeared to be Monopoly money. She held them up and with her bright, enticing smile. "Guess what these are?"

Maxine whispered to Moria, "Oh, crap. I know what she's going to do. It's too late to stop her."

The volunteers, intrigued by Jada's spiel, waited for her answer. "These are rider bucks."

The riders looked confused. One questioned, "I thought you weren't going to pay us?"

"Well, there's pay and there's *pay*. We will keep up with the hours you work on the trail or related jobs. You will receive bucks to put toward your ride entry."

"What if we don't ride? What can we do with the bucks?"

Jada gave a big grin, "Wait until the day of the ride and you'll see."

The volunteer frowned, "Best you tell us now. I don't mind working, but I might not ride." Others in the group waited for an answer.

Jada fanned herself with the rider bucks, deciding what to say. "Okay, you can spend your bucks with the vendors or for food. How's that?"

"Works for me," the volunteer answered.

A puzzled voice from the back of the group asked, "How's the ride gonna pay for itself if we have the rider bucks?"

Jada looked at Richard for an official answer. He stood up, smiled and said, "Your rider bucks will probably not pay for your whole entry. Remember, we'll have entries from people who are not helping with the ride and they'll pay the full amount. Also, vendors will sign up and they will pay for space."

Moria could almost read Richard's mind. *And I'll pay for the rest.*

"Whatever you say. Glad I'm not the manager, but I'm willing to work."

Jada looked at her notes then at Moria and Maxine. "Now, I'm going to turn the meeting over to the trail ladies."

The two women took Jada's place and held up the maps. Moria began, "Rodney's actually the trail boss. We're just helping with the map work. We've visited the Forest Ranger and have a trail approved unless something shows up out there that we're not expecting. Riders will be camping in my pasture. The ride will be two loops, both returning to camp, with no away vet checks." A sign of relief coursed through the group. "We've brought some sketches for you to keep. This way you can write on them as needed, make notes or whatever. This is not written in stone. You'll probably have some suggestions once you get in the woods. You'll get updated copies as we finalize the route."

"Yes, teacher," one of the group teased, knowing that these ladies would always have a plan and be one step ahead. Many of their children had attended fourth grade classes at Cherry Valley Elementary, so these parents and the two teachers were well-acquainted, for better or worse.

Maxine handed out the maps and Moria continued, "Most of what we have to do, the trail clearing, is easy." Laughter followed her statement. "Well, compared to working on the trail tread," she smiled, "but it all has to be done. Remember, the trail needs to be traversed in the six or twelve hour time at a reasonable pace. Take a look at your maps. We've made notes and divided the trail into sections. Choose a section and maybe some of you can work together. Let Rodney know what you decide. Your work hours will be on the honor system and you can call or email Jada so she can keep up with your hours and pay your rider bucks."

Jada gave Moria a wicked smile, and to the volunteers, her phone number.

Moria continued, "If you're not sure what to do, call Rodney and he'll help you get started. My advice, work in the early morning with plenty of water and bug spray." She paused, and glanced at her audience, assessing their interest in continuing the discussion.

One of the volunteers said, "You know, some of us work and don't have a summer vacation. We can only get out there on the weekends."

"We can get this done. Most of the trail is in decent shape. We're very pleased with the show of support for this event..."

Jada stopped Moria in mid-sentence, sensing that she was losing control and said, "Why don't you all come in the dining room for a snack and take a look at your maps. If possible, let us know what you think you can commit to before you leave today. Maybe get some groups together."

Glad for a break, everyone picked up some snacks, milled around, chatted and made plans. The pieces of the puzzle began to fall into place and Rodney started his list.

Moria and Maxine stood at a side table with the maps to answer questions.

"Do we have to bring our own tools?"

"Yes, if possible. We have some tools, if needed."

"How do we know where our section starts when we get in the woods?"

Moria and Maxine looked at each other and laughed, "Uh, we'll put up pie plates. It will take us a day to do this."

Moria pointed to Maxine saying, "Bright and early, we will scurry. I've got markers and plates. Bring a hammer and roofing nails and duct tape. Those will hold the plates better in the wind." No more questions surfaced, and the volunteers left. Only Jada, Richard, Rodney, Moria and Maxine remained.

Maxine looked at Rodney, "Well, what do you think?"

"Seems they're ready to work. Let's see what we got after their first day out. Might have to put the little cowgirlies out there near my house. Bet Rita didn't sign on for trail work. If y'all don't need me anymore, I'll go break the news to my helpers. See ya on the trail."

Maxine smiled at Jada, "And, you can travel with us while we put up the plates. Good way to start your movie."

Jada took a step back, "No, people have sent me pictures of the fireworks and I have to edit these for the beginning of the film."

Richard closed his laptop and stepped away from the desk, "No, go with the trail ladies."

His steely gaze apparently pierced Jada's thinking. She turned to Maxine, "Oh sure, this'll be fun. Tell me time and place." She waited for an answer.

Maxine looked at Moria, "My place? Seven?"

Moria and Jada nodded in agreement. "Bring water, bug spray and food. We may be out there a while."

By now, the two women were out the door. Moria carefully rolled up the maps, "Well, what do you think of that?"

Maxine grinned, "I think Richard's holding something over Jada's head. We don't care what, as long as it works. Why don't we go into town for lunch and get with Cassie about the bridge? The GPS thing is in my truck so we can check it out, too."

Moria followed Maxine into town, her mind already on tomorrow and marking the trail sections. As they arrived in town, Maxine put on her blinker and turned into the pool hall parking lot. Moria soon saw why.

Maxine parked beside Jackson's truck and got out, motioning to her friend. "Looks like we won't have to buy our lunches today. Lucky us." As they entered the pool hall, voices quieted, knowing who the teachers were. The two women waved at their cowboys and the guys motioned them over, pulling out their chairs. No sooner than they were seated, the waitress appeared and took their orders.

"Well, what a coincidence," Jackson said with mock surprise. "Looking for a free meal? It's gonna cost you." Jeremy nodded, winking at Maxine.

"Okay, dudes," Maxine replied, "we got it covered. We're just passing through and you two looked like customers hunting for a good time," she teased.

"Do we need to give you directions?" Jackson asked in a serious tone.

Moria laughed, "No problem. We've got a GPS."

Just as Jackson and Jeremy stood to leave, Pete entered the pool hall. Moria stared, glanced at Maxine, who nodded, *okay.*

Moria stepped away from the table, looked toward him and said, "Hi there Pete, good to see you again." The old codger squinted in the dim light and then recognized his errant visitors.

"Wal, shit, I don't need nothing to do with y'all," tipped his hat and attempted to pass.

Moria took another step, blocking his way, saying, "I just want you to meet our cowboys, Jackson and Jeremy."

Even Pete was gentleman enough to shake hands.

Jackson grinned as he shook Pete's hand, "You must be the mean old man on the mountain."

Pete glared at Moria and Maxine, saying to Jackson, "Yu better keep up with them cowgirls. They could get themselves in a pot of trouble."

Not able to resist, Jackson fueled the fire, saying, "Oh, you have pots of trouble on your farm? Sounds interesting. Maybe we can come visitin'."

Pete turned on his heel, barely avoiding Moria. "You sons o' bitches stay away from my private property!" He stalked away, found a table across the room and sat with his back to the aggravating cowgirls.

Jackson tapped Moria's shoulder. "Look at me. Don't mix it up with that ornery bugger. He's nothing but trouble. I don't want to be getting you out of jail for harassment."

Moria looked noncommittal but said, "I hear you," not quite meeting Jackson's eyes.

Knowing her friend well, Maxine asked, "What are you thinking? I have a feeling you're not giving up on that dude," looking in Pete's direction.

"Yeah, I think we need to talk to him here in the pool hall where it's safe."

"Look around, Missy. These folks would love to see you two go at it. Guess whose side they'd take? Not yours. No matter if you taught their kids. Trust me. Hurry up and eat. We need to get to Cassie's office."

Moria looked over her shoulder as they left. "Are you sure?"

"Come on, we've got more constructive things to do."

~ ~ ~

"Hey, glad to see you ladies," Ranger Cassie motioned toward the two comfortable vintage chairs near her desk and slid the rolling chair over near them. "You look like you all could use a drink. How about some water?"

"Oh yeah, water would be great," Maxine answered.

Cassie reached into the small fridge near the desk and handed the bottles to them. "Well, fill me in. You all look beat."

Moria took a breath. "I hardly know where to begin." The episode at the pool hall, still fresh on her mind, occupied a lot of her mental space.

Maxine, feeling her friend's distress, took over the conversation. "We just had an encounter with Pete, the old homestead guy who lives up on the mountain. Maybe we can talk about that in a minute and look at the maps again. Earlier today we went to another meeting at Jada's."

Cassie smiled, "And ..."

"Actually, it went better than expected. She managed to get the volunteers back and then some."

Maxine continued to relate the morning's events ending with, "She had it together and was reasonably pleasant. At least the volunteers didn't leave. We've got commitments to start the trail work and Rodney seems okay with the plan, so far. The problem is connecting that old logging road to the power line. If we're going to use that route, we need to get on it because it's going to need a lot of work."

Cassie nodded, "I know your time is getting short. Let's look at the maps again. Maybe we've missed something here. Sorry I haven't gotten out into the forest. I'd like to go soon."

Moria had recovered her wits enough to focus on the map. "This is the area where we need to make the connection," and traced her finger from the water crossing to the powerline giving Cassie a hopeful look.

The ranger studied the area for a minute, then said, "I wonder if this would work." She picked up a pencil and traced a line along the bluff at the edge of Pete's farm from the water crossing to the powerline. "Have you all ever been up here?"

"No, we haven't. Looks a little sketchy and dangerous," Moria answered.

They all three studied the maps and proceeded to mark trail possibilities. Cassie said, "Why don't we go up there tomorrow and take a look around?"

Maxine said, "I'll call Rodney. I'm sure he'll have a horse for you. By the way, I have my GPS in the car. Do you have time to help me with it? Maybe we can take it with us on our exploring trip."

"Sure. Go get it and we'll see if it's like mine."

"I have a question, too," Moria added, "about the grant to repair the bridge."

Cassie sat down at her desk and shuffled through some folders. "I was just looking at it the other day. Do you want a copy?"

"That would be great. I've never even seen it. What I want to know is, can volunteers do the repairs if they have building experience?"

"Well, let's get some copies here and see."

Maxine returned with the GPS to see Cassie and Moria studying a sheaf of papers. "The grant?"

"Yeah," Moria answered. I'll take it home and see what the restrictions are. Good luck, you two with the 'toy'. Don't forget to call Rodney. We can meet there in the morning. I don't think we should take Rita and the children on this excursion."

"Agreed," Maxine answered, lifting her shiny, new GPS out of its box.

On the way home, Moria stopped at The Diner to pick up dinner. *I want Jackson's mind to be stuffed with food so he can relax and help me with this.* The driveway into Peace in the Valley Farm welcomed her with the familiar scene, never changing … a comfort to the soul.

Jackson greeted her at the door. "You must have been busy since I saw you at lunch today. I've fed the critters. What have you brought us?" sniffing and opening bags and boxes.

"You'll see," she said, setting the table. "Come over and help your plate."

Moria waited until after dinner and she had cleared the table to say, "You weren't the greatest help at the pool hall today, annoying Pete. We need his help."

Jackson shoved his chair back and took hold of Moria's arm. "Sit down and listen. Stay away from Pete and his farm. There probably *are* pots of trouble up there and you don't need to get mixed up in his business."

Moria jumped up from the chair, "You're not going to tell me what to do. What's the matter with you? I thought you were on board about the ride." She began to pace the floor, then stopped in front of Jackson.

"Whoa, Missy, let's talk about this. I don't want to sleep in the barn tonight," he answered with a tentative grin.

"If you know there's pot up there, you need to tell the sheriff. He can get rid of Pete and then we can cross the property," Moria snapped.

Jackson slapped his forehead and flung his arms out, "Not gonna happen. He's a smart dude. Right now, he's just minding his own business, which you need to stay out of. You've grown up here. You know people do stuff they shouldn't. What about your school kids? How many times have you come home telling me about some suspected situation going on with one of the families, but you looked the other way? What about you and Maxine trespassing on private land because it was convenient? If the Feds took over Pete's property, it could be tied up in court for who knows how long, and you sure couldn't cross it then."

Tears slid down Moria's cheeks. She sniffed and reached for a paper towel to blow her nose.

"Come here, honey." Jackson walked over to his cowgirl and held her close. "I don't want anything to happen to you, us, our friends or the horses …

"What do you mean?" leaning into Jackson's strength and looking into his worried face.

"Couch time, let's write an end to this chapter."

Deciding the fireworks were over, Pounce and Pandora crept from under the table. Pounce's frazzled gray fur stood up on his body as he lashed his tail. Pandora tapped him on the head, *Watch yourself or we're going to spend the night outdoors,* she cautioned. Pounce growled and settled in his usual place on the back of the couch behind Jackson.

Pandora took a chance and jumped in Moria's lap. "Oh, here's my therapy cat, on twenty-four hour call," and scooped Pandora into her arms. Turning to Jackson, she took a ragged breath, "Okay, I know you're right. Maxine and I joked about being buried in the forest by Pete and his cohorts if we got in the way of their business."

Jackson put his arm around Moria. "It's no joke. You know, we see stuff like that on the news every night. It always happens to someone else. I don't want to be on the news, all distraught, because you did …

"Something stupid?" she finished.

"Even in Cherry Valley people can get killed and don't go home at the end of the day. Remember, this is not a TV show. Pete may seem just like a grouchy old man, but word around town is, he's mean as hell."

By now, Moria and Pandora were both in Jackson's lap. "So, what do you think we should do?"

"I know you've got to connect the trail some way. Why don't you all take a few more days to ride around that area? You may see something you hadn't noticed."

"Maxine, Cassie and I are going up on the bluff above Pete's farm tomorrow and check it out. We don't think it'll change the mileage, but it will be slow going and not too safe. Before you ask, no, Cassie's not riding Silver. She's using one of Rodney's horses."

Jackson smiled, "Good girl. Come on, you and the spoiled cats, let's go to bed. I think we're plum wore out today."

The cats trotted down the hall behind their people. *No rodeo tonight.*

Chapter Twelve

At breakfast Jackson said, "At least I know where you're going today. Be sure and have your phone with you. You'll probably have service since you'll be on the bluff. Call me when you get home."

"Here, have some more coffee," Moria poured into both their cups and looked into Jackson's dark eyes. "Thank you for last night. I know what you said is true. I just wanted to believe nothing would happen to me. I love you and our life. Nothing is worth doing damage to us or our friends."

"Okay, just remember that when you all are out there romping around in the wilderness."

She nodded.

Jackson held up his little finger. "Pinky promise?"

"You rascal," she laughed, locking her little finger to his. "Get outta here."

Later at the barn Moria cared for the horses, then put Rainbow in the crossties. "Okay, buddy, we've got to go to work today."

The chestnut stomped his foot and shook his head.

"So, what does that mean?" Moria laughed. "Get the fly spray, or I hear you, or it's too hot to work?" Then she saddled up and headed to Rodney's.

Sassy greeted Moria at the driveway and asked with her most pleading, respectful look. "Hey, Miss Moria, can we go with y'all today?"

"What did Maxine say?"

"She said it might be dangerous. Maybe another time."

"There's your answer. If it's safe and we decide to use it, you can go."

Sassy grinned, "Your voice is our command. Rodney said we're going to work on the ups and downs 'cause nobody will be there today. I can hardly remember when I had friends."

"This too shall pass," *for all of us.* "Before you know it, you'll be back in Atlanta, at school and with your friends like this never even happened. Keep your head down, mind Rita, and ride your ponies so you don't end up dead in a ditch somewhere."

Sassy frowned, "Yeah, there's that."

"Today you will, more than likely, cut back face branches. Rodney can tell us if there's any machine work we can do, that won't make it worse. It's a rough patch, for sure."

Moria winked at Sassy, gave a thumbs up and moved over to Maxine and Cassie. "Ready to ride, ladies?"

"Why don't we use the Rutherford's Road to the power line," Maxine suggested, "since it's going to be part of the plan, we need to see what work needs to be done on the piney woods trail, too."

As they meandered through the pines, Moria said, "We need to straighten this trail out and flag it well."

Cassie and Maxine adjusted their GPSs to the setting they hoped would be accurate to measure the distance and whatever else the mysterious gadgets would surprise them with. Cassie laughed, saying, "Don't forget to hit the home button, too, incase we get lost."

The riders traversed the powerline road at the trot. Moria glanced back at Cassie. "How are you doing? I know you haven't ridden in a while."

"At least, I'm able to use my own saddle. That makes a huge difference, especially on a strange horse." She reached down and petted the Appaloosa's neck."

"Rodney must really trust you. Timex is his horse."

As if on cue, a squirrel jumped onto the trail in front Cassie's horse. The mare swung a one-eighty. Cassie shortened the rein and brought her in full circle. Laughing, she said, "Guess Rodney wants to see if I can ride," then gathered Timex back together. "Wonder how that's going to look on the GPS?" and tightened the strap holding it to the saddle.

The bluff and Pete's farm appeared in the distance. As the panorama widened so did Moria's doubt about the decision to ride the bluff.

"Cassie, let's take a good look before we climb this thing. If you don't feel comfortable, just say so."

The riders stopped in the road and gazed up at the granite cliff looming over them, covered with scrub pines, weeds, and dust blowing in tiny whirlwinds. Cassie took a hard look at Moria. "I don't know you very well yet. It's your call. You and Maxine have ridden in this area all your life. I get the feeling you're a little spooked."

Moria returned the look, saying, "Just to let you know, I've seen visions in the woods near my farm more than one time. There's something about this area. I don't know … her voice trailed off into uncertainty.

Cassie looked at Maxine. "So?"

Maxine grinned, "I say we go for it. We might have the adventure of a lifetime."

Moria looked into the cloudless, sunny sky. *Dear Jesus, please walk with us on this journey*, gathered up the reins and said, "Let's ride!"

The horses' ears perked forward as the riders approached the edge of Pete's property. "Get a grip," Maxine cautioned, "he's got a couple of big dogs. Here they come. Move over to the far side of the road."

The dogs hit the fence running, but it held. The horses lurched forward to escape the danger. Pete came running toward the fence with a shotgun. "Oh, it's the damn cowgirls, again," he shouted.

They stood across the road and faced Pete. Moria glared at him. "Put your gun away. If you'd help us find a way around your farm, we'd mark it and be done with you, except for the ride day."

Pete pushed his hat back and scratched his head. "Where's y'all going?"

"Up on the bluff. Hopefully, we won't fall down on your farm."

He grinned, "Wal, have fun. Don't get caught by the soldiers."

"What?"

"Some say Yankee soldiers camped up there and buried some of their guys who got killed by us Rebs. They don't take very kindly to folks botherin' 'um."

Moria looked at Cassie and nodded her head as if to say, *Told you so. Ghosts.*

Pete peered through the fence at Cassie. "Ain't yu th' new ranger?"

"Yes, I am. You have a lovely farm," and took a long, hard look at the chicken houses. "Glad to meet you. Well, ladies, guess we'll be on our way," and turned her mare toward the power line road.

Moria and Maxine smiled at each other and followed Cassie, glad to have her in their corner.

The ranger stopped to study the terrain. "It's interesting how the powerline makes a turn here where the road stops. Guess they didn't want to drill through the rock. Let's go a little farther along the line and see if we can find a way to climb up."

The riders continued for about five minutes, looking into the under-growth for an opening onto the bluff. Large granite boulders lay along their route as if a giant had scattered them in thoughtless abandon. "Hey, look here." Maxine pointed to a gap between the boulders and a narrow game trail leading upward. "Want to try it?"

"Sure, if it gets too rough we can always turn around, or maybe not," Moria said, looking up through the pines crowding the trail. "Okay, who's got the bravest horse?"

"Not me," Cassie answered, and looked at Maxine. "Catch On Fire," she grinned. "We vote for her."

"Take a deep seat, dudes, here we go." Maxine turned her horse into the wilderness. Moria and Cassie followed close behind to give the horses courage to follow their leader.

The trail twisted in and out between the boulders and trees as the riders climbed with caution. Loose rocks scattered under the horses' feet as they scrambled for footing. Fire lurched forward and branches slapped Maxine's face. She pushed them aside, saying, "I don't see the newbies on this trail."

Timex climbed with zeal, as if on a mission. Cassie leaned forward, holding the mane and said, "If you ever want to train for the Tevis, this trail would be a good place to start."

Maxine looked over her shoulder to answer and Fire began to slide backward. Her rider urged the horse forward. The mare lunged, caught her footing, scrambled up a few more feet and continued into the unknown.

Moria looked back at Cassie, who said, "Go."

The climb seemed never-ending. Silence followed the group as the riders dwelled on thoughts about what lay ahead. At last, Maxine said, "I can see the trail leveling out. I think we've reached the top."

The three explorers breathed a collective sigh of relief as they looked down at Pete's farm in the valley and the forest stretching out beyond. The trail snaked out before them, a tiny ribbon of dusty footing spread on top of the granite. "Okay, folks, no spooking," Maxine said. "Who wants to lead?"

Moria answered, "Why spoil a good thing? If you feel okay, go for it."

"Works for me," Cassie agreed. She looked at the drop-off, "You know, I just thought of something. I'm probably going to be in front going back unless we get all the way down on the other side."

Maxine laughed, "Let's roll." The riders eased along for about ten minutes and began to relax.

"If we end up on the old logging road, guess we'll have a choice of the kudzu bitch trail, which is probably worse now," Moria speculated, "or, we'll turn around. Cassie will be a hero and lead us out."

"I'm praying for the logging road," Cassie answered.

Maxine held up her hand, "Hey, look at this." The top of the bluff widened into a flat, weed-covered field surrounded by pines and hardwoods. "Let's take a break."

Soon the riders found a spot at the edge of the trees to tie the horses. "Too bad there's no water for them. "Let's look around," Moria said. The trio walked the edges of the field and peered into the forest. "That looks like a cleared place," and pointed into the woods. They walked farther and stopped in the opening. A breeze blew through the trees. Pine cones fell and the horses whinnied in alarm.

"We need to watch the horses, or we'll be walking back," Maxine said, turning to see what spooked them. Stillness fell over the field and the horses quieted.

Moria smiled, "The Yankees aren't happy. I'll bet this was their camp." She walked around, scuffling the leaves with her feet. "Here's the camp-fire," kneeling to scrape away the collected detritus covering a circle of rocks. "I don't think many people know about this or it would have been marked in some way. Maybe it's better to leave well enough alone."

"Cassie shivered. "It is weird. So where are the graves Pete mentioned?"

"I'm guessing, in the field. Let's look out there," Moria said, brushing the leaves and dirt from her knees and motioning the others to follow.

The horses' ears flexed forward at the sight of their people, *stay close they seemed to say.*

The women trampled through the weeds in search of any sign of graves. "Did you notice, these piles of rocks? Who wants to dig?" Maxine asked in a serious tone.

Cassie said, "Well, I could turn this find over to the main office and see if they want to send archaeologist out to investigate."

The three looked at each other with a silent thought, *rest in peace.* Moria said, "Let's just say goodbye to the Yankees. Somehow, I don't think it would be a good idea to have this made public."

Everybody mounted up and Maxine said, "Let's keep going. Now, I'm curious about where we'll end up." By now, the sun was overhead, bearing down on the riders and reflecting heat off the stone. "If we make it down to Pete's maybe he'll let us cross one more time and water the horses." They looked back toward Pete's farm, now in the distance and journeyed on in the heat for thirty more minutes. The farm was now out of sight.

Moria took the lead. "Looks like we're on the way down toward the logging road. Hope it doesn't get too steep." The horses trod with care as the trail led them through the woods and then into an open space cluttered with giant boulders. The riders stopped to stare. "Are you sure we're on the same planet?" stopping to face her friends.

Maxine and Cassie checked their GPSs and both burst out laughing.

"What?" Moria looked at them with concern.

Maxine sidled over to Moria. "What does this look like?" she grinned and held the device for her to see.

"Spaghetti?"

Maxine said, "Well, the GPS isn't going to get us home this time. I think we need some lessons! Seriously, we've got three choices. Keep going to the Logging Road and Jeep Trail to Pete's and whine until he lets us through, or backtrack. We'd be out here the rest of the day if we turned around." She gauged her friends' expressions. "And we've got to be sure we're actually going in the right direction since we've wound in and out so much."

Moria reached in her pack and pulled out a three dollar compass she'd borrowed from school. Holding it up for them to see, she said, "I know west is home and east and south are back to the powerline. Let's keep going and get off the bluff. I say try to get to Pete's, then we'll figure out the rest."

The downward trail was treeless with scrub brush and rocks. The sun showed no mercy on the riders as they silently picked their way through the endless loose rocks. Maxine said, "No way is this going to be in the ride. Think about it. Fifty milers will have to do this twice, plus the gullies. We'd probably end up with a bunch of lame horses and pissed off riders because even the front runners couldn't make the cut off time."

"You're right," Moria answered. "We've got to convince Pete to help us."

"Yeah, too bad you got in his face this morning," Cassie commented. "No worries, the humidity and the deer flies will kill us all."

The other two burst out laughing. Then, Moria said, "It's called put your boots on, Missy."

Cassie replied with mock surprise, "I'm wearing my Tevis boots."

"Then, lace 'em tighter," she encouraged with a laugh. "Hey, I think we're nearly here." The dusty path had leveled out and dipped down to a ditch and a familiar sight, the Logging Road. "At last, we know where we are. If we go left, we'll come to the embankment to the Jeep Road and then it's not far to Pete's."

As they continued, Maxine said, "Moria, why don't you see what magic you can work on his ornery hide?"

"Uh, where's Jada when we need her? Okay, I'll try."

In sight of the farm, the riders dismounted and led the horses. Moria said, "Might as well try it. Feel free to coach me or take over." The riders stood back, but in view, and hoped for the best.

A truck parked near house with a small trailer attached, caught their attention. "Looks like he's got company and Pete's got his shot gun again," Maxine muttered.

The horses pulled back as the dogs hit the fence, but the riders were prepared. They stepped back a few feet with their mounts, then gave a snatch on the reins to say "enough." The horses peered at the dogs. *Oh, yeah, been here*, but stayed on guard.

The two men reached the gate and Pete handed the gun to his buddy. "Well, lookie here, the cowgirls must'a not been captured by the Yankees. How was yer ride?" giving them a welcoming smile.

Caught off guard with Pete's changed greeting from just a few hours earlier, Moria mind whirled. *Is this it? When we're going to get kidnapped and buried in the forest? Okay. I'm going to play it his way.*

"No, the Yankees weren't interested in us today. It's pretty amazing up there, but not for us."

His friend spoke up, "Guess you're here to buy some ..."

Pete scowled and elbowed the guy, pushing him aside. "Naw, they just wanna get to the powerline and go home. Right?"

Answering with her most genuine smile, "Yes, and we'd really appreciate it if we could water the horses."

Pete motioned the dogs aside and unlocked the gate. "There's a trough at the other gate. This here's my friend from Atlanta. Comes to visit once in a while."

The three women greeted his nameless friend as they came in and the group started across the yard. Moria walked beside Pete and Maxine and Cassie walked behind with the friend. Pete growled at his buddy, "Go close the doors."

"What?"

"To the chicken house," and picked up his pace toward the gate.

Seeing leafy green plants in the chicken houses as Pete hustled her by, it seemed natural for Moria to ask in her most innocent voice, "What are you growing? Looks like your plants are doing very well."

"Poinsettias … for Christmas."

"Oh, nice," she answered, not wanting to get him riled up.

As the guy ran to the chicken houses, it gave Maxine and Cassie a chance to look through the open doors and give a silent nod to each other. "Hey, Pete, why don't you help us find a way around your farm so we don't keep bothering you? Think about it. Do you have a secret passage we could use?" Maxine joked.

Throwing his hands up in surrender, he unlocked the gate and pointed down the powerline. "There's a deer trail yonder a ways, pretty overgrown, runs beside the creek and comes out on that old road where the kudzu is, 'bout a quarter mile on the right. That's my offer."

The riders mounted up, waved and Maxine said, "Thanks, see ya."

"Be gone," he answered.

As the trio rode away, Cassie breathed a sigh of relief. "This was just like a movie, except we got away. What fun. You all are a clever pair, congratulations. I can't believe Kam left all this intrigue."

Moria answered, "As you said, It ain't over till it's over. Kam's probably in a better place. Thanks, Cassie, for playing your part in our movie, being an observant, intimidating presence. I'll bet that's why Pete helped us on our way. Y'all keep watching for the Deer Trail. We need to come back here and check it out. Speaking of movies, we're supposed to be back at Jada's in the morning to regroup."

"I hate to complain," Maxine said, digging into her pack. "I'm starved." Soon the three riders were snacking as they headed home.

Cassie pointed into the trees. "I think that's it." They stopped, studied the bushes, and rode closer. "Looks like some kind of game trail. What do you all think?"

"It's worth a try. Let's come back tomorrow," Moria said.

Exhausted, but encouraged, the riders continued home with renewed energy from their hopeful success in securing another piece of the puzzle.

Moria reached home ahead of Jackson and went to the barn to care for the other horses. Silver galloped to the gate and whinnied to Rainbow, *where did you go today? Was it fun?*

The chestnut gelding answered with a weary nicker. *We visited the Yankees on the bluff. I think we stirred up their souls. Glad to be home.* Rainbow took a fast roll in the dirt to stretch his muscles and scratch the itches.

"Come on, you dirt ball, to the wash rack. I know you're going to roll again, but it'll be easier to clean you up tomorrow."

She gathered up the feed buckets and put flakes of hay out for the night. "Okay, here you go," as she offered them the treasured rewards.

Later, Moria and Jackson settled in their nightly spot on the porch swing. Jackson put his arm around his cowgirl and said, "Tell me about your day, Missy."

And she did, ending with, "You were right. We're pretty certain Pete's raising more than poinsettias and I think he knew we were on to him. The deer trail he offered might work. We have to go to Jada's in the morning. Maybe we can get some help for the bridge. How was your day?"

"Well, I can't complain. Jeremy and I might have to make an over night trip to check out a water dispute between two property owners up near the Tennessee line. Also, I talked to Fran and set up a meeting with Ranger Cassie tomorrow to go over the grant. Then, we'll have to round up a few people to help. I think we can get it done by mid September."

"Thanks, I know you will. Now I can take that off my to-do list. Just don't upset our people." She thought back to the night Jackson saw the images of her ancestors for the first time as 'her people' crossed the bridge. She knew then he was accepted into the heritage of her family when he was gifted with the vision.

Jackson said, "You know, I miss our training rides. Maybe we can go out for pleasure this weekend, just you and me. We should go at night and see if those old folks are roaming around … or the bear."

Moria smiled to herself, "Count on it," and took Jackson's hand. The tribe of cats and dogs scattered into the night as Moria said, "Be gone."

Jackson studied her face and said, "Where'd that come from?"

"Oh, I've heard it around. It's my new saying."

"Whatever, just so it's not to me. Come on, let's be gone to bed." A welcome trip to 'the land of you and me, baby' ended the day on Peace in the Valley Farm.

Chapter Thirteen

As planned, Moria picked Maxine up mid-morning for the trip to Jada's, saying, "Looks like we've still got most of our volunteers," parking between two familiar trucks and glancing at the other vehicles. She gathered up the maps and approached the house with the usual worry about the meeting.

Maxine secured her laptop in a bag and carried notes in her hand. "After yesterday, I'm prepared for anything. Well, almost."

Jada welcomed them with an excited greeting. "Come on in, I'm just getting ready to show yesterday's filming."

People settled down facing the screen, looking at each other, not sure what to expect. Jada focused the projector and asked, "Any questions before we start?"

One of the guys said, "Yeah, what if we don't like what you filmed of us or what we said?" A murmur of unease ran through the group.

Taken aback, Jada answered, "I don't think that will happen. I thought the shoot was perfect. This was just taken yesterday so I have to add some narration."

The group sat mesmerized as *yesterday* recreated itself in the forest setting. The film rolled and they watched Rodney divide them into three groups, giving directions and tools for those who needed them. Birds chirped and fluttered at being disturbed which added to the reality of the scenes.

Jada started with the first group, filming them doing their various tasks, throwing rocks off the trail, cutting face branches, filling in holes, and a chainsaw could be heard in the distance. Then, a pause as she relocated shooting to the next group.

All seemed well until they heard a strident voice in the film, the guy who had asked the question. *"I don't wanna to take off my shirt,"* he complained.

Jada's voice: *"Oh, this will make a great shot with the rippling muscles across your back and you can look over your shoulder, turn around and wipe your face with your bandana."*

The guy obliged, with a frown.

Jada's commanding directions continued, *"Now, face the camera and wipe your chest and say, 'Anything for the ride.' I deleted 'screw you.' That was inappropriate. Children will see this film."*

The guy jumped up from the chair, hands on hips, and said in a low voice, "I told you to delete that scene, bitch!" Jada took a step back as she and the disgruntled hunk faced each other.

"Now!" he demanded, moving closer to her.

Two of the other men stood on ready.

"Okay, don't get so huffy," she said. "Who knows this might have been your path to stardom," rewinding to the offensive frames and deleting them.

The irate volunteer sat down, looking at Moria and Maxine. "I'll help … but not with her."

On the spur of the moment, Moria asked, "Would you help Jackson and Jeremy repair the bridge? Right now, it's just the two of them. And no filming," she added with a straight face.

"Sure, I can do that," and handed her a business card.

Jada continued with the screening as if nothing had happened. Moria said, under her breath, "Where's Richard when we need him?"

The rest of the film held no discontent and most people seemed pleased with what they saw.

Jada turned to her trail ladies and asked, "Do you all have anything to add to our day?"

Maxine smiled, "Good news, I hope. Ole Pete finally said we could use a deer trail on his property to connect the powerline to the logging road. I think it just has to be cleared of underbrush. The kudzu growth is going to be a challenge. We're hoping the 4-H Club and the hikers can help us on this part."

One of the volunteers said, "The 4-H leader lives next door to me. I'll ask him, if you want me to, and he can call you."

"That would be great, thanks."

Moria gave Jada a thumbs up as they departed. "Keep up the good work."

"I'd love to do some filming with the kids. Let me know where the trail is and when you're going out."

Moria frowned, "It's going to be pretty tight in there. We'll see."

The group disbanded and as they left, people planned for the next day. In the parking area, Rodney walked with Moria and Maxine to their truck and observed, "Wal that was a dust up, for sure. That Jada, she's a piece of work. Guess we'll be out again tomorrow. Rain might be comin' in a day or two. Let me know if you need me on the Deer Trail."

"If you can keep your tribe marching along, that would be the greatest help. Call us tomorrow night and let us know how your day went," Moria answered, giving him a salute.

On the way home, Maxine said, "You know, I think we need a visit to The Juniper Tree. We haven't been there since the Fourth of July. I heard there's going to be a food and drink discount tomorrow night … no fireworks, I hope. Maybe Rita and Cassie can join us. I don't think they've ever been."

"I'll call them," Moria said, turning up Maxine's driveway. "Do you want to take a quick ride to the Deer Trail this afternoon before we drag people up there? I know it's going to be really hot, but we'll just worry about it until we see it for ourselves."

"Here's a thought," Maxine offered, "why don't we drive up, park the truck and walk in? We can get a better idea of the lay of the land, if we're not struggling with the horses into God knows what. About The Juniper Tree, yes."

"Good idea. Don't forget plenty of water and bug spray. I'll bring surveyor's tape. I'm sure we'll need to mark some things."

"I'll pick you up in a couple of hours and I'll drive this time," Maxine answered.

Pounce and Pandora greeted Moria at the door. *Thank goodness you're here. It's past snack time,* Pounce purred, rubbing back and forth between her ankles. Dixie and Hero peered through the screen door and begged in their most charming way, both lifting a paw to say, *please?*

"Come on, you hooligans, here are your rewards for guarding the farm," and opened the treat bags.

"Better call Jackson," she said aloud, reaching for her phone. "Hey, I'm home."

"How was the meeting?" he asked, already knowing it would be story time again.

"We survived and I got you some help for the bridge. Longer version later. Maxine and I are going to walk on the Deer Trail this afternoon and see if it's doable. Maybe we'll be done with Pete and his mischief if this works out. Just wanted you to know where we'll be. I'll check on the horses before I go. What's the latest on your trip?"

"Waiting to see if their attorneys need any validations on the properties. It appears water has been diverted illegally."

"You can tell me more this evening."

"Okay, put the tracker on your phone, just in case."

"Not sure if we'll have service, I'll try. Oh, and one more thing, will you bring food tonight? Please?"

"It'll cost you, Missy," his laughter floated through the phone, a promise to be kept.

"Don't worry. I've got money in the bank, and just waiting to spend it."

~ ~ ~

Early afternoon, Moria and Maxine were on their way to the power line. The road took them through the Cherry Valley village and as they neared the ice cream shop, passing by was not an option. "We need energy," Maxine advised.

They parked in the shade near the Deer Trail and gathered their essentials for traveling the last chance route, as they had named it. Moria ripped off a strand of pink surveyor's tape and tied it to a small maple tree at the entry.

"Here goes." She pushed through weeds, a clutch of briars and stepped over a log. "Jeez." she yipped, as a snake whisked out from under the log and scurried into the bushes. She looked at Maxine and grinned, "Want to lead?"

Maxine shook her head, "No, you're doing fine. Now take another step. You know, John Wayne says, 'courage is when you're scared to death, and you saddle up anyway.' Tighten the girth, Missy."

Moria wiped the sweat from her face and the two 'trail ladies' crept forward. Maxine stepped cautiously over the log in case the snake had a buddy. The trail did not appear to be in current use. Small trees and weeds were crushed and dead from animal travels over the years. Brown leaves were matted on the ground and fallen limbs lay scattered along the way. "We might as well throw these limbs to the side so we don't have to do it later," Maxine said, hefting a sizeable branch out of the way.

The women struggled on for about half a mile, dragging loose limbs aside and trying to avoid poison ivy and unforeseen holes buried in the leaves.

"I think we're near the Jeep Trail," Moria said. "I remember from the map the trail makes a turn somewhere along here. Sure enough, there it is and there's the embankment we slid down." She pushed some branches aside and they stepped off the Deer Trail onto the familiar path which would lead them to Pete's. "Wonder where it goes in the other direction? Let's have a looksee. I don't think it'll help us. I'm just curious." She tied ribbons to mark the trail back to the road and they ventured into new territory.

In about five minutes the pair reached the dead end at a clearing overgrown with weeds which seemed to guard a rustic, abandoned cabin. They stood quietly, listening for any sign of life. The forest lay still. Shadows lengthened as the sun moved farther west. A shiver ran over Moria's skin. *We shouldn't be here.*

"Want to take a look?" Maxine whispered, feeling the weight of the unknown on her shoulders, too. "Let's hope the three bears don't live here," she said, trying to lighten the eerie mood surrounding the cabin.

As they came closer, Moria said, "Watch out, this porch looks pretty rotten," thumping her foot hard on the floor. "Seems okay. Let's give it a try." The porch held their weight and Moria pushed the door open with a scraping sound, adding to their discomfort. Dust motes scattered through a golden haze in a shaft of sunlight as they stepped inside. The tiny room shared the space with cobwebs, leaves and the detritus of someone's past life. A bed stood in one corner, the mattress destroyed by animal invaders and beside it, a wooden cradle.

"Be still, my heart," she said, "who lived here?" and lifted the remnants of a blue baby blanket for a better look.

Maxine walked over to a small cast iron sink and picked up a tiny silver spoon from the wooden counter then set it down with care. Arrayed on the counter near the sink, she noticed a collection of clay pots and a gourd dipper waiting in vain for their owners return. She turned toward a pine table surrounded by four cane-bottomed chairs. A bench and dresser hovered against the far wall, holding their stories forever. "I feel like we're trespassing on someone's life," she said, turning toward the back door which was open.

Moria replaced the blanket in the cradle, rubbed her hand along its dusty rail and wondered, *who was this child?*

They stepped outside into more weeds and noticed a decrepit shed near the woods. "Well, let's take a look," Maxine said. The shed appeared to be on the verge of collapsing into itself; the weathered gray boards covered with moss spoke to a time long gone. Inside the shed they saw a rusted plow leaning against the wall and a leather harness, petrified by time, hanging nearby. Wooden buckets, various shovels, rakes and hoes lay scattered on the dirt floor.

"Jesus," Moria said under her breath, looking into the darkening forest. "Wonder where they planted their crops?"

"We'll probably never know," Maxine answered. "Look over here. These flowers have survived." She walked over to a small patch of mixed flowers. "Oh, man, someone's been weeding the flower bed."

The two women looked at each other, recognition dawning, "Pete," they voiced together. As they looked closer, a flat stone centered in the flowers laid undisturbed for many years.

"We need to go," Moria turned away, unnerved by the tended grave and the baby she knew was buried there. "This is not our business."

As they headed back down the Jeep Trail, Maxine peered into the dusk and said, "We should have hung glow sticks. We can't go up to Pete's. We'll have to hope we hung enough ribbons to get us back." The two trudged on in silence.

Off in the distance, Moria heard Jackson's voice, "Missy, where are you?"

"Joy to the world. The cavalry's here. We're coming to you." she called back.

Through the shadows, they could see flashlight beams in the distance. "We see you. We're almost there." and in a few moments, Moria threw herself into Jackson's arms and Jeremy hugged Maxine as if to never let her go, then laughed, "We thought ole Pete had gotten you two, for sure."

Jackson walked ahead and the others followed single file. Moria said, "We got a little sidetracked. Sorry to cause you trouble. I sound like Sassy. Now I kind of know how she feels."

"Well, I never got to The Diner to pick up supper. Guess we better head that way," Jackson said, as they reached the trucks.

Over a welcomed dinner just before closing time, Moria and Maxine took turns telling about their discovery, and Moria ended with, We don't want people going there out of curiosity. We need to respect Pete's life, especially since he helped us out of a jam. It probably didn't occur to him that we would go there. At least we have the Deer Trail, the last piece of the trail puzzle.

"Oh, there's more to our day," Maxine continued, "the meeting at Jada's," and proceeded to give the short version. Somehow, it didn't seem as important after their adventure at the cabin. She looked at the guys, "How was your day?"

"We spent some time with Cassie this morning, went over the grant again and I called the volunteer." Jackson grinned, "He wanted to know when we'd start and to be sure we weren't on Jada's project list. A friend of his is going to help, too. The grant money's in an account that Jeremy and I can co-sign. Since we're still waiting on the legal case about the water, this is a good time to get started on the bridge. Durant and Durant can manage without us, I'm sure," thinking about the massive environmental office in Wyoming. Our two bridge helpers are flexible, so we'll be out there in the morning and assess what materials we need."

"I think it's going to rain in the afternoon, but we can order our supplies and be ready."

Darla came with the checks and began to gather the dishes, "See y'all tomorrow? We'll be out of business if you ladies ever have time to cook," she joked.

Jackson drove straight to the barn as they returned home. "Remind me how we got hijacked into putting on this ride?" he grumbled.

"Well, Jada…"Moria paused, trying to sort through the chaos that had blown through their lives in the past few weeks.

Jackson grinned, "Never mind, I know you and Maxine didn't think she could put the ride on as well as you could."

"Sort of." Her grudging answer bespoke a portion of truth. "We just didn't want the Cherry Valley Ride to be remembered as a disaster."

"I'll tell you one thing, you all are lucky to have Richard's ability to see the big picture and the money to go with it, plus have some control over Jada. How'd he do that?" Jackson puzzled.

Moria laughed as she got out of the truck to open the gate, "We wondered that, too. He's holding something over her head."

As the motion lights came on, the horses and dogs greeted their long lost people with barks and whinnies, *about time*, and crowded around the feed room.

Pounce and Pandora climbed down from the hay bales, bounced inside and jumped on the counter. *We knew you'd come here first. We're having a spend the night party,* he purred. *You got a rat problem, so we're gonna spend a few nights down here and fix it.*

Moria looked at the cats sitting on the steps and turned out the lights. "Guess they're camping at the barn tonight."

"So there'll be peace in the valley," Jackson said, as the couple walked to the cottage.

She took his hand, "Showers and play time. Come on, cowboy. Jackson didn't need a second invitation.

Chapter Fourteen

Torrents of rain beat against the kitchen windows and thunder rumbled overhead. Jackson gestured toward the TV weather report as Moria brought their breakfast plates to the table. "Looks like you all won't be doing any trail work today. It appears this is going to last most of the day."

Moria sat down and slathered her pancakes with syrup. "Maxine and I talked about the weather probably interfering with our plans. I think we might go over to the school and nose around. Maybe we can see our class lists. We have a meeting and workday next week." She sighed and looked at the calendar on the wall. "I don't think Mr. Baldwin's going to let us take days off any time soon, even if we're sick. He's on to us."

Jackson gave her a teasing smile, "Just remember, your salary pays for the endurance stuff and I handle all the rest. Don't lose your job, Missy."

She laughed, "Well, you could work two jobs."

"And you could hire on at The Diner. Speaking of working, guess you'll need to feed the horses, since I'm dressed in my town clothes," giving her a hug and reaching for his slicker and hat.

By mid-morning Moria had finished the barn work, removed a few dead rats and complimented Pounce and Pandora. As she turned toward the house, the cats returned to their task. *Guess this will be a good day to go to the school and see what Mr. Baldwin has in store for us. Maxine and I need to regroup and be sure we're covering all our bases for the ride. I don't want to be the mismanager.*

Soon she was on the phone with Maxine. "What? Jada's invited us to supper?"

"Yeah, I've already called the guys. We do need to catch up and Richard will be there so we can all get on the same page. Why don't we go on over to the school? I'll pick you up."

Cherry Valley Elementary was nestled under ancient Elm trees, waiting. The soft rose-colored brick building sheltered memories for the old, the young, the laughter, tears, and dreams to come. Moria remembered the past chaotic year as if it were yesterday: almost losing her job when she used a prism to try and hypnotize Michael into learning his multiplication tables; the play they created, "Alice Goes West," with cowboys for palace guards, out of control lassos and the cowboys tying Alice up for a kiss; and, of course, using all her personal and some sick days to take off for endurance rides.

The two teachers walked across the parking lot in silence. Yellow leaves from the Elms scattered on the sidewalk, a reminder that summer was almost over. Moria took a deep breath.

Maxine said, "Yeah, I know."

Moria's mind swirled with thoughts of new children, unknown parents, rules, studies and all other events that awaited them. In her scattered imaginings, trails, riders, more rules, weather and the horses collided in a mishmash of adventures to come. She looked sideways at her friend, "Time to get on our knees and ask for help."

Maxine stopped with her hand on the schoolhouse door and closed her eyes. Moria bowed her head, and Maxine murmured "Dear Jesus, please keep your hand on our shoulders, today and always. Amen."

"Amen." Moria echoed, grateful for her friend's faith.

The entrance and hallways were quiet. A light shone from Mr. Baldwin's office. "Okay, let's go," Maxine said, stepping forward in a determined stride.

"We should have brought his favorite candy," Moria answered, remembering the times they smoothed the troubled waters with pralines from Miss Ella's Candy Store.

"We should probably keep a supply handy," Maxine laughed.

As they neared the office door, the Principal called out, "Who's there?"

"Just us, getting a head start on the year," Moria answered as they stepped into the office.

Mr. Baldwin stood and lifted his hand in a welcoming gesture. "Come on in. Have a seat," as he took his again. "Good to see you. How was your summer?"

"Oh, we had a relaxing vacation. Not too much going on," Maxine answered with a smile.

He looked closely at his teachers. "That so? Not what I heard."

Uh oh. Here it comes. How did he find out so soon? The two women were silent, waiting for what they knew was coming.

Mr. Baldwin, enjoying the moment, leaned forward and propped his elbows on his desk. "From what I've heard, you riders are planning some kind of an event in September."

They looked at each other. Maxine nodded at Moria. *You take this one.*

"Well, yes, we are having a trail ride. It's a community project. Even the 4-H Club will be involved. It will be good for the town, financially too." She waited.

The Principal stood, pointed a finger at them, and in a grim voice said, "This school is being evaluated in September." Mr. Baldwin anticipated the next question. "No, you can not take personal days that month. I need all hands on deck. We never know what day they will appear."

"Well, this is an unexpected surprise, but we," nodding toward Maxine, "will do everything we can to work toward a successful outcome."

Mr. Baldwin managed a smile to encourage his teachers, saying, "Just don't plan to be away before this is over."

They stood up to leave and Maxine said, "Yes sir. We'll be here," and reached out to shake their boss's hand. "Is it okay if we go down to the room for a few minutes to look around and make some plans?"

"Take your time. The cleaners aren't coming until Monday."

Moria turned back at the doorway. "If you don't mind me asking, how did you find about us?"

Mr. Baldwin grinned, "I have my sources. Ole Pete is a friend of mine. We grew up together. He's been keeping me in the loop with what he calls his trouble chiles. I'm impressed with your efforts to have the ride. Let's hope your dedication will come to school with you in September."

"Sure thing, count on it," Moria answered with a wave.

They walked slowly down the hall toward their classrooms. Moria ran her hand along the lockers and Maxine picked up a stray piece of paper. Finally, Maxine said, "Who would'a thought Pete and Mr. B. are friends?"

"Yeah, wonder if our esteemed boss is one of his customers?" Moria answered under her breath. *Humm ... we need to keep this in mind, just in case.*

Maxine opened the classroom door to be greeted by a dark space that seemed to hold no hope. "Jeez. Let's get some light in here." She flicked the switch to illuminate the room. It was just as they had left it, chairs stacked on desks, all papers and books out of sight.

Moria opened the blinds to welcome sun and reached in her desk drawer for the prism and held it to the light. Colors washed into the air and she remembered Michael. "Wonder if Michael and his Dad are still in Texas? It was a good ending that he came back to visit and be in the play," she laughed, remembering him dressed in the gopher suit and how glad the other students were to see him. But most of all, she thought back to their visit in her yard the next day and Michael opening his arms to Dixie's puppy, Rascal, who would have a forever home and a boy to love her.

Maxine took one chair off a desk and handed another to Moria. "Your mind seems far away," she commented.

"Just thinking about last year and closing the memory book. We need to put school and these next few weeks at the top of our list, until the evaluation is over, whatever it takes."

"Agreed," Maxine said, tracing ABCs on the dusty desktop. She looked at the faded bulletin boards. Grinning, she said, "Right now we've got a ride in our face and we've got to be at Jada's this evening to rescue the event.

"Yeah, the last thing we need is Jada mixing into our school business. Hope this evening is productive and she doesn't pull any surprises. We should go to The Juniper Tree tomorrow night and relax."

~ ~ ~

Peace in the Valley Farm and its occupants settled in for the night, except for Moria and Jackson who headed to Jada's.

As they pulled into the Deavers driveway, Maxine and Jeremy pulled in beside them and the four friends trooped up the steps to turn another page in their endurance life.

Jada and Richard, the perfect hosts, had laid out their treasured table settings for dinner. The well-appointed dining room spoke of their heritage with antiques and paintings from the past displayed to tell the story.

"Thanks for coming tonight. I did ask Rodney, but he said just fill him in on what's coming next. I know everyone's hungry. Bring your plates over to the sideboard and help yourselves," she said, removing the lids from the covered dishes.

The conversation flowed smoothly as the wine glasses were refilled. Moria's school life slipped away and the looming ride came into focus.

Richard mentioned that there were some inquiries about the ride, even though it had just been approved. "We've even had some people calling from California."

Moria cringed, *well, that answers that. Bring it on, Doris Weaver.*

Jada interrupted, "Moving on, I've got some ideas for the awards. We can look at the catalogues and perhaps make some decisions."

Moria and Maxine took turns entertaining the group about their encounters with Pete and his final offer of the Deer Trail. "The last piece of the puzzle," Moria ended her account with a smile.

Jackson brought everyone up to date on plans for the bridge, then winked at Jada, "Sorry I stole one of your movie stars."

She laughed, "Well, I'll find somebody else who'll take their shirt off."

Richard looked startled, then said, "That would be me. I always wanted to be a movie star."

"Now's your chance," Jada said, and rewarded his offer with a smile and a tweak of his ear. "Let's sit in the den where there's a coffee maker and get started."

By now, it was nearing eight o'clock. The last rays of August sun streamed into the room. A breeze had cleared the rain away for the promise another trail workday. The lingering light reminded the riders that time's a wastin' and September awaits them, in more ways than one.

Richard took the floor and opened his remarks, saying, "I'm sure I've forgotten some things, but here's what I've done so far: AERC is a great help, very patient. The ride managers I've contacted have made suggestions we haven't thought about and have even called to check on us, knowing this is our first ride."

Moria smiled, *He owns this. Way to go, Richard.*

He opened his laptop and began the list. "All sanctioning require-ments are done. I spoke with Cassie and the trail system is approved, as you know. AERC mentioned measuring since this is the first time we've used this system officially, but they have approved the ride. I told them what you all said about the miles and you have a little leeway here, just to let them know the final measurement."

Maxine, who had her laptop open too, made a note and said, "Measurement is on our list. One of the worst things that can happen is a missed distance. We're going to see if the hikers will use the surveyor's wheel on the tight spots. We can offer them a free meal the night of the ride and completion awards for their help."

Jada interrupted with vigor, "Oh, no! Completion awards are for rid-ers only."

Moria turned to face Jada, "Hey, you're way off track. Volunteers working on the trail get rider bucks for their efforts. Everybody who helps needs a token of appreciation. The hikers don't need rider bucks but we need the hikers, or you can get out there with the surveyor's wheel yourself." *See how long that lasts.*

Richard gave Jada a look and she regrouped, saying, "We can talk more about this when we check out the catalogues."

Jackson leaned into Moria and put his arm around her, with a gentle *back off* squeeze.

Guess this is my "half-halt." Thanks, buddy.

Richard moved on to talk about the paperwork needed to account for the ride statistics. "AERC has a list in the ride packet and I can get copies made. I'll wait until closer to the ride before I print and see how many entries we have signed up. Also, I've contacted Sherriff Bramblett and have signed for the permits. Jackson, let me know what's needed for camp, since it's on your property. I know you all mentioned a generator and," he smiled at Jada, "the tents. I'm sure we'll add to the list, as we go."

Moria looked at her yellow legal pad and began to mark through items Richard mentioned. Maxine tapped away on her list, and said, "Richard, thanks for what you're doing. I don't believe we could have handled all these details and the trail business, too."

He smiled and sat up a little straighter. "It's my pleasure. It'll be good for the community. People will spend money and our little town will get better known for the jewel it is.

Whoa! This is a side of Richard I never knew. Moria added, "Thanks from me, too. The ride entries are going out online but we are mailing in our region too, for those who aren't connected to the internet."

"We are?" Maxine asked, looking from Moria to Richard.

"We probably should," Richard answered. "I'll run the address labels, go ahead and print the entries. Jada can get them out tomorrow. Good idea."

"Richard, I have to film tomorrow." Jada whined.

"Oh, this won't take long, honey. You can film in the morning and do the mail out in the afternoon. I'll have everything ready for you." Jada huffed out a breath, sat back in her chair and crossed her arms.

Jeremy glanced sideways at Jackson, as if to say, *not my monkey, not my circus. You got this one, Richard.*

Richard looked at his watch, "Okay, what about the trails?"

Moria brought everyone up to date on the trail design and progress so far. "There's a lot to do. Clearing and measuring are critical to the ride's success. The 4-H Club youngsters, the hikers, the saddle club people, Rodney's group, plus ourselves," gesturing to Maxine, Jeremy and Jackson. We have enough help it's just getting everybody on their section of the trail. The guys think they'll have the bridge finished in time. We'll make some phone calls tomorrow and be sure everyone knows what part of the trail they're responsible for."

"Lucky for us, most of these folks have done some kind of trail work before. We already have the volunteers for rider bucks hard at work, we hope," Maxine added.

"Okay, now can we plan the awards?" Jada asked, reaching for the catalogues.

Moria handed her a list of the award categories and said, "I'm most concerned about the competition awards. You've been to enough rides to know what people like. Sometimes the ride photographer will do portraits for the winners in each division. Oh yeah, we need a photographer." She paused and looked at Richard.

He nodded, "Got it."

The riders browsed through the magazines, shared, discussed, and decided on coffee mugs for the completions. "There's a local company that does awards for schools and other events," Maxine reminded Jada. "Get as many items as you can from them. Find out how much lead time they'll need. And, while you're in town, why don't you stop by some of the churches and see which of them would be willing to come and cook for us. Offer them the proceeds as a donation for the church."

"Give them the proceeds?" Jada shrieked, jumping up from her chair, waving her arms and spinning around in the center of the room.

Jackson interrupted her antics, saying, "You want to cook for a couple of hundred people for two days?"

"We don't have to provide food."

"Yes, we do. It's a southern thing. Get over it."

Richard nodded in agreement. "We'll take care of it."

Moria said to Jada, "Get back to us in a day or two and let us know how things are going. And to Richard, "It might help to open a temporary checking account so we can pay the bills with money from the ride entries and the vendors. We might be able get some sponsors, too."

"Good idea. Thanks for coming over tonight."

And, thanks for the dinner," Moria added and was echoed by the others.

As the four walked to their trucks, Maxine said, "I feel better that we took the time to meet tonight."

"There's more to this production than I thought," Jeremy commented. "I'm glad our assignment is just the bridge."

"Uh, not quite," Jackson answered. "We have to get the camp ready but that will be the last few days."

Later that evening Jackson took Moria in his arms, "I love you. There's no other place I'd rather be than here," and they tumbled into bed for the reward of the night.

Chapter Fifteen

Early the next morning the phone rang and Jackson handed it to Moria, "Gotta be for you this early."

"Moria, it's Rodney. Got some good news, I hope. The gullies section of the trail we've been worried about, I think there's another way to go … up on the ridge. The Forest Service put a fire break in years ago, but they didn't maintain it that I know of. I'm going up there today and if it's good, let's use the 4-H kids to clear this stretch."

"Thanks. What a great way to start my day. Call me later and let me know what you find." Then she dialed Maxine's number.

Soon they were on their way to work on the Deer Trail. "Looks like the Rutherford's Road is going to be our raceway," Moria commented as they drove toward the powerline. "At least it's in good shape and the footing will be okay … unless it rains. We need to have the finish line a safe distance from where the trails meet."

"Right," Maxine answered. "Where do you think Jada is this morning?"

"I heard Rodney say he was sending people to the Logging Road. Hope she's not there! They're going to have to park near the saddle club and hike in. I'm pretty sure they're carrying Weed Eaters and machetes plus bug spray, food, water, and who knows what else. I think they deserve double rider bucks for clearing that stretch."

Maxine laughed, saying, "Yeah, and if that's where Jada decides to film today those folks might need triple bucks. "Let's hope Rodney's new trail on the ridge is doable. This will be the last hard part. Of course, we'll need to cut face branches and keep the trails in order, especially if we have storms taking trees down. No way could we have had these trails ready for the ride without our volunteers ... and Richard. He's amazing. Who knew? He's always been in the background and managing Jada, well, most of the time."

Maxine parked in the shade and the two trail blazers began to gather their needed items. Moria reached for her backpack, a limb lopper, pruning shears, and a small hoe. "We need to remember to get the high face branches since we're not on the horses."

As they turned into woods, Maxine said, "Hey, wait a minute. What are we going to do about this log? Remember the snake?"

"The horses could step over ... or we can move it to the side."

"Let's move it," Maxine said.

Laying their equipment down, they took hold of one end of the log to drag it off the trail. As they lifted and walked it to the side, a nest of copperheads slithered away. "Be gone, you rascals." Moria wiped the sweat from her face, saying "Let's hope this is the worst thing that happens to us today."

The sun rose higher and as the two women worked. A trail began to emerge, a single track with good footing. Maxine said, "I don't think we can finish this morning but at least we've got a start. Let's come back tomorrow. We need to update the progress of the volunteers since they're all over the place working on their own. Also, be sure we haven't left a section out, everybody thinking someone else is doing it." She reached for a high branch, sure to hit a rider in the face, and used the limb loppers to remove it. "Look here, I think the horses might be able to get to this small creek for a drink. It's a step down, but not too dangerous. There can never be too much water on the trail."

"For sure," Moria answered, "I say we head back. I'm hungry."

Soon they were sitting on the tail gate of Maxine's truck parked in the shade and enjoying their well-earned lunches.

On the way home, Moria said, "Why don't we divide the volunteer list and call them tonight? This afternoon we ought to go around town and see if we can get any sponsors, that is, if you're not busy." Then she laughed looking at her dirty clothes and sweat streaked face. "Maybe we better go home and clean up first."

Maxine said, "Busy? It seems like this ride has become my life. You know, we probably need some information to give the store keepers so they'll know what they're sponsoring. When I get home, I'll run off some copies of "What Is an Endurance Ride?" Part of the article is about benefits to communities where the rides are held. Why don't we meet in town? I'll start at one end of the street and you at the other. We can meet at the ice cream shop." And soon, the ladies were on a mission.

Moria decided to tackle the sandwich shop first. Mr. Brown greeted her with a smile. She launched into her spiel and handed the owner a flyer. "We could really use your support. Be sure and have some extra food because no matter how much we bring to the rides, we always seem to run out and head to the nearest town. Mr. Brown glanced at the flyer and then at Moria. "We could even bring our truck out to the ride site. We'll pay you a percentage of our profits."

Moria smiled and shook his hand. "That would be great. I think some people from the church will provide dinner, but maybe you could be there for breakfast and lunch. Uh, we do get up early."

"No problem, we'll be there. Give me a head count near the time. I realize what you said about people bringing food, but when they smell that bacon frying, they'll line up."

"Thanks, again," Moria said as she reached for the door. *That was easy. Now, who's next?*

The next possibility was just a few doors away, the hardware store.

"Hello, Miss Moria, what can I do for you today?" the owner asked, knowing the Durants were big spenders in his store.

"Well, a couple of things. We're having a trail ride in September," and handed him a flyer.

"Yes, I know," he grinned, "word gets around. We had some of your volunteers in here to rent or buy tools. I asked them if they'd be reimbursed for their expenses and they explained about the rider bucks. That was a good idea. How is it going?"

"I didn't realize they were spending their own money for what they needed."

"Yeah, I just rented out some Weed Eaters for the kudzu trail." He spoke as if this was an ordinary transaction. "Maybe I'll get some pictures for advertising."

"You can contact Jada Deavers. She's filming up there for a few days. I'll let her know what you need."

"Jada? Okay. Or I might just go up to see what they're doing and make my own pictures. Let me know where the kudzu trail is."

By now, both of them were distracted, then the owner asked, "You must'a come in here for something?" Giving her a quizzical look.

"Oh yeah, I was going to see if you would like to donate an award. A lot of our local people will be there. And I need to see about renting a generator for that weekend."

"I've got a better idea. Why don't I donate the generator for the event?"

"Oh, my gosh. That would be amazingly generous! You're sure?"

"Like you said, a lot of locals will be there. I might even show up, too."

"Please be our guest for dinner. Thanks, again."

Moria stepped out on the sidewalk in a daze. Meandering down the way and trying to process her good luck, she noticed the next two stores, the boutique and the dress shop. *Probably not. I'll check them out next time I'm in town.* She looked down the street to see Maxine waving from the ice cream shop.

On the bench in front of the shop they enjoyed a tasty reward and compared their findings. "How was your luck?" Moria asked, between quick licks on her melting cone.

"Well, better than I expected. The feed store offered to sponsor one of the awards and they plan to bring a pickup truck of hay, available for those who run out. Also, they'll bring fly spray and other items the riders might need. I wasn't sure about the drugstore, but they offered to sponsor the completion awards. You know, that's a big ticket item. I gave them an estimate of what it might cost and they were okay with it. Both places said it was the best advertising they could get for the money. I'm exhausted, but it's well worth it. I did offer them dinner." Maxine paused to catch her breath, "How'd you do?"

Moria related her successes and Maxine said, "Maybe we've missed our calling. We could get donations for non-profits. I'll bet United Way would hire us and we've already started on our resumes."

"Well, let's hope it doesn't come to that," Moria said, with a laugh. Just then, Jackson's truck rolled to a stop in front of them, followed by Jeremy.

Jackson called out, "Don't you two ever work? What's this? Hanging out in town when you should be home feeding the horses and cooking dinner?" He threw his hands in front of his face as Moria bolted to the side of the truck, leaned in with a come-hither smile, "I'm just gettin' sweet for you, honey."

"You minx."

"To The Diner, cowboy. My treat. We've got good news."

Maxine, already in her cowboy's truck, waved out the window and pointed toward the restaurant.

As the four entered, Rodney and his new family motioned their friends to an adjoining table.

Maxine whispered to Moria, "Guess the little cowgirlies must have been behaving for Rita to bring them out in public."

"Hey, Sassy, how's it going?" Moria asked.

"Excuse me, ma'am, my name's Alyssia. I just moved here from ..." she glanced at Rita who mouthed Alabama. "Alabama," Sassy finished with a smug look. "And this is my sister, Teresa," nodding at Mousey. "We're here for the summer while our parents are gone to Europe. This is my Aunt Patricia and Uncle Rodney."

Moria realized that the girls had a cover for leaving the ranch, just in case anyone got curious. Wanting to test them, she looked at Mousey, "And, Teresa, how do you like it here, so far?"

Mousey, already exhausted with the pretense, whispered, "Okay. I'm homesick for ..."

"Our hometown, Birmingham," Sassy/Alyssia answered for her sister and took hold of Mousey's hand. The girls smiled at each other, *we rock!*

Maxine decided to continue the conversation and give the youngsters some more practice. "Alyssia, do you have trails in … where is it you live?"

"Yes ma'am, we live in Alabama and yes, we have trails. Would you like to know my favorite one?"

"Sure. Do you hike or ride?"

"We do both, but riding is our favorite. We love the trails in Bankhead National Forest and the camping's to die for. When we get home you should come visit." Sassy sat back with a satisfied grin and winked at Maxine.

"Well, bless your heart, little dude. You get an A plus. Now, tell us about your day."

Darla interrupted the conversation to take orders and then Sassy continued, "We hiked a looong way," giving a dramatic gesture with her arm. "And …"

Mousey couldn't stand it any longer. "And we found a new trail up on the ridge. Rodney says it will be the best ever." Her voice dropped, "when it's cleared."

"Yeah, and we'd already worked on the ups and downs gully section, but I guess we won't use it," Sassy picked up their tale. "And the best part, the 4-H kids are going to work with us." Her eyes gleamed, "Friends at last."

Jackson and Jeremy's heads swiveled back and forth taking in all the information, true or false. Moria and Maxine looked at Rodney and Rita who seemed to be on board with all these revelations.

Moria turned to Rita. "You're going to let them be around those kids? What if their story slips?"

Rita gave a confident smile, "They've got too much at stake to mess up. We've practiced and they are calling each other by the second set of assumed names all the time. When they finally get to go home, it's doubtful if they'll know who they really are."

A tear ran down Mousey's cheek. "We won't know who we are?" and began to cry in frightened gulps.

Rita leaned over to give the sobbing child a hug.

"Don't worry, we'll write your name on your arm when this is over."

Mousey's face brightened, and Sassy said, "Can I get a tattoo with my name, in case I forget?" she grinned.

"Thank God, here comes the food," Maxine said, reeling from the conversations. "Let's eat."

Moria and Maxine filled everyone in on the successful outcome of their plea for donations.

Jackson had stopped eating, to listen. "You all got that done in a couple of hours? And the generator? Richard is going to be a happy camper about the money he's saving."

Rodney chimed in, "I've got some good news, too. Mousey was right. Rita and the girls hiked up with me and we agree, it'll take some work so why don't I sign on for this stretch? We'll call it the Ridge Trail since all the trails seem to have names." He paused for a sip of tea, and said, "Looks like we've got ourselves a trails system. Uh, what about the measuring?"

Moria reached for another biscuit, gazed around at the group and observed that no one raised their hand. "Relax guys, the hikers have already asked about helping and have everything they need. They're on the list for competition awards, too. Jada's going to have a hissy fit but look at the money we've saved them."

"And we're not done yet," Maxine added. "The tack store in Drapersville has a whole trailer of items they bring to horse events."

"Tune in tomorrow for the latest news," Jeremy said with a laugh, reaching for all the checks. "My treat."

Later in the evening Moria and Jackson sat in their winding down place, the swing. Night lights shone near them and sifted through the tree branches to cast shadows back and forth over the gathering on the porch.

"Well, another day in the books," Moria said, as Jackson folded his arm around her. "I can't believe it's ten o'clock. The poor horses probably thought we'd abandoned them."

Yeah, so did we, Hero whined, licking her hand.

Dixie put her paw on Jackson's knee, *please, can we have a snack?* her eyes pleaded.

He rubbed Dixie's head as if he read her mind.

Pounce jumped in Jackson's lap and put his paws on his cowboy's shoulders, *I know you keep treats in that jar.* Pounce looked steadily at the jar decorated with paw prints.

Pandora sat in the rocking chair, letting her friends do all the work. *Now,* she meowed. *Three, two, one ...* and, Jackson reached for the treat jar rewarding the adorable tribe.

Moria took the treat jar and set it aside. "Now for my treat," turning Jackson toward her and wrapping her arms around his neck. Burying her face on his shoulder, she said, "I never dreamed I'd be married to a Wyoming cowboy ... lucky me ... being rescued ... by you."

Jackson answered, "All because of an ad at the store advertising you needed help during the snowstorm. Remember when your daughter answered the door and she said, "Can I help you?" seeing my motorcycle stuck in the snow.

"And you answered, No ma'am, I've come to help you ... and so it all began."

Jackson waved to their furry audience, "Sorry, the next scene is R rated and not for your innocent eyes. See ya in the AM."

Pounce glowered and ran around the side of the house to the bedroom window followed by Pandora. No sooner had Pounce jumped into the flower box at the window than Jackson dropped the blinds. "No peeking."

~ ~ ~

As Jackson left for work the next morning, he gave Moria a hug and held her close, "Thanks for last night. I love the way you make every time seem like the first time and add a few surprises."

She laughed, "Well, if you remember, the first time wasn't the greatest since you were only the second person ever ... and I was a wreck. Then you put Rainbow's neck strap around your neck and told me to hold on tight. The rest is history, as they say."

Jackson grinned, "By the way, do you think you might find time to do the laundry today?"

"Why of course. Maybe while you get the oil changed in my truck? Late this afternoon we can make an appointment to do chores," she laughed, handing him his hat. "No excuses."

As Jackson drove away, Moria pondered on her recurring thought, *Am I lucky or am I blessed or am I blessed to be lucky? I am grateful, for sure.*

Pouring a second cup of coffee, she reached for the phone. When Maxine answered, she said, "Okay, boss lady, let's make a plan."

"We should finish the Deer Trail this morning. Shouldn't take too much longer. We can hike over to the Logging Road and see how it's going. I know some of these guys have taken vacation days to do this work. Jada better not complain any more about rewards for the volunteers. I've never slapped anyone silly, but I might try if she doesn't shut up about this," Maxine finished with truth in her voice.

During the morning, deer flies and other flying pests hummed around the trail ladies, taking bites where they could. Sweat streamed down their faces and spider webs seemed to drop down from nowhere to spread sticky webs on their prey. Brambles impeded their progress and poison oak was rampant. As the trail veered toward the stream, Moria said, "Time out," knelt down on the bank and rinsed her face and arms.

Maxine joined her, saying, "We're almost to the end. Let's git 'er dun."

The two women finally emerged onto the Jeep Trail and Moria looked back at their work. "Well, this is one for the books. Let's hope Pete keeps his word and leaves us alone," she said, as they scrambled up the embankment. "Listen, I hear the Weed Eater brigade. I think they're not far away." After about a ten minute walk the workers came into view.

Upon seeing the women, they shut off their tools. One of the volunteers wiped sweat from his face, saying, "Hey y'all, out here to check up on us?"

Moria looked at Maxine then back at the workers, "No, we finished the Deer Trail so we came to help you. What can we do?"

A look of surprise crossed his face. "You're serious?"

She laughed, "Might as well." Maxine gazed down the road. "This looks really good." Piles of kudzu and tree limbs lined both sides of the trail, leaving a clear path for their endurance guests. "Let's hope it doesn't grow back before the ride. So, what can we do?" The guy reached into the tool pile and with a grin, handed them each a machete and gloves.

Soon Moria and Maxine were whacking away with the best of them. A voice down the trail yelled, "Heads up, ladies." They turned to see a copperhead slithering their way. Everyone gave the snake a wide berth as it crawled into the underbrush off the trail.

Moria grinned and said to one of the men, "It's not my first rodeo. I've been living in these mountains all my life. In fact, you look familiar. Didn't we go to school together? I remember you, Wilton Bowers, right? You sat behind me in math class and you were always pulling my hair. Remember the day I pulled *your* hair?"

Wilton rubbed his head, laughing, "Oh yeah. I thought you'd never let go. We got in a shit pot of trouble." He paused, staring down the trail and gave her a wink. "We even dated a few times. If I was cleaned up, maybe you'd recognize me … and you married a guy from Wyoming. I've seen y'all at The Juniper Tree."

I do remember you, Wilton. You were my first real kiss. We could have gotten into another shit pot of trouble that night.

"I remember Jeremy, too," he said, nodding toward Maxine, "when he was a bouncer at The Juniper. Ask him, if he remembers Wilton."

"I'll do that. I hope you're using your rider bucks to enter the ride."

"Sure am. This'll be my first ride. Been reading up on conditioning my horse. Haven't had much time to ride lately," nodding to the pile of kudzu, "but we're almost done. You remember Cade? We're teaming up together for the ride."

Moria's ears perked up hearing the words, first ride.

Surprised, she asked, "How do you know Jackson?"

"Oh, I've seen him around."

"At the pool hall?" she asked, already knowing the answer.

"Yeah, it's a happening place. Maybe you'll join us there one of these days."

"I'll think about it. If you and Cade need any help with your riding plan, Jackson and Jeremy will be glad to offer advice."

"Maybe I need lessons from the teachers," he answered with a hopeful, teasing smile.

"We'll see you all on the trail before the ride, I'm sure," Maxine answered, beginning to see where this tale was headed. "Looks like we better call it a day. Don't work too much longer in this heat, you all are doing an amazing job."

"Join us any time," Wilton answered. "See ya' around," and turned back to his task.

The two women walked back down the Deer Trail to the truck, admiring their handiwork and tossing a few more branches to the side. "It'll be interesting to see if Wilton and Cade get through the ride. Maybe Jackson or Jeremy could ride with them," Moria said.

"Somehow, I don't think those two guys are going to want any help. Let's just hope they come to the first time riders meeting and *listen* to the vets."

Yeah, and there's a chance that more of the volunteers are first time riders, too. We can only give advice and hope for the best."

As they reached the truck Maxine asked, "What's the rest of your day like?"

"I'm going to clean the barn, then Jackson and I have a work date," she answered as if this was an ordinary part of their routine.

"Huh? That's a new one."

Moria proceeded to explain and when she finished, Maxine couldn't help but laugh, "So, this adds excitement to the bedroom?"

She smiled, "We'll see. I think we'd do better dancing at The Juniper Tree."

Chapter Sixteen

A s Moria approached their shed row barn, the horses came out from the shelter to greet her. Rainbow pressed his head against her for the hands he knew and trusted to rub and scratch his neck. Silver pushed his way close for attention. The chestnut's ears laid back *not sharing.* Silver stood his ground and managed to get his share of attention. "Someday I'm going to be in the middle of a horse fight with you two. Be gone."

The heat of the afternoon was barely noticed as Moria cleaned stalls, swept cobwebs from the corners, raked the aisle, scrubbed the water troughs and prepared the night feed. Taking a moment to rest, she sat on a hay bale and looked across the field, over the creek and beyond into the forest.

A thoughtful look crossed her face as she remembered Mousey's fear of the Indians. *Wonder what she'd think if she knew we have Indian graves on our property. Maybe I'll show her sometime.*

The crunch of gravel let her know date work time was almost here and soon Jackson came through the gate. "Hey, Missy, what have you been up to today?"

"Do you really want to know?" she patted the hay bale, "Sit."

"Do I have to roll over?" he grinned.

"Not quite yet. Don't wear yourself out on our date so you can't do your tricks later," she answered, rubbing his leg.

Jackson sat beside Moria and soon Rainbow and Silver returned, looking for treats. "Okay, okay," he said.

Moria gave the short version, ending with, "Do you know Wilton and Cade?"

"Yeah, I've seen them around. Why?"

"They'll be first time riders. I'd appreciate it if you would keep an eye on them during the ride."

Jackson looked at Moria in disbelief. "Excuse me ma'am, we're having over a hundred people on our property that weekend. I'm not riding. Somebody's got to mind the store, so we'll have a place to live when the circus leaves town."

"Well, there's that," she answered, as if only just realizing the depth of their commitment.

Jackson took her hand, "Come on, let's get our chores done so we can roll over and do our tricks."

Pounce and Pandora followed their people to the house and Pounce gave a grim meow, *guess we're sleeping on the porch again.*

Pandora reached over and rubbed her face against him. *Don't worry, I'll be there.*

Yeah, once upon a time ... Pounce winked and flicked her with his tail.

~ ~ ~

The next morning Maxine's kitchen became the war room with lists and maps covering the table. Moria held her cup out for a refill of coffee as the evidence of their work swam before her eyes.

"You okay?" her friend asked, noticing Moria's glazed expression.

"Yeah, just overwhelmed. We've got to get this right. Even if we never have another endurance ride in Cherry Valley, I want people to know that this was a classy event."

"Hey, you know what, Missy? We all want the ride to be successful. You're not the only one stressed."

"You're right. Maybe we should go to The Juniper Tree tonight."

"Works for me. Now let's get busy. We need to get back to Jada's soon. Let's get our shit together and maybe we can go over there late this afternoon."

Moria picked up the map and the trail list. "Okay, let's decide which trails are ready. On the Red Loop … you know, I just thought of something. The fall colors will be coming in and red ribbons won't show up very well.

"Let's not borrow trouble. We'll see what the leaves are like when it's time to mark the trail. Maybe we'll have a storm that'll strip the trees."

"Works for me. From the start of the ride to the water crossing is a 'moving on' trail. Rodney seems to know what he's doing on the Ridge Trail above the gullies."

I don't know why we didn't explore that part before," Maxine said. "He's got Rita, the kids and some of the 4-Hers working every day. We should get up there and take a look."

Moria slid the map toward Maxine, "The trail from the Rutherford's seems easy to us because we know it, but when you get out among all those planted pines, if any ribbons are down a person could get turned around."

"At least, our worn path is there if people will pay attention and follow it. I think we should have a spotter where the Blue and Red Trails come together." Maxine wrote down, spotter at red and blue."

"The powerline's easy and we better have lots of turn ribbons into the Deer Trail or they'll end up at Pete's. He'll be mad and come down and block the trail."

Maxine laughed, "Does this go on our borrowing trouble list?"

"The Logging Road will be slow going because of the footing. Red clay and rolling rocks don't add up to speed but it's doable and at least, no one will be hung in the kudzu," Moria said, remembering her decent into the wall of green vines *seems like so long ago.*

Maxine waved her hand in front of Moria's face. "Hello?"

"Sorry, I was just remembering … Let's call Jada and see if Richard's home.

Soon they were out the door. "Why don't we have lunch at the Pool Hall before we go to Jada's," Maxine suggested.

"Call the guys?" Moria asked.

"No, let's surprise them if they're there."

Moria and Maxine walked into the Pool Hall to an unexpected scene, Jackson and Jeremy having lunch with Cassie.

"Uh oh," Maxine said, as the two guys smiled and motioned them over to the table. "Stay cool."

The men stood and reached over to the next table for chairs. Cassie smiled, saying, "Glad to see you. We're talking about plans for the bridge. Why don't you all catch me up on the trail work? This was quite a surprise when I came to lunch and your guys were here," Cassie continued, reacting to their startled faces.

When everyone was seated and their orders filled, Jackson said, "I was just telling Cassie that the volunteers helping on the bridge are doing most of the work. They own one of the construction companies and I trust them to get it right. Cassie says that the Forest Service will send an inspector out to certify it safe for horses to cross. We need to be sure the volunteers get rider bucks, even if they spend them with the vendors or maybe they'll become first time riders."

"Wait till Jada hears this one. She may be having second thoughts about the rider bucks. Too late now." Maxine laughed.

Jackson turned to Moria, "I'd like to restore the bridge to its original design. Do you think your parents have any old pictures or drawings, since your family was the original owner of the land where the bridge is?"

"Good idea," Moria said, thinking of the many boxes of historical information stored in the attic. "That's a rabbit hole for me on a rainy day."

"Don't depend on the weather, Missy. I'll help you tonight," Jackson answered.

Moria smiled, "Uh, we have other plans tonight. The Juniper Tree, remember?"

"Oh, yeah. We've been trying to get there for a while. Well, our adventure into the attic can wait a day."

"Cassie, you ought to meet us at there tonight," Moria said, and her invitation was echoed by the others.

"Are you sure?" Cassie asked. "I wouldn't feel right, just wandering in."

"Because you're the Forest Ranger, or you're single? Don't answer. We'll pick you up. Being a California girl, you'll fit right in."

A look of relief passed over Cassie's face as she said, "You don't mind? I'd love to go." She hesitated, "How did you all feel going as … teachers?" looking at Moria and Maxine.

Maxine took up the story, saying, "We were living here when The Juniper Tree was built and attended the grand opening. Everybody went and some of us just kept going because we wanted to be supportive. We tried not to dance with the fathers of our students and not get knee-walkin' drunk." She winked at Moria.

Cassie grinned, "But sometimes you did?"

"Well, once," Moria answered, glancing at Jackson, who covered a smile with his napkin. "Okay, it's settled. We'll pick you up around 7:00."

Moria turned to Jackson in the parking lot, "We're going to Jada's. Richard's home today. It's easier to regroup without half of Cherry Valley being there. Which reminds me," she said, "we probably need to have an Introductory Ride. There's going to be more newbies than I thought. It's probably not too late to add it to our agenda."

Maxine looked at Jeremy and raised her eyebrows.

"Yes ma'am, I'm on board to run the intro ride."

"Done and done," she laughed. "Probably the easiest thing you'll have to do." *You think?* whispered the breeze through the trees.

~ ~ ~

Settled in Richard and Jada's den, Moria opened the conversation with encouragement, saying, "Considering it's the first of September and we've still got almost a month to tie up the loose ends, I think we're doing pretty well."

Richard, all business, opened his laptop and announced, "A hundred riders, signed up and paid."

Moria gasped, "Hope our field will hold everybody. That's great. I guess the overflow could be at the Rutherford's. It's a good thing they travel so much and let us house sit. 'Course there's not much to do but cut the grass. And we can seed their pasture if needed."

She stopped for breath and Richard continued, "There have been lots of inquiries, too, since this is a new ride."

"Since this is a new ride, we need to add an Intro. Ride, if possible. Will you check with AERC and see if it's not too late? We can always do an informal one. Jeremy said he would do it."

Richard nodded and tapped away. On the spur of the moment Moria said, to him, "Thanks so much for all your work. We couldn't have done it without you."

He smiled and Jada frowned, as if to say, *What about me?*

Seeing her expression, Moria added, "And, just think, Jada, if it wasn't for your idea, we wouldn't be having The Cherry Valley Ride. Thanks for your hard work, too." *They should be thanking us.*

Jada took the floor, saying, "I've ordered the awards from our local store but haven't given them numbers on the completions. They have some really nice trophies. The ones I liked for top ten were glass water pitchers with the inscription, a mountain range and horse running. The 50-milers get a larger size and the Limited Distance riders, a smaller one of the same design." She waited for the expected blowback.

With a determined look, Maxine glared at Jada. "No, we need same size trophies. The LD people work just as hard to prepare and compete. Some of these people are sponsoring new riders, some are bringing horses back from injuries, or their own injuries, or it might be the first ride for a new horse."

Jada clenched her fist saying, "You all agreed that I could take care of the awards. I think people should always go 50 miles."

"And how did that work out?" Moria asked, nodding toward Jada's barn.

"Well, sometimes you have to take a risk," Jada answered with less confidence. "Okay, you win. All trophies the same size, ribbons for the weight divisions." No contest on the ribbon choice." She reached onto the table behind her and brought a sample of the completion awards, a coffee mug, light green with the same design as the trophies.

Maxine and Moria agreed about the coffee mugs and Richard gave a sigh of relief.

Moria excused herself to the restroom and soon came flying out with a sheaf of papers and envelopes in her hand. She dropped them in Jada's lap, "What is this?"

Jada looked at the papers and anger flashed from her eyes. "Where did you get these?"

"You know very well. They were under the bathroom cabinet."

Jada stood, hands on hips as the ride entries scattered to the floor. "So, you were snooping into my cabinets?"

"No, you were out of toilet paper. I thought that's where I'd find some. Instead, I found these entries you were supposed to mail *last week*."

Richard flinched at this revelation, "We'll get them in the mail tomorrow."

Moria sat back down, picked up the maps, and tried to focus on the purpose of their visit, to update Richard on the latest trail change and be sure items needed for the camp were available. *Even though Richard's not a rider, he needs to know about the trails.*

"You know, Rodney's worked relentlessly on the latest trail change." She offered the map to Richard and Jada peered over his shoulder. "His summer visitors and the 4-H kids have worked really hard."

Jada said, "Show me where this is. I need to film some children. Maybe they'll be available for a photo shoot."

Realizing Mousey and Sassy did not need to be filmed under any circumstances, Maxine said, "The kids are finished with their work and Rodney said the 4-Hers are going to camp, since school is starting soon, and the visitors are going sightseeing in the area."

Moria nodded in agreement, changing the subject. "Richard, let's hear your list for camp."

"Well, let's start at the road. We'll need signs on the main road and the turn into camp. Do you and Jackson want to mark off parking spaces?"

Moria made a note, "Yeah, maybe we should. It's going to be tight. We'll get out there and do some estimates. I guess it'll be first come; first served."

Richard continued, "The Porta Pottys will be between the vendors and the vet check and one by your barn. Where is the vet check?"

A blank look crossed Moria's face. "Oh, the vet check? Jackson and I can figure it out and get back to you."

Don't forget the tent," Jada added. "There's always a possibility of rain."

Maxine, said, with a straight face, "Is it too late to rent the fairgrounds?"

"Okay," Richard said, "Let's finish up. I'm hungry. We've rented trash cans and the generator is donated. I think between us we can supply water troughs. You all can go to the hardware store for surveyor's tape and what other trail markings you might need. We have a running account with them right now. I think between all of us we can come up with temporary fencing for the vet check."

"We'll need another tent there," Jada said. "Most people bring chairs, but we might have to supply a few."

"Richard, I believe you said at our last meeting you have the paperwork in order, vet cards, and all else?" Moria asked. He nodded, and she picked up the completion mug sample. "Here's your award for your dedicated service," handing him the mug.

With a rare smile, he said, "I will treasure this forever," setting it on his desk. "Are we done?"

Maxine closed her laptop, saying, "Will we see you all at The Juniper Tree tonight?"

Jada glanced sideways at Richard, who said, "Not tonight. We've got some work to do," looking at the abandoned ride entries on the floor.

As they drove away, Moria let out a sigh. "That Richard, he doesn't joke around and, you know, he's saved us a world of trouble."

~ ~ ~

At Peace in the Valley Farm, the furry friends watched as the taillights of Jackson's truck disappeared into the night.

Don't our people ever stay home? Pounce whined, sitting on the steps with Pandora.

Hero nudged Dixie off the porch. *They had their dancin' boots on. I don't think they'll be back for a while. We're goin' huntin'. Wanna go?*

The cats brightened at the invitation and the four guardians of the farm dashed away into the night.

"Let's not forget Cassie," Moria reminded Jackson, as they turned on to the highway. "I hope she has a good time tonight. It must be hard, moving to a new town and region. Plus, since she's an official, she's got to be careful about not getting knee walkin' drunk."

"Yeah, like teachers," Jackson commented, remembering Moria's meltdown during a scrap with Jada in the bar restroom last year.

"Well, lesson learned," Moria laughed. "Here's Cassie's house. Why don't you go to the door?"

Just then, Cassie came out to the truck. Jackson opened the back door and said, with an admiring grin, "Looking sharp."

"You're wearing the buckle. That'll be an impressive conversation piece, for sure," Moria added. "You're dressed for the occasion," noticing Cassie's boots, snug jeans, standard cowboy shirt and western style silver earrings.

Cassie laughed, "If I don't watch what I eat, you won't be able to see the buckle and thanks for picking me up. I never would have gone by myself."

"We've got your back. Hope you have a good time and don't get overwhelmed by all the 'suits' who become cowboys on Saturday night. Actually, lots of these people are our trail workers so this probably won't be the only time you'll see them," Moria encouraged.

The parking lot at The Juniper Tree overflowed into the nearby field. Trucks and cars settled down for the evening, their engines ticking to silence as they cooled down.

At the door, the bouncer greeted the trio, "Let the games begin," and gave Cassie a whistle. "Welcome. We've been thinking you'd show up one of these nights. Save me a dance, yu hear?"

"You got it, Mr. Bouncer. I'll be waitin,'" sliding into southern talk. She winked at him and entered into what Moria realized was not uncharted territory for her friend.

Jackson led the way to the tables where most of the horse people gathered. One of the guys pulled another table into the group giving a big grin to the trio. "Looks like we got company tonight," he announced and pulled a chair out for Cassie. Jackson seated Moria and several people waved to them.

The waitress appeared, saying to Jackson and Moria, "The usual?" Jackson nodded and she moved to Cassie, "And for you, ma'am?"

Cassie placed her order and the waitress asked, "Are you from California, ma'am?"

"Well, yes. How'd you know?"

Your accent gives you away, no offense," the waitress added.

Cassie looked at the waitress with a smile. "Honey, I'm your people now. Bring me what Moria's havin', please."

By now, Maxine and Jeremy had joined the group. Maxine greeted Cassie with, "Glad to know you're one of us. We can always use another down-home gal," she said with a grin. "Hope this will be a night to remember."

Cassie reached for her drink, "Depends," she smiled as the band struck up a familiar song, "Always on My Mind."

Maxine and Jeremy headed to the dance floor. The spinning lights, country songs and friends gave Moria a moment to reflect, *it doesn't get any better than this, except, maybe on the back of a horse.*

Jackson reached for Moria's hand and pushed his chair back. She nodded slightly toward Cassie.

Jackson got the message and turned toward the ranger. "May I have this dance?" he asked with a bow.

"Of course." Then Cassie and Jackson joined the others on the dance floor.

Moria watched as they whirled away, remembering the first night Jackson visited The Juniper Tree. *My leg cast from the ski accident kept me seated and the next thing I knew, Jada whisked Jackson right out the door. I barely knew him, but something told me he was worth the chase. Where is Jada tonight? Home mailing out the entries!*

Moria felt a tap on her shoulder and looked up to see Wilton with his hand out.

"Well, hey there. You clean up pretty good," she said, as they headed for the dance floor. "No hair pulling tonight?" she teased.

Wilton nodded toward Jackson, "I guess not. I'd rather face the principal than your Jackson. I hear he's quite the cowboy."

Moria laughed, "He thinks so."

Wilton held Moria close in a 'friends with a history' embrace. She relaxed in his arms as they swayed to "Lookin' for Love" *in all the wrong places*, Moria hummed, remembering again her time with Wilton in their younger years.

As the song ended, Jackson maneuvered close to them and tapped Wilton on the shoulder, saying, "Meet Cassie, our new ranger," and reached for Moria as Wilton took Cassie into his arms.

Almost no one sat during this set of their favorite songs. Many dancers changed partners, or with a shake of the head, some couples stayed together. When the band took a break, thirsty dancers flocked back to the tables.

Cassie took a swig of her beer, saying, "Man, I think I've met all the cowboys in the county tonight. Don't worry, y'all will be the ones taking me home."

Moria said, "So, *y'all* is your new word now?

Cassie signaled for another beer, "I'm just gettin' started, honey," she laughed.

Moria leaned into Jackson with a worried look, "I think we've unleashed a tiger."

"She's fine," he replied. "Remember, she's not one of your students. Just let her roll."

The band struck up "Rocky Top" and the dancers were on the floor again, dancing like pros. "This'll get her back to herself," Jackson commented. "Come on, Missy let's show 'em how it's done."

The night blazed on, the music louder, voices scrambled over each other to be heard, dancers drew closer as their favorite songs enveloped them. Then, the last call for alcohol herded them back to their tables.

Cassie held up her hand with a no as the waitress reached her. "I'm Junipered out," she grinned.

The waitress gave her a smile and a wink. "Yeah, I believe you are one of us. Welcome to Cherry Valley."

Later, Maxine walked out with Moria as they headed to the parking lot. "If you're feeling okay tomorrow afternoon, why don't we ride to the ridge and check out Rodney's trail?"

Moria laughed with bravado, "Speak for yourself." Then, she turned to Cassie, "What about you? Up for a ride tomorrow?"

"Sure, after noon. I'll call Rodney and see if I can get Timex again. Maybe they'll want to go with us."

"What about you two?" Maxine asked, turning toward Jackson and Jeremy.

"We've got some help on the bridge tomorrow. Don't stay out after dark, and maybe take a compass just in case," came his teasing answer.

"Moria whipped out her reply. "You think we'll get lost?"

"Take it easy," Jackson said pulling her close. "Sounds like the beer's talking."

Cassie let herself into the back seat and soon the trio was on their way. Jackson turned on the radio and the road rolled out before them, a reminder that 'tomorrow is another day' full of Southern adventure.

Chapter Seventeen

Peace in the Valley Farm awakened to a bright pink and gold sunrise, all except the cowboy and his cowgirl wrapped in a tangle of covers. Horses whinnied, dogs barked, and Pounce and Pandora snuggled with their people. The phone rang. Moria answered in her 'I've been awake for hours' voice.

"No, you haven't been awake for hours," came Cassie's reply. "Neither have I," she laughed, "but I did call Rodney. He said I could use Timex. They can't go today. Didn't say why. Just said, you'll see, wait at the gate. I checked with Maxine. She's going to meet us at Rodney's about two this afternoon. I'm not meaning to mind your business, here. Just glad to ride and see the new trail."

"You can mind my business anytime. Remember, you're one of us now."

As Moria mixed the pancake batter, Jackson poured his coffee, saying, "I'll feed the horses while you finish up here. Give Rainbow time to eat before his easiest day ever."

Later Moria groomed the chestnut gelding and commenced a one-sided conversation with him. "Sorry you're going to miss some rides while we're getting ready for this one. In fact, you're not going to get to run down the road until after this circus. I don't even have to do your body clip for a while yet." Dropping the brush back into the grooming kit, she laid her face against Rainbow's shoulder, breathing the horse aroma she treasured. "You'll be my go-to horse, for sure, if we have to rescue somebody."

Then she whispered, *Dear Jesus, please guide us safely down the Cherry Valley trails in the coming days and through the ride. Is this a meant to be? Guess we wouldn't have gotten this far with our plans ... or maybe this is your teachable moment for us. I pray that I remember, it's not all about me.*

Maxine's voice brought her back to the moment. "Hey, shake a leg, Missy. Time's a wastin'. Catch On Fire whinnied from the gate, anxious to be on the way.

As the two riders trotted toward Rodney's, Moria asked, "Why do you think we have to wait at the gate? It's usually open."

Maxine pointed toward his farm. "There's Cassie's truck parked outside. Guess we'll find out in a minute."

Two serious German Shepherds leapt off the porch and raced to the gate.

Rainbow and Catch On Fire skidded to a stop. Rainbow looked at his companion saying, *Those dudes look familiar. Remember...*

Rodney hurried around the side of the house and called to the dogs with authority, "Sitz. Platz. Bleib." (Sit, Down, Stay) The dogs dropped obediently to the ground but stared at their suspects with unnerving attention.

"Guess you're not wanting any company today," Moria joked, and remained mounted.

"Oh sure, come on in," pointing to the porch and commanding the dogs to "Geh." (Go)

"You're sure?" Moria asked, peering at the dogs. I think we've seen these guys before at Pete's."

"Sho' nuff," Rodney answered with a grin. "We had a little trouble on the farm last night while y'all was rowdyin' around at The Juniper Tree. The cowgirlies thought they was gonna take a midnight walk with the 4-H kids. Lucky for me and Rita, the horses kicked up a fuss. I went out to see if there were a coyote prowling around. When I turned on the light, the visitors took off and there stood our young'uns, just about to leave the property."

"So, what happened?" Moria asked, wrapped up in the tale but eyeing the dogs.

"Rita gave the girls 'what for' and restricted them to their room. First thing this morning I asked Pete to borrow his dogs until I can get my own."

Maxine studied the dogs, commenting, "That's pretty amazing that they can just go off to a strange property and guard it like it's their own. Pete spoke English to them."

"These doggies speak two languages," Rodney said with pride as he reached to open the gate. "It's called training. They've been around the military. I should have my own dogs soon. Besides keepin' track of the young'uns, they'll watch for coyotes and any strangers lurking around. I don't want to be the one that lets a bad guy get to these girls before the trial. Come on in," he invited.

You're sure? Rainbow appeared to question, pricking his ears forward and eyeing the dogs. *We are prey animals, you know.*

"These dogs only attack on command or in a threatening situation. I trust them," Rodney said as he opened the gate, winking at Rainbow's wide eyes.

"What are the dogs' names?" Maxine asked, "Or do they even have names?"

"Yeah, they do. One's named Bad and the other's named Worse, he laughed. "I'm gonna call my dogs Frenzy and Fire."

"Give us a heads up when you get them," Maxine said, not wanting to ride by the farm and be surprised with an unexpected horse spook.

He led his neighbors around to the barn area where Cassie was finishing saddling Timex. Moria glanced toward the back of the house to see bars on a bedroom window and Mousey's tearful face pressed against the barrier. "Hey, Miss Moria, can you get us out of here?" the youngster moaned.

Moria smiled and thought, *not my monkeys, not my circus,* but said, "Remember Winnie the Pooh's advice, "You're braver than you believe, stronger than you seem."

"Oh yeah, that," Mousey sighed and turned away from the window.

Cassie mounted up and grinned saying, "Let's ride," and turned to the gate.

The three riders travelled side by side on the road to the forest. Moria said, "What do you all think about the dogs?"

"Well, I'm not going to be creeping around Rodney's property and I'll bet that's the end of the midnight visitors," Maxine answered. "Rita's taken on a challenging job to keep these two kiddos safe and secluded. I don't know if I'd have the patience. School's hard enough."

By now, they had reached the gate where the road became trail. Cassie dismounted and opened the gate. "Sounds like we're near the bridge. I can hear hammers and saws. I don't think it's the three bears helping us out," she laughed.

Jackson waved to them and called, "Come on over and see the progress."

"Wow! This is really good." The next few minutes became a lesson in carpentry, history and pride as Jackson described the bridge's historical past.

"Looks like you've kept to the original design. How'd you do that? Moria asked, now doubly impressed.

Jackson grinned, "When all else fails, go to the library. Jeremy kept the office and Sadie, the librarian, was more than happy to help me. She's quite a historian and was pleased that we were restoring a part of Cherry Valley's past. It's going to be a while before we're finished to specs though. Come on over. Let's see if it's going to hold the horses."

"Surely you jest," Maxine said, looking into the interior of the bridge. The sides had open spaces to provide light to the interior, but the floor was new wood, a slip and fall waiting to happen.

Jeremy walked over to her, saying, "Come on. I'll go with you all."

The horses followed Jeremy to the other side with no mishap. The three riders breathed a sigh of relief and then were distracted by a rider coming down the trail.

Jada, mounted on her latest horse, Mayhem, came around the corner waving her camera. "Hi. I was out getting some trail pictures and heard something going on here. I'd love to get a few shots of y'all working on the bridge." She paused, smiled, and said, "Continue on."

The helper threw down his hammer and glared at Jackson. "I thought you told me she wouldn't be coming around." Then frowned at Jada, "You need to leave. Nobody's taking their shirts off for your pictures."

Taken aback, Jada scrambled for an answer. "Not you, buddy." She came closer and stood near Jackson and Jeremy. "I have some other prospects in mind," winking at the two guys.

Moria said, "No ma'am. Come on, you can ride with us and see Rodney's new trail." The trail ladies surrounded Jada, moving her forward with them. "See ya' later, guys," Moria called as the group disappeared up the trail with their captured rider.

Soon they reached the turn off to Jada's house. The silence was broken when Jada said, "You bitches can let me off here," as if this was an ordinary trail ride.

Moria looked at Jada's narrowed eyes and knew she would go right back to the bridge. "Oh, come along with us. I'm sure you'll see some beautiful scenery from the ridge." Jada pushed Mayhem against Rainbow, who pinned his ears and leaned into the offending horse. Jada reached for her phone, Rainbow gave another shove and the phone dropped to the ground.

"Damn it. This is kidnapping! Where is my camera? I need to record this outrage," she screamed, searching for the camera. "It's back on the trail. I've got to look for it. You all are going to jail."

During Jada's rant, Maxine dismounted and scooped up the phone, putting it in her cantle bag. Maxine gave Jada her 'schoolteacher' look and said, "Let's ride, dude."

Rainbow reminded Mayhem with laid back ears, *Move it. We've got a long way to go and a short time to get there.*

The contingent of four continued up the trail, Jada huffing and puffing as the riders corralled her. Ignoring Jada's whining, they chatted about the progress for the ride and complimented Jada on her hard work.

Cassie took the lead from her friends, "Just think, Jada, if it hadn't been your idea to have the ride, we wouldn't be having so much fun getting ready. I'm sure this will be a ride to remember."

By now they had reached the water crossing. The kidnappers looked at each other, not sure how they would get across and keep Jada with them. Their captive took the chance, wheeled and bolted back down the road.

The three looked at each other and laughed, "I don't think Sheriff Bramblett will buy her story, if she gets that far," Maxine said. "I'm guessing she's either going to look for the camera or skedaddle home. Poor Richard, he's in for a night." She hesitated, "We've got to return her phone. That's a legitimate theft."

Moria looked at the rushing stream and then at Maxine.

No, Missy. We're not throwing the phone in the water."

"Let's take a look at Rodney's trail," Cassie encouraged them. "I'm exhausted with all this drama."

Oh, yeah, the trail," Moria said, and began to look for the entrance. "Here it is," pointing to red ribbons tied to a tree sheltering a small opening just across the creek. This crossing's going to be a mess with two trips of fifty-milers and one of twenty-fives."

"Well, they would have done the same if they had gone through the gullies," Cassie commented. "If we have another ride here, we'll have to harden the crossing. I should have seen this. Too late now."

Another ride here? Uh, no. flashed through Moria's mind. She glanced at Maxine, to see her friend's wrinkled brow. "Well, let's git 'er dun," she said, crossing the creek and beginning the climb to the ridge. The narrow one-track trail serpentined back and forth to prevent erosion. "Somebody knew what they were doing. Looks like this path's been here a long time. I guess we never thought to explore here since it was so overgrown at the entrance. Rodney's crew did a great job, so far.

"I'm thinking the rangers cleared it originally since it was part of the fire break. Or, it could have been an Indian trail. I'm going to check this out," Cassie said. Heavy breathing announced her effort, standing in two-point, clinging to her horse's mane as they climbed. "I need to do more riding if I'm going to hang out with y'all."

The trail leveled out as they reached the top of the ridge. The riders halted to let the horses breathe and took time to gaze down into the forest below. Looking ahead, Maxine said, "I don't think we should trot since we don't know the trail." The others agreed and they moved along, single file.

A thin barrier of trees marked the edge of the trail on one side and sparse, twisted pines and hardwoods filled in on the opposite side. Through the trees they could see the sky on the other side of the ridge. Cassie pointed to blackened stumps from a long ago fire. "At least it cleared out the underbrush. Looking at the size of the regrowth, it's been a while, probably from a lightning strike. Do you all remember any forest fires up here in the last twenty years, or so?"

Moria and Maxine looked at each other. "Moria said, "We had just finished college and into our first year of teaching. There were fires up here off and on. None threating us or I'd remember. They must have gotten them out quickly."

Now the history of the ridge had Cassie's attention. "I'm going to do some research about this area where the trails go for the ride. It might be interesting for the riders to know who went before them."

As they continued, the trail became more tangled in vines and the horses stepped over logs and scrambled through a rocky section. "What's this all about?" Maxine asked, taking a closer look at the scattered rocks. "Oh look, there's an arrowhead. This must have been an Indian cache for defense. Hold up, I want to get this arrowhead," she said, dismounting and reaching for her treasure. Just then, thunder grumbled in the distance and lightening flashed.

Moria yelled, "Never mind. I don't think these folks want you stealing their stuff. Come on, let's ride." Another stab of lightening punctuated her angst and thunder rolled across the mountains.

Maxine scrambled to control her frightened horse as he whirled away from her. Cassie grabbed the bay's rein and Timex backed up. Her hind feet slid off the edge of the trail pushing loose rocks down the hillside. Cassie let go of Catch On Fire's rein and kicked her horse forward, calling above the storm, "Here comes the next act." Wind and torrents of rain lashed across the ridge.

Maxine managed to re-mount and the three riders hustled down the unknown trail, going slowly, not knowing what lay ahead. The storm continued to pound the travelers, a tree crashed behind them, the horses bolted forward and jumped over whatever detritus lay in their path. At last, thunder drummed in the distance and the riders realized that their problems were behind them and belonged to others now.

A brisk wind blew through the trees, scattering leaves and sending the clouds on their way. "My body and soul," Moria said in relief, "We could have died back there."

Maxine laughed, "Let's get off this mountain before another storm tracks us down," glancing over her shoulder at dark clouds looming on the horizon. About the trail, it is better than the gullies. This last part just needs to be finished."

The riders descended with care, sliding in the mud and soon came out at the Rutherford's. "Almost home," Moria sighed. "What a ride."

When they reached the turn to Rodney's, Cassie said, "I need to return this pony and head home for a hot shower. Will I see you all tomorrow?"

"I wish," Moria answered. "We're in school from tomorrow forward. "Let us know any history you discover. Thanks for going with us today. Now, you're *really* one of us."

"Take care," Maxine called to Cassie and she and Moria turned toward home. They approached Maxine's farm to see Jackson's truck and Richard's SUV parked in the driveway. The two women looked at each other with foreboding and Moria said, "This can't be good."

Just then, Jeremy stepped onto the porch and waved the women to the house. Maxine said, "I think you're going to be here a while. Let's put the horses up and face the music. At least, the sheriff's not here yet," she said with a dubious smile.

Jackson came out to the barn to help them, giving Moria a hug. "Stealing people's phones and kidnapping them is against the law, you know. Lucky for you all, Jeremy and I sweet talked Jada into letting this go, with the promise of a shirts off photo shoot."

Moria winced and Maxine stared at Jackson saying, "You better be joking or all hell's gonna to break loose."

"Well, there are consequences for breaking the law," Jackson said with a grin.

"And there are consequences for Jeremy if there's a photo shoot with Jada." Maxine shot back in a grim reply.

Horses forgotten, Moria and Maxine stood before Jackson in defiance. Moria poked her finger on Jackson's chest saying, "This had better be a joke, buddy."

Jackson backed off, seeing he could end up in the water trough. "Let's finish up here, get in house, and sort everything out."

Before long, they headed inside, Jackson holding a lady with each hand. The smell of the fired up grill went unnoticed as they reached the porch.

"Okay, you two missies put your boots on. Here we go," Jackson encouraged, opening the door and walking behind them into the sunroom.

Richard and Jada sat on the couch glaring at the two miscreants. Richard broke the silence, "Well, what do you two have to say for yourselves?"

Speechless, Moria stepped closer to Jackson. Jeremy nodded to Maxine. She reached in her pocket for the phone and handed it to Jada, who snatched it, pressing the button to see if it still worked.

Moria recovered enough to say, "Jada harassed the guys who were working on the bridge."

Jada raised her hand, "Objection. I just wanted a few pictures. This would have been great." She sighed with feigned disappointment, covering her face.

"You should have asked first," Moria continued. "That volunteer had already left the trail work group because you offended him about taking his shirt off. He only came to work on the bridge because you wouldn't be around. You need to respect other peoples' feelings." She paused, thinking of what to say next. *Where am I? In the fourth grade?*

Richard ran his fingers through his hair, stood up and spoke again, "I think we're done here. We'll be returning the work we've completed so far and you can take it from there. Moria, you need to respect people's feelings, too." Jada began to cry. Jeremy and Jackson shifted uncomfortably, looked at each other and the door.

Maxine reached in her pocket, approached Jada, and got down on one knee. Extending her closed hand to Jada, she said, "Here's a peace offering. We're turning in our weapons." She opened her hand and offered Jada the arrowhead.

Suspicion clouded Jada's face. "What is this? A dirty rock?"

With a straight face, and genuine concern for the ride, Maxine continued, "No, this is a priceless piece of warfare … an arrowhead. It's valuable. Treasure it."

Jackson, Jeremy, and Moria barely restrained themselves from laughing and Richard looked on with interest. Jada examined the arrowhead. "Can I wear it?" she asked.

"Of course," Maxine answered with a sigh of relief. "I'll even put it on a leather string for you. Peace?"

"Peace. No shirts off. I get it."

Richard reached for Jada's hand as they prepared to leave.

Jeremy said, "Hey, don't leave. Stay for dinner. We're having burgers."

Richard looked at Jada, who nodded yes.

Maxine gave Jeremy a panicked look.

"No worries. Jackson made a trip to The Diner for fixins'. Let's hope they never go out of business." Everyone laughed as the group trooped out to the porch for supper. Maxine grabbed a couple of throws off the couch, tossing one to Moria, who was shivering from her wet clothes and, no doubt from their misbehaviors. Banding together again as friends on a mission will do, they toasted the day goodbye and enjoyed the evening as if nothing had ever happened.

~ ~ ~

Later in the evening after Moria rode Rainbow home and the horses were tended to, Jackson said, "Let's sit on the porch for a while and make a plan," smiling and putting his arm around his cowgirl. "I know you like plans."

Moria leaned into him, "Well, at least we didn't lose Richard in the chaos. Maxine saved the day for sure, giving Jada the arrowhead."

"Is that really where you all found the arrowhead?"

"Yep. It appeared this was a weapons cache for the tribe who lived around here. Every time I think about the Indians, I feel sad and guilty. My people were a part of this history."

Jackson held Moria closer, "My people were just as bad." Jackson rubbed his face from tiredness and perhaps sadness and guilt, too. "At least we can take care of their land, as best we can."

Pandora crept into Moria's lap, sensing her distress. She mindlessly scratched the cat's ears and stared out into the night. "Maybe we can give a donation to the Indian village outside of town. They make beautiful jewelry, leather belts, vests and so much more. In fact, I've bought some of their jewelry. You think they would like to be one of our vendors?"

"Not a bad idea. On second thought, people from out of town would probably buy something. Why don't you go talk to them and let Richard know if they want to join our circus."

Moria smiled, "Maybe I'll even buy something to encourage them." Pandora jumped to the floor sensing the trouble was over for the night and wandered to the barn in search of mice.

"It's your money, Missy." Taking her hand, he opened the door, "I've got a freebie for you in the meantime."

"Now, that's enticing," she teased.

Chapter Eighteen

The alarm jangled way too soon for Moria's comfortable self, snuggled up to Jackson. In the morning shadows she reached for the clock. "Okay, here we go, one hundred eighty days …" She reached for her shirt, pulled it over her head and mumbled, "Till summer."

"Hey, cheer up. At least you have a job and you're done at three o'clock."

"You must have a short memory about all the nights I brought my work home with me," she grumbled.

Jackson winked at her, "I think you need a shower," he said, leading her toward a great start for her morning.

Cherry Valley Elementary waited, serene as the trees sheltering it. The building's blank glass eyes stared into the parking lot awaiting the onslaught of children and seemed to laugh, *not my first rodeo, bring it on.*

As Moria entered the school, she remembered her prayer, *Dear Jesus, please keep your hand on my shoulder. Amen.*

The familiar ritual of greeting her friends and going into the library to hear Mr. Baldwin's plans for the new school year provided Moria with peace of mind. Time for someone else to make decisions, she thought, sliding into a seat beside Maxine.

Mr. Baldwin walked to the podium with purpose, welcomed everyone back and introduced two new teachers, Amy Styles and Rose Sampson. "Please welcome them." The group clapped and the new teachers smiled and waved. They will be the 5th grade team to replace our two retired teachers. They are right across the hall from you ladies," nodding at Moria and Maxine. You all can get acquainted after the meeting. When we finish, Ramona will hand out your class lists and the schedules."

Mr. Baldwin continued, "The most important task facing us in the coming days is our school evaluation. This year I know it will be in September. First, be sure your classrooms are in order and your students are on task at all times. I will speak with the parents at the PTA meeting to impress upon them to have their children here every day. We don't know the exact day they will come. Second, no personal days will be granted until this is over and if you are sick, I expect you to return with a doctor's excuse."

The teachers offered their reasons for needing to be away in September but the principal stood firm. "No," he answered again and again as people's lives were changed by his decision.

"My son's getting married in September …

We're going on a cruise for our anniversary …

My daughter's having a baby …

I have surgery scheduled …"

The new teacher, Amy, said, "I'm getting married in the middle of this month. Sorry, you'll have to get a sub. I won't be here for three days." She crossed her arms and glared at her new boss.

Maxine rolled her eyes and muttered, "Another Jada. What a way to start the year."

Moria watched Mr. Baldwin, knowing his experience would carry him through this crisis. He raised his hand to quiet them. "First of all, as I said, we won't know the day or the hour when we will have the visit. That is part of their purpose, to surprise us. I don't make the rules and neither do you. There's a good chance your personal plans will be spared. You can make an appointment with me, and we'll see if there are options for you. Now, please go to your classrooms and prepare for Open House on Thursday night and, as you know, the children will arrive on Monday. Good luck." With these final words, he left the room, returned to his office and closed the door.

Moria and Maxine picked up their papers and started toward the classroom. "Well, guess we'd better introduce ourselves since the two of them are new to the school and our ways. They might need a little help getting started," Maxine said, as they reached the 5th grade classroom and she knocked on the door jam. "Hi, we're your neighbors from across the hall. We're just stopping in to see if you all need any help."

"Thanks, come on in, if you can find room," Rose answered in a cheerful voice.

Moria looked over Maxine's shoulder into a room filled with large boxes from Office Depot, Target, Walmart, Dollar Tree and other stores. "Looks like you'll be well-prepared," Moria commented, as if this were an everyday occurrence.

"Well, we didn't know what to expect, being up here in the sticks," Amy answered, continuing to unpack a Walmart box holding a globe and a coffee maker, among the school supplies. "Rose and I just met a few weeks ago and decided to order things we might need."

"Have you just moved here?" Moria asked, choosing to ignore Amy's attitude.

"Well, sort of. My fiancé is an avid hunter and didn't want to get married unless I was willing to move to the mountains. He's quite a catch. I don't know how long we'll be here. If I have a baby, we're going back to Atlanta."

Can't be too soon for me, Moria thought, but said, "Hope all your plans work out. In the meantime, let us know if you have questions we can answer."

Turning to Rose she asked, "How'd you end up in Cherry Valley?"

She smiled, saying, "My story's a little different. We moved up here to take care of my parents. They live at home and we're building a house on their property. My children will go to this school." She hesitated, "They're in second and third grades. Are the teachers …?"

Maxine realized her concern. "Don't worry. In fact, would you like to meet them now? I'm sure they're working in their rooms. Come on, we'll run down there right quick."

Moria nodded in agreement and said to Amy, "I need to get busy."

Later, as Moria and Maxine began to pull items out of drawers and closets, Maxine said under her breath, "We need to keep our voices down," she glanced across the hall, "from unwanted ears. Not that we would gossip or be critical of other people," she grinned.

By the end of the day, the 4th grade classroom was decorated with the familiar back to school theme. Looking around the room, Maxine said, "You know, our stuff does seem worn out. Maybe we should do some shopping on our way home.

"Seriously?" Moria answered, taking a second look at the walls, the reading corner and the window decorations. "Well, it wouldn't hurt to make a pass through Walmart." Two hours later and a hundred and fifty dollars gone with the wind, the two teachers emerged into the late afternoon sun, arms laden with their finds.

"Guess we'll have to start over in the morning," Maxine laughed. "Nothing like keeping up with the Joneses. It's a good thing I don't have to buy any new endurance stuff right now. Also, remember to keep the receipts for taxes."

On the way across the parking lot, Moria said, "I forgot to tell you we might be adding the Indian Trading Post to the vendors."

Maxine stopped in her tracks. "What? Is this a joke?"

Moria shared the conversation with Jackson and the two women decided to visit the Cherokee Village the next afternoon.

~ ~ ~

The evening sun sank behind the trees, the last glimmers of light cast the horses' running shadows as they raced to the barn. Moria smiled, *Thank you, God, for my horse gene.* She put her arms around Rainbow's neck and took a deep breath, saying, "You never disappoint me, and you always smell good." She brushed his forelock to the side and put her face against his muzzle.

With a huff the chestnut gave her a push. *Enough already.*

"You're so romantic," she laughed, and began to scoop out the feed.

Later in the kitchen, Moria realized she had the ingredients for shrimp and grits, one of their favorites. "At least Jackson won't have to go to The Diner for us tonight," she announced to the cats. "There might even be a smidgen left for you."

"Great job, Missy," Jackson said as he scraped the last of his dinner onto his fork. "Uh oh," he said in mock surprise, dropping two shrimp to the floor. Yellow and gray streaks snatched their prizes and raced to the loft. "Got to keep on their good side," he teased.

Moria came to sit in his lap. "Guess it's just as well we didn't have children. They'd be spoiled rotten." Then she shared the happenings at school that day, but Jackson seemed distracted.

"What's the matter?" she asked, knowing him well enough to sense all was not right with him.

"I need to make a trip to the Wyoming office for a few days. Dad is making some changes and it's just easier if I'm there. Jeremy's going, too. It's a good chance for him to do a five-day course in the field with the Forest Rangers."

"When will you be back?"

Don't worry, Missy. We'll be back well before the ride." Then he tipped her face to his, saying, "Don't get in any trouble while I'm gone."

~ ~ ~

The next day at school Moria and Maxine redid their room and smiled at each other at the result. "Maybe the new decorations will inspire our students," Moria said.

"Or, not," Maxine countered, stapling the last poster in place. "Guess we'd better make some new lesson plans with our old books. Maybe we should rewrite a little history here, about the Indians."

Moria tapped her pen against the table and gazed out the window into the nearby field. Squinting her eyes, she could almost see the inhabitants of long ago crossing the field on their way to forage in the forest.

"Hello, Missy?" Maxine said, waving her hand in front of Moria's face.

Startled, she shook herself back into the classroom. "Uh, somehow, I don't think Mr. Baldwin would appreciate our efforts, especially not right before the visit," she paused and reached for her notebook. "But we could have somebody from the University come and give a talk about Indian history in our area. Maybe bring some artifacts and we could ask them to tell the story straight, not a movie version. They could get away with it and we wouldn't be in trouble." Looking up from her notes and across the hallway, she said, "Wonder if our neighbors would want to join us?"

Now, Maxine began to make notes. "We could have the kids do a mural for the hallway and research how the Indians lived. Maybe the art teacher could have them make clay bowls…"

"And, weave baskets," Moria added. "We should try it. If we can do it, they can, too."

Maxine doodled on the edge of her paper, "We need to get some Math in here. We'll be sure our speaker talks about how they traded. You know, we could even have a trading post."

"Disney, here we come," Maxine laughed.

As soon as their school day was over, the two teachers drove to the Cherokee Trading Post. As they crossed the parking lot, Moria said, "We might even do a field trip here."

"Let's not push our luck," Maxine answered as they entered the store. The head of the tribe, Running Deer, came from behind the counter to greet them. "Well, hello, ladies," he smiled and reached out his hands, one for each of them. "Good to see you. What's up?"

"We're getting ready for school but most important, we're having an endurance ride in the forest in a few weeks."

"I heard about it. Are you here for donations?"

"No, we have a better idea. We could use another vendor. Would you like to set up shop at the ride? We think a lot of people from out of town would love to purchase from you. You would keep all the proceeds, a donation to your school."

Surprise flashed across Running Deer's face. "You're sure? We could use some money for new books and some supplies."

Moria smiled, "We think it would add to the flavor of mountain living."

"Thanks," he answered. "I'll talk to the others. I'm sure they'll agree."

As they reached their trucks, Maxine said, "You know, they use a homeschool program approved by the state. I think it's a lot like what we do. It's interesting how they have a village and neighborhood on their own land. I've heard they bought it a long time ago. I'm sure Mousey would love to meet them. When the girls come to the ride they can get acquainted with some real Native Americans."

"Guess the girls will be at the ride unless something happens. They've been training all summer. Those young'uns have learned to take the horses' pulses and they've got a pretty good eye for lameness and ear for gut sounds. Rodney's doing a good job with them. I think the barred windows and the dog visitors, Bad and Worse, have made them pay attention to what they do. Rita's doing a good job with her charges. I really like her. Too bad she'll leave when the girls do."

"Maybe she can come back to visit," Moria answered, cranking her truck and heading for home.

The driveway to Peace in the Valley Farm seemed lonely without Jackson's truck in its parking space. *Hurry back, cowboy. I miss you already* Moria thought as she changed clothes and went to the barn for the nightly chores. Her furry companions trailed along with her, dashing to and fro in the bushes searching for imagined critters. "We need to order winter hay soon," she said aloud, "and I need to call the farrier. Glad he's going to be available for the ride." Twilight passed into darkness as Moria tried to focus on plans for the coming events, lessons for school and tasks for the ride.

~ ~ ~

A few days later, the Cherry Valley Elementary staff welcomed parents and students to Open House. Mr. Baldwin spoke about the visit for the yearly evaluation and encouraged the parents to be sure their children were in attendance each day. Then, dismissed the parents and children to the classrooms.

When the children and parents entered the classroom, Maxine said, "Please sign our list if you don't mind. And, before you leave, take one of the folders by the door. This information will help you understand our expectations for your child's behaviors and academics. Please feel free to contact us. If you have a computer, you can e-mail or call to schedule an appointment."

As Maxine spoke, Moria prowled the room with the children, showing them games and activities used to teach and entertain. She listened to their conversations, getting a read on their personalities as they interacted with each other. The youngsters, unaware that she was spying on them, seemed comfortable in the setting. *No new students. They all know each other. Thank goodness their last year's teacher pointed out the trouble spots, bullies, slackers and liars. Sometimes teacher parking lot meetings are the best. Who knows? Maybe we can change some hearts and minds.*

Later Moria and Maxine walked down the empty hall toward Mr. Baldwin standing at the door. Maxine saluted, "First to arrive. Last to leave."

Mr. Baldwin returned the salute, "Just remember, ladies. No naps in your trucks during planning time."

~ ~ ~

Saturday morning Moria and Maxine drove to Jada and Richard's to tie up any loose ends for the ride. Richard settled at his desk and opened his laptop. Moria and Maxine sat on the couch ready to check off items.

Maxine said, "We need to add one more vendor. We want to handle this one a little differently."

Richard became attentive, waiting for the good news.

"It's the Cherokee Trading Post. Running Deer and his families can bring genuine items they make to sell. I don't want to charge them a fee because they are a part of our community and could use the help. Our riders, especially those from out of state will love this." She waited for the expected complaint.

To her surprise Richard nodded and smiled. "We're going to make money on this ride. If not, as I said in the beginning, we'll take up the slack."

Jada looked pleased. "Maybe I could go up there and do some filming at the Trading Post. It would really add to the story."

"No shirts off," Maxine teased. They reviewed various aspects of the event and the two women left, feeling confident all was right in their world.

As they drove away Moria said, "Let's stop by Rodney's and see what they're up to. Remember to call when we get there."

Bad and Worse met them at the gate, standing in a watchful stance, prepared to discourage whoever breached the gate.

Maxine reached for her phone, calling Rodney. "No answer. Guess they don't have a signal where they are."

Moria checked her phone, "I've got a message. They're up on the ridge for the day, finishing the clearing. Why don't we grab a sandwich at my house and hike in to meet them? We can take some tools with us. If I remember, the trail work just looked tedious. Nothing we can't handle. Then, we can check this off the list."

The afternoon sun shone down through the forest, highlighting the beginning colors of foliage. Moria picked up a leaf, "Look at this. It's as if this was painted by an incredible artist."

Maxine took the leaf, "It was." And flicked the leaf into the air, watching it spiral slowly to the ground. "Let's hope we can protect these mountains. Our property is to be a nature preserve when we're gone."

"So is ours. Of course, it will be Sarah's for the time she might choose to live there. But somehow, I think she's going to be living on a horse farm in northern Virginia. She and Will seem pretty attached to each other."

By now they had reached the beginning of the trail. Moria opened her backpack to retrieve the clippers. "Okay, let's get to work. This entrance needs to be widened." Brush and downed limbs were cast aside. Loose stones tossed away, and face branches removed. "We need to ride through here sometime soon to be sure we cut high enough on the face branches."

The women continued to clear the trail as shadows lengthened on the mountainside. "I think we should be meeting up with Rodney's crew unless they've headed back," Maxine said, giving a shout. "Hello, the trail. Anybody out there?"

Rodney's answering call sounded nearby. "Up here. We're taking a break."

The two women topped the rise to see Rodney, the girls and Rita relaxing and having snacks. Moria and Maxine settled down beside them, sharing their day's efforts. Rodney wiped the sweat from his face with a tattered bandana. "Wal, we dun all we could back yonder," pointing over his shoulder. Suddenly he leaped up shouting, "Hell's afire. We got company," as the resident black bear and cub lumbered into view, coming up the trail toward them.

Everyone *but* Rodney scrambled behind the nearest trees and Mousey's shrill scream echoed into the forest, "I don't want to die."

Rodney yelled, waved his arms and ran toward the bear, flapping his hat in the air. The startled animals, growled, wheeled and crashed through the underbrush, disappearing from view. Rodney laughed, slapping his hat against his leg, "Thars bears in them thar hills, for sure. She must'a smelled our snacks."

Mousey crept from behind a tree, hands on hips. "Where's your gun?"

He grinned, "At home," and waited for her response.

Instead of the expected backlash, Mousey wheeled around and started up the trail, "I'm going home."

"By yourself?" he asked. "Come here. I'll make you a deal if it's okay with Rita."

Sassy walked closer to hear about the deal, as did Rita and the others. Rodney continued, "How would like to learn to shoot?"

Mousey's eyes sparkled as she turned around and faced the group. "A real gun? I would like that." She looked to seek Rita's approval.

Caught off guard, Rita hesitated and grinned at Rodney, "Thanks for the warning. I'm not sure how that fits into child protective custody. I don't want to lose the race before we reach the finish line. Let me check with a couple of people. Not a bad idea."

"What about me?" Sassy asked, already looking forward to a new adventure.

"You, too," Rodney answered, "if we can figure out how to do this without wrecking your protection. Kids in the mountains pretty much grow up with guns and learn how to use them safely. We'll see."

Everyone began to gather the scattered tools, water bottles, and snack papers. Rodney said to Moria and Maxine, "Why don't y'all hike back with us and I'll drive yu home? Don't want yu to meet that bear on yer way home."

"Hope not," Maxine laughed, "we don't have our guns either."

The discussion continued during the hike back to Rodney's truck parked at the water crossing.

The girls' questions centered on the guns: what kind they will use, when can Rita find out if they can proceed, and can they see the guns tonight?

Rita finally got a word in, asking Rodney, "Are you prepared for this?"

"Yeah, I am. A couple a yers ago I had a shootin' range for the campers if their parents agreed. They learned about gun safety and I bought some rifles they could handle. The local gun club was lots of help." He laughed, "They like tu git um early."

Moria said to Maxine, as they walked at the back of the group, "You never know how the day is going to end. Who would have thought we'd meet a bear and our smallest trail blazers would be picking up rifles and learning a new skill?"

The last rays of light filtered through the trees casting shadows to guard the forest for the night. "Rodney, thanks for the ride. Good luck with your Annie Oakleys," Moria said as she opened the truck door to be met by Hero and Dixie barking and spinning in circles.

The house seemed quiet without Jackson's presence, his boots in the corner or hat on the deer rack. "I need to get out to the barn," she announced to the cats. They padded softly after her, silver and gray keepers of the barn.

We caught a rat today, Pounce meowed, to get her attention.

As Moria reached the tack room, Pounce's offering awaited on the top step. "Can't you learn to drag these guys away from the barn? I'm sure the vultures would appreciate your prize," she smiled, scooping Pounce into her arms.

~ ~ ~

Early the next morning the phone rang, jarring Moria out of a dreamless sleep.

"Good morning, Missy. Rise and shine. The horses are hungry. You're layin' abed? The day awaits."

"Good morning to you, mister." She glanced at the clock. "Jeez, it must still be dark in Wyoming. Did you stay up all night? Never mind, I don't want to know."

"Yeah, we have been up all night, herding cattle that escaped their grazing area. We're back at the ranch now and heading to the office. What's going on with you?"

"Sounds like typical cowboy life."

Moria could picture his grin as he said, "Well, I'm glad I don't have to do this every day. But it was fun. What's been going on in the valley?"

She elaborated on the meeting at Richard's, ending with, "I was surprised he liked the idea of offering Running Deer a free vendor spot. And there's more. We met a bear up on the ridge. Rodney saved the day, thank goodness. You won't believe this. He's going to teach Sassy and Mousey how to shoot." She paused to take a breath.

Moria could hear Jackson laughing. "No bears for us yet. Jeremy is getting a lot of information we can use in our forest. I hope he doesn't decide to become a Ranger!"

"We're okay, but I miss you," Moria said, running her hand over Jackson's pillow.

We're coming home earlier than we thought." Jackson said.

Moria poured a cup of coffee and settled at the table, but barking dogs brought her to the front door. "Maxine, what's the matter? Why are you dressed up?"

Maxine came in and sat at the table. "Coffee? Appears you just got up." Observing her friend's disheveled look.

"Why are you dressed up?" Moria asked again, with concern. "Did somebody die? Not joking."

"No, Missy. We're going to church."

"Huh? Now?"

"Yes ma'am. I tried to call you. Guess you were talking to Jackson."

Trying to make sense of the morning, she said, "Church? I haven't fed..."

"I'll go down and feed while you get dressed. We've got time."

You never know what the day will bring, Moria thought as she searched for a suitable outfit and looked longingly at her boots. *Later,* she smiled and reached on the shelf for her hat.

Sun brightened the kitchen as they sat at the table later to have coffee and muffins. "Okay. What's this sudden decision to go to church?"

Maxine poured a second cup of coffee, "By the way, your horses are fine."

"Thanks for feeding, especially in your nice clothes. Help me out here, about church."

"Here goes. The horses, the ride, school, and all other happenings have distracted us from who matters most, God."

Moria studied her friend's face to gain some sense of her mood and waited for her to continue.

Pounce and Pandora leaped into the extra chairs as if to say, *It's about time.*

Maxine continued, "To tell the truth, when I was growing up we went to church and I took everything for granted. You and your family went, too. After I was baptized it just seemed like a free pass to go on with my life. I've decided to be a grownup, as we say, go to church, contribute and help out."

Moria stared out the window, lost in thought. Pounce, meowed, *so what do you think, Missy?*

"What about the weekends we're on rides?" she asked, not knowing what answer to expect.

Maxine smiled, "I'm thinking, as long as we take care of the horses, don't cheat and be supportive of our competitors, we could get a pass once in a while. Come on, time to go."

On the drive to church Moria pondered Maxine's declaration. *Be supportive of our competitors? That's a stretch.*

Maxine glanced at her friend and looked up at the cloudless sky. *I'm bringing you one today, and two more are in the queue.*

The church service was what Moria remembered as a young person. Sunlight shone through the stained glass windows, reflecting over the congregation and reminding her, *these are my people and I get to be a part of Cherry Valley, by the grace of God.*

After the service the pastor greeted everyone at the door and gave his unexpected attendees a welcoming smile. "Looking forward to your event in September. We've got a great meal planned and thank you for your donation of the proceeds."

Moria shook Pastor Will's hand saying, "Thank you for helping us out. This will be a treat. Let us know what you'll need."

"Just some space. I believe your friend Jada said you'll have tents, tables and chairs."

As they walked to the parking lot, Maxine said, "They'll do well because the riders' dinners are covered in the entries so we'll give the church a check at the end."

"What should we do this afternoon?" Moria asked, lifting her skirt as she climbed into the truck. "I feel like we need to be doing something constructive for the ride and we have the munchkins showing up tomorrow. We could work on lesson plans ... or not. Maybe we should take some of our special iced tea for lunch on Monday?"

"Somehow, I think Mr. Baldwin would sniff us out ... or we could share." Turning into the Peace in the Valley Farm driveway, Maxine said, "If you have some food besides muffins, we could have lunch and map out the camp. We need to draw a map on poster board and put it at the barn for whoever will be greeting arrivals and parking them."

"Good idea. Why don't we go outside and walk the areas to be sure we're okay on parking, especially space for trailers."

Soon they were off in the world of endurance ride camp, a puzzle with many pieces. Maxine with her laptop and Moria with her legal pad walked into the pasture. Then looked wordlessly at each other, realizing the circus was about to begin and all the monkeys needed a place.

"Let's start at the gate by the barn," Moria suggested. "I can see right away that extra cars and trucks will have to park along the road or at the Rutherford's unless something is being unloaded. We'll need at least two people at the gate for parking since the riders haven't been here before."

Two hours later they were back at the table studying their notes. Moria brought out a white board and markers. "This will be better because I have a feeling this camp will be a work in progress. Let's put the vet check in the center, vendors by the highway fence and the farrier along the fence line near the vet check." She sat back, smiling with confidence.

Maxine ran her hand through her hair and looked at her notes. "We've got a hundred entries, according to Richard. Some rigs will be hauling two or three horses. That'll help. Maybe we should have had a limit ride. Too late now."

Moria's smile faded. "It seemed like this would work when we were outside. We've got too much stuff going on. What were we thinking?"

"Well, standing in the pasture waving our arms around isn't going to translate to a camp. We forgot about the tent for registration, meals and the riders' meeting. Maybe we can squeeze it in the corner by your house."

"This is harder than lesson plans." Moria pushed her chair back, saying, "Let's not forget the Porta Pottys. Want some more coffee or special iced tea?"

"Yeah, tea."

"Coming up. I always keep some in the back of the fridge, for emergencies. This task qualifies, for sure."

A few glasses later, Maxine looked at the map and laughed, "It's a good thing we wrote on the white board. Let's take a look at this tomorrow.

Maybe our guardian angels will work on this project tonight. I need to get home and feed the critters."

Moria stood at the door as Maxine's truck made the turn onto the highway. Dixie and Hero wagged their tails, hopeful for some attention. "Okay, you've been patient all afternoon. Why don't we count our blessings?" She sat in the swing scratching the dogs' ears and receiving thank you licks. The dogs moved away as Moria put the swing in motion and soon fell asleep.

Later that night, loud whinnies snatched her awake. Sitting up from her cramped position in the swing, disoriented and needing to go to the bathroom, she realized she hadn't fed the horses. Hero and Dixie gave her a look that only Weimaraners can show. She ruffled their heads, "Why didn't you wake me?"

Hero shook his head. *We tried. No more special iced tea for you.* And he jumped off the porch. *We gotta feed the horses, missy!*

"What a day, and night," Moria mumbled. She looked at her watch and frowned. "I have to be at school in four hours. No call in for a sick day?" She laughed as the horses greeted her at the gate, "Some days are diamonds; some days are stones. Glad I have my boots on."

Chapter Nineteen

M oria took a deep breath as she entered the school. *It's a wonder what a hot shower, makeup, and some coffee and muffins will do for your spirit.*

Maxine's cheerful greeting made her laugh. "You made a quick recovery."

"All in a day's work," her teammate replied, placing folders on the children's desks. "Same as last year for our speeches? At least we know the children from notes and observations. I like the way Mr. Baldwin lets us spend a few hours in the classroom of our up and coming students. That's the advantage of a small school."

"I'm glad we didn't have to change grades. Let's check on our neighbors. See if they need anything."

Maxine opened the 5th grade door and stepped in, Moria, close behind. "Hey, ladies, how's it going?" The classroom could have been a movie set, perfectly appointed and the two teachers appeared to be outfitted in the latest fashions.

Moria whispered, "Wonder if they ever sit on the floor?" She sensed an air of uncertainty as the new teachers stood up from their desks.

"Hi, come on in," Rose motioned to the chairs, "Have a seat if you have time. Thanks for checking on us."

Amy gave a nod and a tight-lipped smile. "Well, I guess we can knock on your door if these kids don't measure up, and you all can tell us why they were passed to the next grade."

So that's how it's going to be, Moria thought, but smiled and said, "You've seen their records. Their test scores were average and above. Sorry you didn't get a chance to observe them in our classroom last spring."

Amy continued, "Just to let you know, if they're not up to our standards, we're sending them right back to you."

"I don't think so," Maxine replied, turning toward the door. "Have a good day."

The two 4th grade teachers crossed the hall, closed the door to their classroom and burst out laughing. Moria gave Maxine a thumbs up. "At least we know what to expect. I think Amy's got Rose wrapped around her finger for some reason."

"I'm guessing Rose is here for the long haul and Amy's going to get pregnant as soon as she's married and go back to Atlanta, so she says."

The sound of chuffing school busses announce the beginning of a new adventure, sure to be as intriguing and challenging as an endurance ride. Moria and Maxine stand at their door with welcoming smiles. The thrill of the chase begins as they herd their charges into the classroom. Now to follow the trails of learning, called The September to May Ride.

"Things went pretty well for the first day," Moria said as she and Maxine left that afternoon. "Let's just hope the State doesn't throw more stuff on us. The workshop in June gave us plenty of new ideas and techniques."

"I say we get back to your house and finish our camp plans. We need to stop by the hardware store and get the trail ribbons and other supplies. Let's go with red, even though the leaves are still abundant. I think you and I should mark the trails, don't you?" Maxine asked as they reached their trucks.

At the hardware store they were unprepared to find no red ribbons. Plenty of blue, yellow and pink were the choices. "Oh, crap. What now?" Moria said under her breath. "I guess we could use pink. What do you think?"

"Yellow won't work," Maxine said, gathering up a basketful of blues and pinks. "We've got plenty of Styrofoam plates but I forgot we can't nail them to the trees. We'll have to punch holes and tie them. Maybe we won't even need plates. Grab some duct tape for whatever. This'll do for now. I'm sure we'll be back a few more times."

At the checkout counter, the owner asked, "How's it going for your ride?"

Moria laughed, "always one more thing to do. Thanks for your support, especially the generator."

"It's on hold for you. Jackson said he would pick it up."

"Thanks, we really appreciate the donation of its use."

Later the two women went out again into the pasture. Maxine said, "I think we can finish up the campground plans today. No tea."

"For sure, coffee and cokes will be fine. Jada said she would order the tent, chairs and tables. We might need to check with her on this, she's been so focused on the filming."

Dusk was falling as they called it a day. "We've done all we can on the campground plans for now," Moria said. "Tomorrow is another day."

In the evening Moria sat on the couch scanning through the papers the children had written on the assigned topic, "Making a Difference in My World." She was surprised to see the varied ideas from those so young. Their thoughts ranged from being an astronaut to rescuing animals. Smiling as she put the papers away, announcing to the cats, "This is going to be a good year. I think I can make a research project out of this. Come on, let's go check on the horses."

Seeing the lights come on, the horses raced to the barn. One look at their dirty coats and she opened the tack room door, "I can't believe I've been so neglectful. Sorry, dudes." The horses poked their heads into the tack room as she gathered the grooming tools and handed them each a treat. "It's showtime. Who's first?"

Rainbow came closer, flicking his tail at Silver. The gray horse, unconcerned, ventured over to the hay ring snatching hay out and flinging it around as if to say, *who cares?* But kept a watchful eye, not to miss his turn.

Dust flew as she scrubbed the chestnut with the curry comb, then brushed, noticing the beginning of Rainbow's winter coat. "Oh, man, your feet look terrible. When were you shod last?"

~ ~ ~

The classroom became new territory as her workday began. During planning time while the children were at PE, the two teachers sat down to organize for the rest of the day. "These kids are almost too good to be true," Maxine commented, looking over the papers the children had written about "Making a Difference in My World."

"Well, it's only been a couple of days. I'll be glad when the other shoe drops, and we'll really know what we've got here. The day we visited their class they were on their best behavior. If this trend keeps up, maybe we should buy lottery tickets to complement our good luck."

Moria laughed, "I hear hoofbeats in the hall. Let's do So You Want to Buy a House? It's one of our favorite activities. At least, when we finish the game and the worksheets, they'll know what their parents went through, what they might face, how to plan a budget and so much more. I'm always surprised at their interest. Just goes to show you even kids know there's a real world out there waiting for them."

As the children settled, Moria stood in the front of the room with a tiny house in her hand. "Who wants to buy a house?" All eyes turned to the sparkly Christmas decoration and puzzlement clouded their faces.

"For a Christmas tree?" Jerry asked.

Moria smiled, knowing she had their attention. "No, a house to live in when you grow up. Are you planning to live with your parents forever?"

Brenda, on the next row, said, "Well, I guess not … I'm planning to get married."

Just what I hoped you'd say, Moria thought, remembering the child's dreams for "Making a Difference in My World," *I plan to marry someone rich and have lots of children and a fur coat.*

By now Maxine had turned away to keep from laughing and gathered supplies the children would need.

Moria continued to engage Brenda, saying, "What if you don't get married?"

The child's answered, "My mother said I will because I'm so cute and she 'knows people,' whatever that means." The youngster crossed her arms as if to say, *So there.*

Challenged by the girl's attitude, Moria said, "But what if no one will marry you, or you get married and your husband dies? What then?" trying to lead her to the conclusion, *I would need to take care of myself.*

Maxine saw where this dialogue was headed, cleared her throat, looked at Moria and pointed to the clock.

Jerry chimed in, "Yeah, what if no one would marry you?"

Brenda burst into tears and ran from the classroom, right into Mr. Baldwin, with Moria close behind.

"Hey, what's the matter?" he asked, taking hold of the student's hand.

"The teacher says I won't get married and if I do, my husband will die. I want my Momma!"

Mr. Baldwin glared at Moria with that *not again,* look. "Let's go to my office and straighten this out," nodding for her to follow.

She glanced over her shoulder at Maxine standing in the doorway and waved goodbye. Her teammate closed the door and said a little prayer.

The principal handed Brenda a tissue and looked at Moria. "Mrs. Durant, do you have an explanation for this?" gesturing toward the distraught child, who was now even more upset, knowing she was sitting in the principal's office.

Just then, Rowena, the secretary, opened the door and with an encouraging smile, handed Moria the lesson plan for "So You Want to Buy a House?"

Thank you, Maxine. "This is what we are working on today." Then, proceeded to do her best show and tell about their goals for the children.

When she finished her presentation, Mr. Baldwin said, "I'm impressed with your creativity. We need to share it with the 5th grade. Perhaps they can expand it for their grade levels." He paused, staring out the window, "We could have people from the community come to speak."

Moria barely breathed. "We're glad to share and welcome more input. Sounds like a good idea." *Okay, what about Brenda?*

As if reading her thoughts, he looked at the child, who seemed to have forgotten why she was upset. "You go back to class and listen to your teachers. I'm sure you'll get married and I'll come to your wedding," he smiled, ushering them to the door. "Mrs. Durant, "I'll call Brenda's mother and explain that there was a misunderstanding and she's welcome to look at the project. We'll talk more about this later. May I keep this copy?"

"Of course, let us know when you want to pursue this," she answered, in her most professional voice.

Brenda reached for Moria's hand as they walked back to class. Looking up at her teacher's face, she asked, "Are you married?

"Yes, I am."

"Is your husband rich?"

"Yes, he is." *Tread lightly.*

"Why are you working?"

"Brenda, I love my job, but something could happen to him and I would have to take care of myself."

As they opened the classroom door, Moria thought, *What now?* The children looked up from where they were seated on the floor with the game, and Jerry said, "Did you get a whuppin'?"

"No, and let me tell you this," Brenda answered, taking a bold stance to get their attention. "The older kids are going to use our game and I'm going to help because," she paused and smiled at Moria, "someday I might have to take care of myself and you might, too. Where is my game piece?" she finished and sat down beside Jerry.

Maxine grinned, motioning Moria to the other side of the room. "How'd you pull this off?"

"Guess my guardian angel must have been close by," she said, sitting down at a nearby desk and relaying the events in the office.

"So, for now, we're on Mr. B.'s good side. It would be great if something comes of this. We could invent more games," and the conversation drifted into: "So You Want to Buy a Bike?" "A car?" "A horse?" "Take a trip?" Maxine opened her laptop and typed in "board game life skills" and began her search. "The market seems slim on this subject," she said after a quick glance.

Moria leaned over to take a look and the bell rang, signaling a five-minute call for the busses. The startled children jumped up from the floor.

"Sit." she commanded, pointing to the scattered game and motioning the children back to the floor. The youngsters scrambled to get everything in order, then she followed with, "Okay, get ready and line up at the door. Have a good afternoon."

"What a day," Moria said, as she glanced at the papers on her desk. "No work is going home tonight," she laughed. "Welcome home, cowboys."

"Oh, yeah." Maxine replied. "I do need to make a stop by Piggly Wiggly so we'll have something for breakfast besides Jimmy Dean frozen biscuits."

"I have two eggs left and some pancake batter. Guess that'll do."

In the early evening Moria and the furry tribe sat on the porch awaiting Jackson's arrival. Pounce whined to Pandora, *Guess we're sleeping in the barn tonight. You know the drill.*

Might be more than one night, Pandora purred. *This was a long trip.* She licked her golden fur and rubbed against Pounce.

Day late and a dollar short, Pounce answered. *You won't get nothing from me. I fought the vet, but the vet won. Nothing's gonna change, no matter how many times you ask.*

Sometimes I forget 'cause you're so cute, Pandora said, licking the gray cat's face.

Jackson's truck turned into the driveway, to be met by Hero and Dixie, leaping and barking a joyous greeting. Rainbow and Silver raced along the fence line knowing their giver of treats was home at last.

Moria ran to the truck, "My turn," she said to her four-footed friends, as Peace in the Valley Farm was peaceful no more.

"Did you miss me?" Jackson laughed, holding his girl and swinging her around. He glanced toward the road and asked, "What about the kids' parents? They might see us making out in the driveway."

"Screw them," she answered giving him an X-rated movie star kiss.

"Speaking of screwing … Jackson teased, and the two lovers headed to the house.

The furry tribe dispersed to the barn for the night, knowing that peace can be stirred up in many ways.

Rain lashed at the kitchen windows as Moria and Jackson sat down to breakfast. "Let's draw straws to see who feeds the horses," she said, pulling a straw from the nearby broom.

"Never mind the straws, good news," Jackson answered. "I told Jeremy to come in at noon today. So, I can be the good guy and feed," he answered, looking out the window. A crash of thunder echoed across the valley. "Maybe I'll wait a little while. What about chapter two?" he added, with a hopeful gesture toward the bedroom.

"You forget, I need to go to work, *even if you are rich*, Moria thought. "Besides, Mr. Baldwin would come looking for me."

Jackson fastened his raincoat, saying, "After I feed the horses, I'm going up to the water crossing to check on the stream flow during the storm so we'll buy the right materials to harden the crossing. Whatever we put in will need maintenance from time to time, depending on the traffic. Do I need to bring food tonight?"

"If it's not too much trouble. Why don't we have Maxine and Jeremy over so we can catch up on things."

~ ~ ~

Moria and Maxine readied the classroom for the day as the storm whipped up against the building, *I'm a comin' for you.*

"This is not going to end well," Maxine said, going to the window and watching the trees thrash back and forth.

The loudspeaker came on and Mr. Baldwin's anxious voice sounded throughout the building. "Attention, there has just been a severe weather warning. The first busses are due any minute. I also got word that the bus from the Overland neighborhood is stranded at the other end of the valley at a mudslide. They're okay for now, but don't expect them anytime soon. When the busses arrive, get your children in the hall. Follow the procedure unless you hear differently."

Just then, the 5th Grade teachers' door flew open. Rose and Amy's distraught faces told it all. "Oh, my God," Amy's raised voice predicted she would be no help.

"Calm down." Moria said, "Haven't you all been through weather drills?"

"Yeah," Amy choked out, "but not for the real thing."

"You?" Maxine asked, looking at Rose's pinched face and knowing this was going to be a long day.

"We've done drills a hundred times, and I've seen wrecked schools." the teacher answered.

"We don't know how bad this will be. It's a warning. You all do know the drill. Our job is to get them into the hall, sitting as close as possible and arms over their heads. We'll have them pull their jacket hoods up if they have them. They know what to do."

The busses pulled into the driveway, lined up and let children off under the portico. Moria closed the classroom door and motioned for Rose to do the same.

"No running," Maxine called out as the school filled with anxious, excited children pushing toward the safety of the hallway. The constant wail of sirens added to the angst.

Chills swept over Moria as she thought, *Heels down, eyes up. Follow the ribbons, Missy. You know what to do.* With those encouraging words to herself, she directed the children to sit and put their bookbags on the floor in front of them.

Maxine took a moment to say, "You'll get an A plus in Science today if you follow what we've practiced." As one, the youngsters crowded together, pulled their knees up, placed their heads face down and covered their heads with jackets.

Maxine took her place at one end of the crouched students and Moria, at the other end. Taking a breath, she looked across the hall at the 5th graders. All eyes were on her and Maxine. Over the roaring wind, she gave a thumbs up. Some of them smiled, *you haven't forgotten us,* and gave her a thumbs up in return. The power went off and the hallway blackened. The children screamed but stayed in place.

Moria saw that Rose was in place at one end of her class. *Where is Amy?* Then, she knew and crossed the hall into their classroom. Amy was crouched under her desk but looked up as Moria approached.

"What are you doing?" Moria yelled over the rain beating on the windows and wind raking the shrubs against the wall. "Get your sorry ass up and get out in the hall."

Just then, the downspout swung loose, twisted, and shattered the window. Amy jumped up, crying, "Our stuff!" looking at their recent purchases, soaked by water pouring into the room.

Moria grabbed Amy's arm and dragged her to the door. "Go."

Amy got the message. Walked back to her place and acted as if nothing had happened.

"Keep your mouth shut," Moria warned.

Amy shot her a bird and buried her face on her knees.

Moria took her place again and called to Maxine, "We're good."

Somewhere down the hall, shrieking sounds penetrated the building as the roof ripped off the lobby. The staff and bus drivers scrambled into protective halls and crowded in among the frightened children as water and debris cascaded into the now roofless space.

Above the chaos, a child's voice echoed up and down the lines, "Our Father who art in heaven …," and others joined in, "Hallowed be thy name …"

As the prayer ended a hush fell over the disaster at Cherry Valley Elementary. The storm had passed. Children and grownups looked at one another, and with childhood innocence the youngster who had begun the prayer said, "See, we're not alone."

Just then, Moria and Maxine's phones rang, as did for the other adults nearby.

"Thank you, Verizon," Moria said as she answered, grateful to hear Jackson's voice.

"Yes, we're okay, I think. I hear Mr. Baldwin coming this way. How's the farm?"

"Tree on the fence. The animals are safe. Call if you need me. I think the community is going to be out helping to check and clear the roads. Jeremy and I are involved in that so the kids and parents can get home. He paused, "Steaks on the grill?"

Moria sighed in relief, "You got it. We can't leave until the children do. Also, we have to try and contact the parents to be sure somebody will be home, or where they need to go, because some parents work in Atlanta. Since the internet is down in some places, we are responsible for calling our kids' parents or emergency numbers on our cell phones as long as the tower works. Hurry and clear the roads so I can come home tonight. Stay safe." she looked down the line to see Maxine nodding her head and pointing toward the lobby as if Jeremy could see the damage.

The children became restless, realizing the storm had passed. "I need to go to the bathroom," came a voice from somewhere down the line.

Maxine got up to address both groups. "Sit tight. Here comes the principal. He'll tell us what to do," thus giving Mr. Baldwin her problem.

Their boss approached and observed the two huddled classes. By now the bus drivers and others had left to survey the damage. In a sober voice, he said, "Check your rooms. Double up if you need too or stay in the hall. The cafeteria is providing sandwiches for lunch." Then, with a grin, he added, "I don't guess the State officials will be visiting us anytime soon. I'll check on you all in a little while." He looked into the 5th grade classroom, saw the water damage, and then checked Moria and Maxine's rooms. "Looks okay in here. Mrs. Styles and Mrs. Sampson, double up with the 4th grade. Any questions?"

A wavering voice came from the group. "Can I go to the bathroom?"

"Ask your teacher," he answered, giving the problem back to Maxine.

As Mr. Baldwin walked away, Moria said to Rose, who looked shell-shocked and Amy who looked grim, "Why don't you bring chairs over here and we can share desks. We'll watch the kids while you all take turns seeing what you can salvage from your room. I think we've got plenty of supplies. We need to start calling parents, too."

Maxine placed a stack of computer paper on the table and gave the assignment, "The Storm. Here's a chance to tell it your way. What you thought, what you saw on the way to school, how you felt, what you imagine the world will look like when you arrive home and anything you want to put in your book. Every time you fill a page with a picture or story, come up for another sheet of paper." Chastened by the events of the day, the students settled down and got to work.

The hours seemed never ending to the teachers as they contacted parents. They too, wondered what would become of their upside-down lives. Some parents came to pick up their children and the bus drivers ran their routes to see if the roads were clear.

After school was dismissed, Mr. Baldwin gathered the teachers and staff in the cafeteria and said, "You no doubt realize we're going to be closed for some time for repairs. The county is bringing mobile units for some of you. The power should be back on soon so we can give you an update."

"What if the power doesn't come back on for a while? How will we know what's going on?" a perplexed teacher asked.

Mr. Baldwin looked at Moria and Maxine, and said, "Maybe we'll have to use the Pony Express."

As the two teachers crossed the parking lot to their trucks, Maxine grinned and said, At least we're going to have time to finish up for the ride. Thank you, God, but this was a little extreme."

Moria answered, I can't believe we've only been in school a week. Come on over to the house when you've checked out your place. Thank goodness Jackson and Jeremy got home when they did."

When Moria arrived home she could see Jackson repairing the fence. Walking into the pasture, stepping over fallen branches and the worst of the mud, she called to him, "Can I help?"

Giving her a hug, he said, "Hey, glad you're okay." Looking out over the field, he continued, "What a mess. Just hope our ride is spared a storm. We'd be pulling every trailer out and it would take a year to reclaim the pasture."

"Yeah. And think about the farmers who might have been hit with this one. It's harvest time, too."

The couple stood in silence for a moment, holding each other, grateful Peace in the Valley Farm was spared from no worse than a broken fence. A clearing wind blew across the valley offering streaks of blue and sunlight pierced the clouds.

Back to the moment, Jackson said, "Why don't you go ahead and feed the critters? There's minor damage at the barn but it's not too bad."

"Sure, I'll change and get down there. Remember, Jeremy and Maxine are coming over soon. I'm going to call Rodney and see how they're doing. He's been through worse than this. They're probably okay."

Jackson picked up the chain saw and turned back to the fallen tree. "I saw Cassie in town. She has help from work and she's going home with one of the Forest Service people who has power. What about Richard and Jada?"

"I'll call them, too," she answered. On the way to the house Moria's mind whirled as if on a merry-go-round.

Around and around we go, and where we stop, nobody knows. School, the ride, the horses, friends, and most of all, Jackson, my steady rock. The merry-go-round spun faster in her mind as the colorful horses jumped off an on and off again, cantering into the circus of her life. The barn the animals greeted her, each with their own stories.

Hero ran to his mistress with a shingle from the roof in his mouth. Dropping it at her feet, he barked, *we nearly lost the barn.*

Dixie lay at her mistress' feet panting a message, *There's a leak in the tack room.*

Pounce gave a grim meow, *no mice today.*

Pandora finished his thought, *we're hungry.*

Rainbow and Silver whinnied greetings and twirled in their stalls. *Let us out of here.*

She looked in their stalls, knowing they would need a thorough cleaning. Then released the horses, who raced away, skidding to a stop near Jackson. Soon the chores were finished, and the animals settled and peaceful.

Maxine and Jeremy arrived with extra lanterns and a box of cookies. Jackson put steak, potatoes and corn on the grill and, as the food cooked, the four friends relived the day, ending with the common thought, voiced by Jeremy, "We were damn lucky … this time."

"And, blessed," Maxine added, with a wink at Moria.

As they sat around the picnic table, Jackson said, "I never got up to the creek crossing this morning, but Jeremy and I can check it out tomorrow. Cassie said they have some stored supplies we might be able to use. Jeremy, did you bring the drawings?"

"Of course, they're in the truck. Be back in a minute."

Maxine smiled as he walked away. "Jeremy is smitten with the Forest Service and being involved with the environmental law business. Good thing he loves the outdoors."

Jeremy returned with the various plans to harden the creek crossing. In the lantern light, he explained the pros and cons of each possibility. "Cassie is going to help us decide which approach is best. She's seen the crossing a couple of times but wants to get a better look at it and has some resource people to call if needed."

Moria studied the plans and said, "I'm impressed. Jada needs to document this in her video to let people know putting on an endurance ride is not just about hanging ribbons and getting some awards together."

Jeremy gathered the information. "Uh, no. I don't need her directing this operation so she can shoot more movies."

"Seriously," Moria continued, "it would add to the reality of what managers are faced with sometimes."

"No."

Maxine jumped in, saying, "What if Moria and I go with you all when she plans to film?"

"Well, maybe." Jeremy hesitated, seeing the value of having the creek work in the film. "We'll see." He glanced to Jackson for support.

Jackson grinned, "It's your party. Maybe if we have M and M Security on board to manage Jada." nodding to Moria and Maxine. They're not going to be busy at school for a while. We'll see what damage was done during the storm. Someday we need to get back to real work. There's a pending case in Townsville where the city wants to build fairgrounds and the plot is near the river. The Department of Natural Resources is questioning some of their plans. The city hired us to represent them. I don't want to go up against the DNR. We need to stay on good terms with them if we can, but business is business." He handed Jeremy the lanterns and looked at the sky to see the remaining clouds whisking away, uncovering a half moon. "Guess I shouldn't borrow trouble."

Jackson and Moria walked their friends to the driveway and she said, "We won't know the latest about school until tomorrow. Mr. Baldwin said at least a week." She checked her phone for a message. We could drive over tomorrow and see what's going on."

"Why don't we saddle up the Pony Express and ride over instead? Maybe around nine o'clock?" Maxine suggested. "We can go the back way. Then later, check to see if there are any downed trees on the trails. Bring a lunch."

Moria looked at the scattered branches and another tree down near the road, "I think we're going to be at this for a while. At least, we'll have more time do last minute things for the ride. I want this to be an event to remember." *Be careful what you wish for, Missy.*

Jeremy rolled the truck window down, waving his car charger at them. "Don't forget."

Jackson headed to his truck. "Get your phone, Missy."

As the couple sat in the truck listening to the radio and charging their phones, Moria leaned into her cowboy, savoring his strength and steady heart. "Are you worried about the ride? The creek, our pasture …," she sat up, jarring Jackson from his nap against the window.

"What?" disoriented, he looked out the window into the night.

She repeated her questions and paused.

He untangled his hand from the charger cord and rubbed his face. "Of course, I'm worried. Even with ride insurance and signed waivers, shit happens. Yes, the pasture's going to be an ordeal, too.

"Are you sorry we started this?"

"Well, *we* didn't start this, you and Maxine did."

"No, Jada did."

"No excuses. You know as well as I do how this came about. You girls let your egos get in the way of common sense. Richard and Jada could have managed this ride and *we* could have helped."

Tears trickled down Moria's cheeks. "Can I ever make it up to you, this out of control journey?"

Jackson grinned and wiped her tears away, "We could begin tonight."

She gave a sniffy smile as he said, "A million things can go wrong at the ride, or with a little bit of luck and the creeks don't rise, a million things can go right. Come on, Missy, bedtime."

Chapter Twenty

G ray light seeped through the blinds as the day struggled to re-create itself for another adventure. Moria glanced at the clock. Glad it was a wind-up and she had her 'takes a lickin' and keeps on tickin' Timex watch. Jackson's sleeping form appeared to have not a care. No lights shone inside or out. *Power, where are you? Guess I'd better feed the horses and bring in the camping stove, I gotta have some coffee.*

By the time Moria returned from the barn, Jackson was busy at the fireplace, bringing some warmth and encouragement into the room. "Thanks, for the fire." Looking into the refrigerator and shuffling a few things around, she said, "I don't think anything's spoiled," bringing out eggs, bacon and coffee creamer. "Glad I learned how to grill toast on this tiny stove."

Jackson laughed, "Now I know why I married you. Nothing like a home-cooked meal. Sounds like you and Maxine have a busy day planned. Jeremy and I can go ahead and check out the creek crossing. That reminds me, I need to get a couple of loads of sand for the bridge flooring. Cassie was adamant that we couldn't use creek sand. We could put a spotter at the bridge if we need to use it and let the riders cross one at a time. What do you think?"

"How could I have forgotten about that crossing?" Moria replied. "If the water's not high, the riders will want to go through the creek to sponge the horses or let them drink. Maybe we should plan to use the bridge."

Jackson added, "Since we have the bridge, guess we'd better try it out first or we could get sued."

Moria busied herself making sandwiches. "There's a job for you and Jeremy. Y'all have better insurance than Maxine and I do." Giving him a kiss, she said, "Here's your lunch since you'll be out there somewhere and Little Red Riding Hood won't appear with your lunch, or cookies."

They both laughed, remembering the time Moria scratched on Jackson's window screen in the night offering him a cookie with the well-remembered words, *Hey, Mister Big, Bad Wolf, it's Little Red Riding Hood. I brought you a treat.*

Jackson hugged his storybook girl, saying, "Happy endings unfold somewhere every day, even at the Cherry Valley Ride. We're cool, Missy," and gave her his signature cowboy kiss.

Moria and Maxine met at the turn to the Rutherford's. Rainbow Chaser and Catch on Fire whinnied greetings to each other and looked down the road, eager to be on their way. A spritely breeze blew through the valley, encouraging the horses to pick up the pace. This trail through the pines would lead to the powerline and to the back of the school.

"Hold up," Maxine called. "There might be trees down." At the opening to the trail, the riders stopped in dismay. The planted pines had taken a hard hit, many were on the ground and others lay against each other, waiting to fall on unsuspecting animals or people.

"We'll never get this cleaned up," Moria wailed. "I'm not even sure it's safe for us to go this way to get over to the school."

Maxine urged her horse forward. "Let's go easy here. We're going to have to see how bad it is soon anyway, so what better time?"

Pine sap scented the air as the riders picked their way down the path toward town and the school. Cones, needles and branches littered the ground, and soon they had to give up following what once had been a trail.

"Most of this stretch is on Forest Service land but that doesn't mean they're going to be in any hurry to clear it out." Moria said. "Maybe Cassie has some pull and can get some help for us."

The sun was high when they reached the school. "Time for lunch," Maxine said with a laugh, glad to be out of danger, at least for now. Where do you think we should tie the horses? Glad you mentioned bringing halters and lead ropes. That's all we need, the horses running through town. Not a good way to advertise the ride."

Moria dismounted, saying, "Let's tie them in the ball field. Then, if they do get loose, they can't go far. We won't be here long anyway."

As the two teachers walked across the ball field, Maxine said, "Looks like the power is on in the school. There are a lot of cars here, probably people coming in to see what they can save or throw away. Too bad about our 5th grade friends and all the money they spent on supplies. Maybe we can help them regroup. Our room's okay for now."

Entering through the back door brought them into their hallway. A jumbled pile of classroom items were piled outside Amy and Rose's door. "Well, let's check it out. Looks like they got here early," Moria said, stopping at the open door. Rose, on her hands and knees pulling more supplies from the cabinet, turned around and sat on the floor.

"Welcome to Hell," she muttered, pushing her hair out of her eyes. "Come on in."

Moria glanced into the room, not seeing Amy. "Where's your partner in crime?" she asked, trying to make light of the situation.

Rose got up from the floor, easing down into a chair, "Who knows? Mr. Baldwin came down a little while ago and said Amy quit." Her discouraged face caused Moria and Maxine to bring their chairs closer to comfort her.

What to say? "Can you tell us what happened?" Moria asked. *Maybe she wants to talk about this, or not.*

"Yesterday was a little unusual, granted, but she was a wreck. Amy's been teaching, been through storms and all that comes with this job, but I could tell there was something else upsetting her. Finally, toward the end of the day she confided to me that she is pregnant, and her guy had left for parts unknown."

Moria and Maxine looked at each other. Finally, Maxine said, "What a train wreck." and waited for Rose to continue.

"Yesterday we were just trying to survive and keep the children as calm as possible. No time to talk about her turn of events. When we left, she said she'd see me this morning. On the way home, I wondered how she would resolve the crisis, knowing marriage was a big deal, in her eyes, anyway." Rose paused, "So that's what I know. Mr. Baldwin said try to save what I can of materials because the workers will move the furniture and throw everything else out. They've got to deal with mold besides the cleanup and reflooring. He said the county is sending out a doublewide mobile and he'll get a sub for me until they can hire a fulltime teacher."

Moria felt a sadness for Rose, new to the school and the area. "We'll be glad to help you finish up today. You can store whatever we salvage in our room for now. Oh, the horses. We left them tied outside."

Rose did a double take, saying, "You rode horses here? Can I see them?"

Startled, that the teacher would want to see the horses with all the chaos in her life right now, Moria answered, "Sure. We need to check on them, anyway."

The three walked out to the ball field. Rainbow and Catch On Fire began to paw and whinny, seeing their riders approach.

Maxine laughed, "This is new territory for them. Looks like they've made a mess with pawing and manure. Guess we're going to have come back later and clean up." She glanced at Rose's face to see that look, a horse lover, for sure.

The horses quieted for attention. Rose asked, "Is it okay to pet them?" The two women nodded and observed her confident spirit as she walked to Rainbow and leaned her face against his neck. Then, he turned his head to hug her as best he could with the short line. "I used to ride hunt seat when I was growing up." Taking a deep breath and stepping back, she continued, "I need a horse!" The three women burst out laughing and a bond began to form, that only horse people can share.

The two riders looked at each other with a common thought ... *Rodney.* Moria said, "If you'd like to ride sometime, we have a neighbor who has several horses." *Mousey and Sassy. I don't need to be bringing a stranger to the farm. What was I thinking?*

Maxine finished Moria's sentence, saying, "We'll check with him and see what we can work out. We'll find you a horse, count on it."

By now, the teachers had forgotten the disaster awaiting them in the school until they turned to go back to the building. Rose said, "You all need to go on. These guys don't need to be tied up any longer."

They stopped and looked back at the horses. "You're right, but you need some help here," Moria said, knowing Rose was right.

"Mr. Baldwin said he'd send someone down to help me. Don't worry. Just find me a horse," she said with a longing gaze over her shoulder at the chestnut and the bay.

"We'll be back tomorrow and see what's going on. Maybe Amy will change her mind and return," Moria joked.

"My worst fear," Rose laughed. "Hope to see you all tomorrow. Thanks for making my day."

Moria and Maxine returned to the horses and looked at the manure mess again. Maxine said, "We can clean it up tomorrow. Nobody's going to be out here today." Just then, two vans pulled up with a scramble of youngsters who piled out and ran toward the football field. "Thank goodness, they don't need home plate today. Let's ride over to The Diner and eat our lunch on their outside tables in the back."

The horses danced, as only Arabians can, around to the front of the school, across the parking lot, behind the stores and to the back of The Diner. The two riders tied them to the fence and settled down for lunch. "You know," Moria said, "we're not going to have time to continue checking the trail today. If we leave from here going on around the loop, we don't know what we'll find … and who wants to ride home in the dark over damaged trails?"

"You don't have to convince me," Maxine said, throwing her trash away and looking at her watch. "We'll have to backtrack. At least we know what to expect and can take a better look this time."

As they rode beside the creek, back toward the school, Moria stopped and peered down the bank. "What do you think about crossing here? The water's not too deep. It would save us some time."

Maxine pulled up short. "Huh? Here? What are you thinking?"

"Saves time," and headed Rainbow toward the bank. "We can do this." The chestnut horse slid down the muddy bank into the creek. Moria looked up at Maxine and said, "Come on in, the water's great," then, grabbed Rainbow's mane and the two lunged up the far bank.

Catch On Fire followed. When they reached the opposite bank, Maxine looked at her friend, "What brought this on?"

Moria laughed and turned her horse toward the trail, "I'm training myself to be brave."

Maxine, riding behind, rolled her eyes and mumbled, "Okayyy. Carry on."

On the way back the riders looked at the number of downed trees and began to think about who could work on this project. As they picked their way, Maxine said, "Let's check with the 4-H dads, and Wilton and Cade might be available. We only need the trail to be about eight feet wide. It might be better, a straight path instead of weaving in and out."

The two riders began to estimate the number of trees that would need to be cut and soon gave up on the count. "At least we've been here and know what needs to be done. I can manage a small chain saw if I have to," Moria said. "Our guys are going to be busy with the crossing. We need to go on a help wanted search." In an 'aha moment', she continued, "Why not give Jada chainsaw lessons? We could film her doing real work."

Maxine burst out laughing and said, "You're serious? On second thought, that's an interesting picture. Let's think about it. We need to get up to their house before too long anyway. Now I know what it's like to have a list a mile long." When the Rutherford's house came into view, she said, "We've got a little time left in our day, why don't we ride on up to Rodney's, see what they're doing and if there's any way Rose can come up to ride. If that doesn't work out, maybe he'll know someone else with extra horses."

By next Spring we'll have Rose scattering dust on the trail, just like the rest of us."

The horses picked up a trot, urged on by the riders' excited voices. "But we have be careful not to spook our new endurance rider. Maybe she can help at the ride and see what it's all about.

They reached Rodney's gate to be met by Bad and Worse. The two guard dogs sat at attention, barking and waiting for their leader's command. The cowboy came around the corner of the house, called the dogs to him, and gestured to the porch. They turned and obeyed without a backward look.

"Rodney, how long are you going to keep those dogs?" Maxine asked, as he opened the gate for them.

"Probably till I get my dogs or when the young'uns leave, whichever comes first. What y'all been up to today?"

"We've got stories," Moria said with glee.

They dismounted and Rodney led them around to the barn where Rita, Mousey, and Sassy were grooming the horses. The girls waved and continued with their task. Rita stopped and came over to visit.

Moria and Maxine took turns describing their day, from the forest disaster to finding a horse for Rose. Maxine ended with, "Do you think she could come up here for a ride?"

Rita and Rodney looked at each other and Rita nodded toward the girls, "Probably not. We've had too much exposure as it is. I'm going to take them through the ride and then we're leaving town from your house."

"Oh, Jeez. What was I thinking?" Maxine said, slapping her forehead. "We're just glad y'all are going to the ride."

"When Rita leaves," Rodney speculated, "Dillon will be available for lease. That'll give her a chance to decide if she wants her life to change forever. This way, I could give her some basic endurance information and go out on the trail with her."

Moria thought a moment, realizing Rodney would be looking for a project to occupy him after his company left, and knowing he would get Rose off on the right foot. "That sounds like a plan. You're close enough that she can even ride during the week. Nothing like arranging someone's life ... but she did seem adamant about finding a horse."

Startled about this turn of events, Rodney said, "Wal, tell me a little about her. Is she experienced?"

"She's been in the horseshow world, so she knows dedication and probably has a competitive spirit. No doubt, her parents were in charge her early horse life." Moria continued, "I'm guessing that *was* her life. If this is a meant to be, it will happen," she ended with a smile.

Sassy and Mousey put their ponies away and came to join the conversation. Rita said, "Want to see the girls do some target practice?"

"That'd be great," Maxine said. "Can we put the horses in the barn? Then, we can enjoy the show."

The sisters ran to get their rifles and Rodney called after them, "Bring your box, too."

Soon the group assembled at the edge of the shooting range and Rodney said, "Okay, dudes, you know what to do."

The two girls opened the box, placed fresh targets on the boards, loaded the guns and reached for their ear protectors. Rodney stood aside, grinning, and nodded to them.

Sassy motioned for Mousey to go first. All business, the youngster sighted the target and fired several times.

"Sorry I don't have anything for your ears," Rodney said, not taking his eyes off his students.

They watched, transfixed, as the girls took turns firing at their separate targets. Sassy took a well-practiced stance and emptied her rifle.

Moria raised her voice, "Man, I'd hate to meet her if I was on the wrong side of the law. Who knows? This might be her calling."

Rita said, "Their parents are aware of the shooting lessons and that they've earned the rifles to take when they leave. They're okay with this. But I think they have other plans for their futures."

Sassy and Mousey raced to get their targets and presented them to Rodney. "Well done." he said, "We're gonna stop for now. Gather up your things and we'll meet you at the house."

"Yes sir," they answered in unison and began their task.

The others walked across the yard and Moria asked, "How'd you do this?"

Rodney grinned, "It's called straight talk. No bribes ... well ... I guess the rifles are a bribe. They're good young'uns." He looked at Rita and said, unexpectedly, "I'm gonna miss y'all."

Taken by surprise, she answered, "We're going to miss you, too. Don't lock the door," she winked.

Maxine raised her eyebrows at Moria and they glanced away.

"We need to be getting home," Maxine said, looking at the lowering sun's last rays slanting over the mountain.

Just then, Sassy and Mousey came to say goodbye and accept congratulations for their performances.

"Good job, girls. Watch out for bears." Moria teased.

Mousey flinched, remembering meeting the bear up on the ridge, but said, with a steady look, "I can handle this … and that bear, too, if he comes around."

Maxine laughed, "Just remind me not to get on the wrong side of Rodney's cowgirls. By the way, how are your school lessons coming along?"

The two youngsters looked toward Rita as if to say, *you answer.*

"Well, they've done a lot of research on endurance riding, care of the horses and where the rides are. We managed to get a little math in by measuring the feed. They're keeping detailed training records, and they've learned to read maps and routes. And last, but not least, we now own a special measuring tape to check the horses' weights."

This information took the teachers by surprise and Maxine said, "Keep up the good work. You can never know too much about horse care. By the way, you might want to wait a day or two before you get out on these trails. They're not too safe right now after the storm. Work hard, girls and maybe you'll get a day off," she laughed, turning toward the driveway.

"Hey, wait a minute," Moria said, "The horses, remember?"

On the way home the two women rehashed the day's events, their plans for Rose, Sassy and Mousey's change of attitudes, and the hint of something going on between Rodney and Rita.

Maxine pondered about their friends' relationship. "They're brother and sister? I don't think so."

Time will tell," Moria said. "I just hope the girls are going to be able to put the Oscar trial behind them and live happily ever after when that nightmare is over."

"I can't help but think their time in Cherry Valley has been good for them. Let's hope it ends well, with a finish at the ride." Maxine added.

As the two riders reached Maxine's driveway, Jeremy pulled up from the other direction. His weary face and bedraggled appearance told the story of his day. "Jackson said to meet at The Diner. Just change clothes and hurry before they close."

"Works for me," Moria said, mentally peeking into her pantry with poor results. "See y'all soon."

When she reached the barn, Jackson turned off the water for the trough and came over to help her untack. "You look like you been rode hard and put up wet."

Moria returned his comment with a tired smile, observing his muddy appearance. "And you, Mister?"

"Yeah, this was a hard day. Let's get changed and head to The Diner. Maybe we can unravel ourselves and figure out where we're going next. I called Richard and Jada to join us."

Moria frowned, but said, "It'll save time for us to get together with them now, I guess."

When everyone was seated, Darla came over to take orders, saying, "I'm thinking you won't be finished by closing time. It takes about an hour to clean up. We'll lock the front door and you can stay till lights out."

"Thanks, we'll wash our dishes," Jeremy joked.

Darla said, over her shoulder, "No problem. You'll love our paper plates."

Sweet tea flowed like wine as the group waited for their meal. Moria and Maxine described the condition of the connector trail from the Rutherford's to the power line and ended with Maxine's comment, "We'll get on the phone tomorrow and round up the troops. We didn't get to check any more of the trail."

In a most casual voice, Jada said, "Pete called and said he and his friend moved a couple of trees off the Deer Trail." She paused to see their reactions and smiled.

The two couples looked at each other, then at Jada. "Are you joking?" Moria choked out her response.

"Pete and I've been friends for a long time."

Maxine cut a sideways glance at Richard, who was enjoying his dinner, totally unconcerned. "Well, that's great. Tomorrow we'll ride the Blue Loop from the Rutherford's to the water crossing and check out the Logging Road. You're welcome to go with us."

Moria nodded in agreement. "We need to go back to the school early in the morning and see if we can help Rose, but we should be ready by noon. We'll call you." Jada flashed her a grateful look and Moria realized their devious neighbor might be lonely for riding companions . . . who didn't steal her phone.

Richard focused his attention on Jackson and Jeremy, "So, what's the latest on the creek crossing?"

The two guys looked at each other and Jeremy gestured to Jackson and grinned, "Your turn."

Jackson smiled and said, "Well, it's a crap shoot right now. There are several possibilities. Cassie has someone coming tomorrow and we have the information Jeremy collected from the Rangers in Wyoming when we were there."

"That covers it for the time being. It is a work in progress, for sure." Jeremy said.

Darla came with the checks and Richard said, "Can we have a trash can? We'll clean up for you."

Moria turned to Richard, "How are the entries coming along?"

Without his laptop to prompt him, he hesitated, saying, "We're still at a hundred riders, pretty evenly split between the fifties and twenty-fives. Most people have paid their entry fees and a few have cancelled for various reasons. I've returned their money. We'll keep the 'no-shows' money unless it's a last minute emergency."

Not wanting to ask directly about the California riders, she said, "So, where are the cancellations from?"

Richard smiled an apology, "I'm not very good without my records. I'll e-mail you tomorrow.

Back at the farm, Moria and Jackson sat at the kitchen table with the maps and lists. "I'm worn to a frazzle, but I'll sleep better if we get our plans sorted out so we're not doing something twice and something else, not at all. Why don't we each work on our lists for a few minutes and see what we've got?" Moria suggested.

"Yes, teacher," Jackson winked at her, saying, "The sooner were done, the sooner we can go to recess."

She laughed, going to the fridge for a Coke. "Maybe I'd better get a good dose of sugar and caffeine. "Want one?"

"Guess I'd better, so I can keep up with you." he answered, reaching for her offering.

Pounce prepared to leap on the table and Pandora meowed anxiously, *I wouldn't do that if I were you.*

The gray cat lashed his tail for takeoff, *You're not me.*

Out of the corner of her eye Moria saw his intention. "Naughty Pounce. Don't even think about it."

Announcing his discontent with a whine, Pounce stalked away to the loft.

Pandora stretched out on the window seat for a nap and looked at her friend. *Pounce, you're so spoiled. You can't always sit in someone's lap. Get over yourself.*

The clock ticked the minutes away and the house settled for the night. The couple worked in silence, until Moria said, "Are we at a stopping place?"

"Yeah. Tomorrow we're spending the day with Cassie and the Ranger from the head of the district. Best to be sure we're getting it right the first time, before we spend wasted time and money. He's going to check out the bridge, too. The other thing that's preying on my mind is space in the camping field. Jeremy said we could keep our horses at their place. There's no way they would stay in the barn with the ride going on all around them. He'll turn them out in the back field and thinks we should also put them up at night. Maxine said they're not bringing their trailer over to the camp to save space."

" Okay. I'm rounding up a chainsaw brigade to clear the connector trail. There are a massive amount of pine trees down."

Just then, Jackson's phone rang. *Who would call this late?* Moria wondered, attentive to see what new problem awaited them.

"Hey, Dad. No, we haven't gone to bed. Is everything alright?" Concern clouded the cowboy's face, as his mind flashed to the Wyoming ranch.

"There's no problem. We know your ride is next weekend and we were thinking about coming for the event we've heard so much about. That is, if it's okay?"

"Sure, come on. You're welcome anytime." Jackson smiled, knowing that Ben and Molly would not be guests, but workers.

"Thanks, Son. We're flying into that small airfield near you. Our pilot is looking forward to the trip and says he would be glad to help, too."

"The more, the merrier, as the saying goes."

"Not to worry. We'll be staying at that cute bed and breakfast, Molly's description. Is it okay to arrive on Thursday?"

"Bring your boots and we'll look forward to seeing you. Catch me up on happenings at the ranch."

Moria could see that conversation would go on for a while. She moved over to the computer to check her e-mail. A message from Mr. Baldwin appeared first. "Teachers, this is an informal notice to meet at the school in the morning around nine o'clock, if you're available.

She responded a "yes," and saw the next message was Maxine's. Another yes response and see you in the AM. *Wonder what's up?*

Next message: from Richard with the list of cancellations. *Don't see my California people on there. Good.*

Jackson came to look over her shoulder, read the message and commented, "Well, it appears that your friend, Doris, is still planning to pay us a visit. You're not worried, are you?"

Moria pushed the chair back and unsmiling, faced him. "About what?"

Jackson gave a teasing grin, "About her thinking she's coming to collect her cowboy."

"Get over yourself, buddy. I'm glad the California bunch is coming. If they do well, and have a good time, it will strengthen our brand, don't you think?"

"What? We have a brand? First I've heard of it," he answered with a laugh.

"Of course, we do. The Cherry Valley Ride. Who knows what will come of this?"

"Okay, I'll take your word for it. Are you going to quit school and promote the brand?" he asked with raised eyebrows.

"No. I can do both," she answered with innocence, going along with Jackson's taunt.

Remembering about tales of his escapades with Doris when the two of them lived in Wyoming, she continued, "About Doris. I beat her to the finish line where it counts, and she doesn't have a chance." Moria smiled and took Jackson's hand, "Let's see if I've been a good student. I believe I've graduated from the neck strap."

The bedroom door closed behind the cowboy and his girl as jeans dropped to the floor. The moon winked at Peace in the Valley Farm saying, good night to another day of adventure.

Pounce peered between the railings of the loft and purred, *It's gonna be along night."* and curled himself into a comfortable grey fur ball.

~ ~ ~

Moria awakened to the buzz of the alarm clock, remembering last evening as the couple discovered a well of untapped energy in their joint endeavor.

The smell of coffee brought her to the kitchen, saying, "Thanks for last night … and the coffee," putting her arms around him and resting her face on his back. "You smell good."

Jackson laughed, "Only a horse girl would love a man's sweaty back."

"That's me, lover of sweaty backs, two-legged and four." Reaching in the freezer for a Jimmy Dean's biscuit and putting it in the microwave, she said, "Want one?"

"No thanks," picking up his lists and maps. "I'm meeting Jeremy, Cassie and the Ranger at The Diner. I hope we can make a decision about how to secure the creek crossing today. There's not much time left and we want the materials to have time to settle, whatever they are."

"I need to get over to the school. Mr. B. is going to let us know the latest and Maxine, Jada and I are going to check some more of the trail for damage. Keep in touch."

Jackson gave a salute and said, "Don't forget the horses, Missy."

When Moria arrived at school the front entrance to the building was blocked off and workers were assembling to begin their day. The back parking lot was full and Moria noticed people on the ball fields measuring areas and marking them with stakes. "Guess that's where the mobiles are going.

"Thanks for saving me a space," Moria said to Maxine as she settled down in the cafeteria to learn the plan. The teachers became attentive to their boss and managed to face toward him in spite of their awkward seating at the lunch tables.

Mr. Baldwin announced, with some relief, "There will be two mobiles on the ball field for the duration of the repairs. The damage is more severe than first thought to the classrooms and especially to the entrance. It will be at about ten days before the children can return. I want you all to prepare assignments for them for this period of time. Be sure book bags and needed books accompany the assignments unless the children already have them at home. The busses will run the routes in two days and deliver the assignments. Please have some lessons ready. We'll return to school as soon as possible."

Moria and Maxine looked at each other with smiles and Moria said, "Good news, we're free from school to finish the ride plans. Bad news, we've got to take time to get the assignments together. Let's get started."

Maxine said, "Let's go down to our room. I see Rose ahead of us and someone's with her. He looks young, maybe her son, come to help her. We need to call Jada and tell her our plans have changed for the day and we'll go tomorrow."

When the 4th grade teachers reached Rose's dismantled classroom they stopped at the door to see what might be needed.

She motioned them into the room, saying, "This is my new teammate, Dale Bice.

Moria's first thought, *what a hottie.* Reeling herself in, she smiled and reached out a welcoming hand. "Rose got the worst of it on our end of the hall. Glad you're on board."

Maxine echoed the greeting, adding, "Bring us up to date on what's happening here," waving at their room.

"We've moved the rest of my stuff that could be saved into your room, as you offered. Our mobile should be here tomorrow, along with one for the lower grades. We'll be occupying the ball fields until whenever." Looking to Dale, she continued, "at least I have a teammate who's planning to stay."

Dale appeared friendly and anxious to help, saying, "I hope we can get everything out of your way tomorrow. We're making some plans with what we've salvaged."

Moria looked at the two teachers and said, "The kids won't be back for a couple of weeks, as you know. Take your time. Glad the county's bringing y'all a house. By the way, we're planning a project and wanted to offer it to the 5th grade, too. Social Studies for our grade is Georgia history, but you could use it too, for the US History. We want to focus on our local past to gain the students' interest. One of the things we'd like to instill in them is to use the term Native Americans, not Indians. We had planned to do murals in the hallways. Guess that's out for now, but we could do them in the classrooms. Also, we'll do research and assemble booklets about historical activity in our area, possibly right in their back yards," she finished with a laugh.

Rose looked at Dale and grinned, "Tell them."

Dale's face broke into a huge smile, "Maybe I can help *you.*"

Moria and Maxine realized they had struck gold as the young teacher continued, "I have a degree in Archeology, specializing in Native American culture. I wrote my thesis on the tribes who lived in the Southeast." Observing their startled faces, he continued, "And I have a teaching degree. This project would be right up my alley. When do we start?"

"Let's get the kids back and settled. There's no rush. We want this project to go well," Maxine answered. "We'll get our lesson plans together and share them with you. More than likely you'll need to get the kids adjusted to being in a new location. By the way," turning toward Dale, "we have a Cherokee trading post right up the road. You should meet Running Deer."

"You might not believe this, but I interviewed him for my paper. He's quite a guy. I'd love to catch up with him again."

"Well, you might get a chance sooner than you think," Maxine said, giving a brief version of the endurance ride and that the Trading Post would be a vendor.

The mention of the ride brought more explanations. "Rose, we have a surprise for you," Moria said with a smile.

"You've found me a horse?"

"Well, sort of. We have a friend who has some horses ..." Moria launched into their conversation with Rodney and that they had vouched for her to be an excellent rider. Then she gave Rodney's qualifications, ending with, "Come by on ride day and you might be able to meet him. Rita will be riding Dillon because she's sponsoring the girls, so you'll see him too."

Rose answered, "I'm thrilled. Can't wait to meet Rodney and Dillon. Thanks, more than I can ever say."

Maxine laughed, "Stay topside on the horse on your new adventure, that'll be thanks enough."

Moria glanced at her watch. "Guess we'd better get started on the lesson plans since we're here. You all are welcome to work in our room."

"What a morning," Maxine said as the two teachers left the school later in the day. "Divine intervention is what I say, for Dale to appear just when we need him."

Moria stopped and turned to her friend, "Maybe the Native American spirits sent Dale to enlighten our children. We just started the ball rolling."

Maxine took a hard look at her, "I think you may be right."

~ ~ ~

The warm September sun shone on the three riders as they trotted past Rodney's the next day and headed toward the bridge. Moria smiled and lifted her face to the sky.

"Fall is my favorite season," Moria declared. Acorns rained down from a nearby oak tree as a squirrel leapt from limb to limb. Rainbow seemed to say, *be gone* and skidded to a stop. His rider left the saddle, clung to her horse's neck, slid to the ground, and landed on her feet.

"Well, that was lovely," Maxine laughed.

Moria smiled with relief and said to Jada, "Too bad you didn't catch that on your camera. Maybe I should be in the movies," stroking Rainbow's neck and looking up the trail.

Jada grinned, "Uh, I did. I was filming our progress when your 'event' happened. We'll take a look at it during our next screening."

"So be it. Seriously, I'd love a copy, if possible," Moria answered. At least, I kept my shirt on!"

By now they had reached the bridge. "Let's cross it instead of going through the creek. We're going to have to check it out before the ride, anyway."

Maxine looked doubtful. "The sand's not down yet and we don't know the whereabouts of the bear. This seems to be her hanging out place." She peered into the ravine, trying to see under the bridge. Now the riders were off the horses, eyeing each other. "Okay, who's first? We need to lead them, for sure."

Moria grimaced, "Guess it's me since I seem to be attracting danger today." The horse and rider walked to the entrance and Rainbow stared into the scary thing. The sun's slanting rays through the open sides distorted the interior vision of the bridge, and swaying branches cast moving shadows on the floor. Moria realized she would have to take the first step.

"Come on, buddy, we can do this." She walked a few feet ahead and entered the bridge. Rainbow followed and came up beside her. "Steady, one step, then another . . ." The rushing water caught the horse's attention and he scrambled in place, looking for the water source.

"Maxine, come on. Surely this will hold the two of us. Jada, why don't you wait a minute?'

Maxine and Catch On Fire followed with caution. The bay mare flinched at the sound of the water but continued across to the other side. Jada and Chaos made a cautious crossing and the riders gave a sigh of relief.

"We're definitely going to need a spotter here," Maxine commented as they trotted on up the trail.

As the riders neared the water crossing, Moria said, "I hear people at the creek. Must be the heroes preparing the crossing for the herd. Can you believe the ride's just ten days away?"

Jada reached for her camera, "We're ready. Every night Richard and I go over the check list and he gives me a list of tasks to follow up on . . .tents, tables, Porta Pottys and everything else."

What is Richard holding over her to make her mind him? Guess we'll never know. Moria speculated to herself but said, "I think between all of us this will be a ride to remember, for sure. You and Richard are doing a great job."

Horses' ears perked at the sound of humans. The riders urged them forward and Rainbow whinnied at the sight of Jackson. Catch On Fire moved toward Jeremy, *I know you.*

Jackson eyed Jada's camera and gave her a thumbs down, "No ma'am," and looked at his companions, who shook their heads. "This will not end well."

Moria hesitated, not wanting to override Jackson's pronouncement, then Maxine said, "It wouldn't hurt to include a few shots for Jada's video since it's supposed to help people learn about all the issues that go into putting on a ride."

Jackson frowned, but said, "Hurry and don't tell us . . ."

"I know, Jada laughed, "to take off your shirts."

The visiting Ranger looked askance at the group for a moment, perhaps wondering what he had gotten himself into.

Cassie quickly intervened, "Just a joke. Let's get this done. I gather you are going to ford the creek here. Give me the camera. Go ahead and I can film the crossing and how the ground appears when you've gone back and forth a few times."

The riders agreed and Jada handed the camera to Cassie. They crossed the creek several times, with Cassie filming. She informed the Ranger that this would be a massive crossing and handed the camera back to Jada.

He looked at Cassie with displeasure. "You signed on for this?"

Cassie stood her ground, "Yes, I did because I knew we could get advice on securing the footing for this crossing. I've seen way worse. We can construct it to acceptable standards, but I thought you would have some helpful suggestions." She paused and searched his face for an answer.

He frowned but said to Jeremy, "Let's see what you've got here. My question, is this a onetime event, or will the crossing have this wear and tear on a regular basis?"

Moria took the lead, "No, sir. This is a onetime event. Mostly local riders use these trails." smiling to herself, *until next year.* "We can maintain them once we see how they're going to hold up. Cassie can check the crossing as she needs to." Then, in her most Southern hospitality voice and innocent look, she continued, "You're welcome to come and hike or ride anytime. It's your forest, too."

The Ranger grinned and said to Cassie, "You need to hire this lady for your PR work. Okay, let's get busy."

They crossed onto the Blue Trail and Maxine said, "We'd better walk here, because of storm damage. I haven't been on this part of the trail in a coon's age. I figured it would be the least of our worries because it's at the foot of the ridge and then the land levels out at the foot of the ridge."

As the riders progressed, Jada laughed, "Moria, you sure cooled that ranger down with your charm. He'll probably want you to go hiking with him."

Moria smiled, "Not my type. Now if he had on a Stetson and some boots . . .that might be another story. Seriously, let's hope they have a plan when they're finished today. I can hardly believe the ride is only nine days away."

Maxine ventured, "At least we're not in school." By now they had reached a section covered with fallen limbs. "Let's walk this part and throw brush." The riders dismounted and Jada reached for her camera. "Oh no, you need to work harder than that. Give me the camera and I'll film *you* working." Jada reluctantly handed Maxine her prized possession, dismounted and began to throw the fallen limbs to the side.

Maxine returned Jada's camera as they reached the end of the trail. "Thank goodness, there were no downed trees. Let's head home. Maybe I'll cook tonight."

The riders said goodbye at Maxine's driveway. Moria called to Jada, "Good job today. Now, you've got a bunch of film to edit. Enjoy."

Jada turned toward home and waved. "See y'all tomorrow?"

Maxine commented as Jada grew smaller in the distance, "Guess we have a new best friend. Somehow, I think we'd better watch our backs."

"Surely not," Moria replied. "Any devilment she pulls is only going to look bad for the ride and her as manager."

"Don't count on it." Maxine turned into her driveway as Artic Cat raced down the fence line to greet them.

Silver Dollar whinnied from his pasture as he cantered up to the gate. "Don't worry, big guy, your time's gonna come next month." *I can't wait to get to a ride where I'm not responsible for anything but getting to the finish line with a sound horse.*

Chapter Twenty-one

Jackson lit a fire in the stone fireplace and settled down on the couch with his cowgirl. Dixie and Hero stretched out on the hearth. Pounce and Pandora hovered nearby and settled with their people; Pounce on the back of the couch and Pandora in Moria's lap.

"This was our lucky week," Moria said, "Dale Bice is an answer to our prayers." Then she proceeded to talk about about his background and plans for the project. "And the best part, Rose is going to lease Dillon and probably become an endurance rider."

"Whoa, don't get ahead of yourself."

"Rose, her husband and Dale are coming to the ride to help and learn about endurance."

"Missy, I think you're asking for trouble to bring these people to our circus. We don't need any more monkeys."

"We'll see. Now, about the trail we rode today. It's clear with no trees down. Tell me the latest on the water crossing."

Jackson could see he was outnumbered by Moria's swirling thoughts. "We finally have a plan. The easiest thing to do right now is use bags of Sackrete to brace the banks and fill the entrances with gravel, to make a long story short. Also, we're going to use the bridge because the ravine's too steep for a hundred horses to navigate. All of us felt like it would be an accident waiting to happen." He paused for her reaction.

"That sounds good. We crossed the bridge today. But, it's going to need some sand."

Jackson shook his head as if to say *what's next?* "Bedtime for you, Missy."

~ ~ ~

Moria drove up to the school in the early morning light. The mobile classrooms were set up on the ball field and appeared ready for use. Rose and Dale came out of the building pulling carts loaded with their salvaged supplies.

Maxine arrived and joined Moria as they walked toward the 5th grade's new mobile house. "Let's see if they need help. If not, we better get on with our ride business."

"We're lucky we didn't have any damage to our room. I feel kind'a guilty, don't you?"

Maxine gave a short laugh, "Yeah, that's what they call survivor's guilt. The best we can do is help where we can and not cause Mr. Baldwin any trouble."

Rose and Dale's room looked ready to go. "Wow! How'd you all get ready so quick?" Moria asked, looking in amazement at their efforts."

Rose sat down on the step, wiping her face on her sleeve. "The mobile people worked through the night. Somebody higher up must have leaned on them pretty hard to get this done so soon. They even moved the desks and all the furniture. I think they brought some prisoners in to help. I saw their bus leaving earlier. Dale and I've been here since daybreak. Mr. Baldwin had already opened the building."

She paused for breath, and Dale said, "Rose's husband, John, helped us, and a couple of my friends who don't live too far away came by. Guess we're good to go. We need to rest up this weekend." Giving a grateful smile he added, "Thanks for letting us store things in your room."

"No problem. You all would have done the same," Moria replied. Then with a wicked grin, "Well, maybe not with Amy. So, if you all are okay, we'll see you at the ride. God willin' and the creeks don't rise."

"For sure," Rose replied. "Take care."

~ ~ ~

"Let's have a late breakfast at our watering hole," Maxine suggested.

"Sounds good. I had a message from the hardware store to come pick something up. Be there in a minute."

Seeing Moria's smiling face as she returned with a prized possession clutched close to her chest, Maxine asked, "What's in the box?"

"You'll never believe this. When I went to the hardware store the owner handed me this …" and she opened the box to reveal red surveyor's tape, enough to mark the trail.

"What a gift. So now the trail's going to be marked as it's named, not pink or white."

"Yeah, he didn't charge us and, remember he's also donating the generator. I love this town."

Maxine grinned, "Are we lucky or are we blessed?"

As the two women waited for their food, Moria glanced at the box of ribbons sitting between them and said, "We haven't made any plans about marking the trails. I want to be sure even a deer could follow it."

Maxine laughed, "Yeah, if the ribbons are tasty, they will follow and snack along the way."

"Seriously, will it just be you and me? You, me, Jada, Rodney and our guys are the only people who do endurance and know how to mark the trails. J and J are going to be busy setting up camp and being sure the crossing and the bridge are ready."

"Marking the trails will probably be just us. Although, we need to do a special request for as many volunteers as we can get, including those that are not riding. Let's meet at Jada and Richard's and be sure we've got spotters, vet check help and maybe train some people about trail marking."

The two friends looked at each other and Moria said, "As far as *this* race is concerned, we're at the last vet check, only a few more miles to go. The sun is low in the sky and the ribbons are blowing in the wind, leading the way to the finish line."

"When this is over, maybe you should write a book. Call it, Follow the Ribbons, Missy," Maxine teased.

"Or, what about The Dog and Pony Show?" Moria laughed. "Come on, let's get busy."

The grandfather clock in the cottage on Peace in the Valley Farm counted the hours as Moria and Maxine rounded up volunteers. "Glad it's okay to meet at Jada's farm on Sunday afternoon. You know, I think we've ended up with plenty of help," Moria said. "Now, we need to give them jobs they can do, and be sure not to forget where we've left them when the ride's over. Maybe we should have a drag rider to follow the last riders, pick up lost items, and start taking down the ribbons. Let's clear our heads and take a quick ride to the water crossing. You can ride Silver. It'll save time," glancing out the window at the lowering sun.

"Good idea," Maxine said, closing her laptop. "Jackson's saddle won't do for me. What else do you have?"

"Sarah's huntseat saddle should work. We need to check the stirrup leathers and be sure the leather hasn't rotted. That was her pony, Tick Tock's saddle. I'll need to search for a girth that would fit Silver. Sarah used breakaway stirrups, so you'll be safe," eyeing Maxine's tennis shoes.

"Yeah, and I guess I'm riding in my tennis shoes since we haven't changed clothes from this morning," Maxine noted. "at least we wore jeans to school. Okay, Missy. Let's go."

Soon they were saddled up and the two riders started up the road at a walk. Moria, asked, "How are you doing?"

Maxine's grin said it all, "Who knew I'd end my day in a tiny English saddle on a stunning gray Arabian? Not complaining. Ready to trot?" As they passed her farm, she called out, "Heads up, here comes trouble."

Catch On Fire and Arctic Cat raced along the fence, whinnying, as if to say, *What about us?* Maxine saluted the bay and the gray, "Your turns will come."

As they approached Rodney's house, the German Shepherds, Bad and Worse, paced the fence, ever watchful. Rodney, Rita and the girls were on the firing range. They waved and Rodney's voice sounded across the pasture as he called to the youngsters to stand down.

Now, the bridge loomed in the distance. "What about Silver and the bridge?" Maxine called to Moria.

"He's a brave one. I can take him, or I can go first with Rainbow. Your choice."

Maxine looked at Silver, who eyed the bridge then nudged Rainbow with his nose. "Guess that answers that. Carry on."

Moria shortened the reins and urged Rainbow forward. Silver pawed, huffed and tried to turn around. Maxine brought him full circle and asked him to go forward. Rainbow whinnied encouragement and Silver followed him to the other side.

The horses picked up a trot and soon reached the water crossing. Jeremy waded out of the creek with a hopeful look, saying, "Hey, the lunch ladies are here."

Moria dug in her trail pack and found two Nature Valley food bars. "This is the best we can do," tossing one to Jeremy and one to Jackson. "Have you had any help today?"

Jackson walked over from the truck with the last bag of Sackrete and settled it into the bank. "No help. We had to go all over the valley to get enough bags. Tomorrow we're going to try and get some good-sized rocks to finish the banks and we've ordered gravel for the entrance and exit. Pray that we don't have any rain next week so all our efforts can settle. We got a tamping tool to seat the gravel. Thank goodness it runs on gas and not by hand." He munched on his food bar, saying, "I guess Richard is glad I offered to pay for this endeavor. I can write it off as sponsorship from my law firm."

The two guys began to gather up tools and empty bags and toss them into the bed of Jeremy's truck. Jackson looked at the two women, "Y'all riding back?"

Maxine jumped off Silver and handed Jackson the reins. I brought you a horse." She smiled and took Jeremy's hand. "We'll take the truck."

Jackson squinted at Silver's tiny saddle. "I don't think so."

Maxine unbuckled the saddle and put it in the back of the truck. "You'll have fun. I'm sure this is not the first time you've ridden bareback," she answered with a straight face.

Jackson pointed to Moria. "What about her?"

Maxine motioned to Moria to dismount.

"Oh, no," she answered with a startled look. "I'm good to go," reaching for the pommel of the saddle.

Jackson looped Silver's reins on his arm, walked over to Rainbow and held his arms up for Moria. "Come on, Missy."

Moria sat still and shook her head, "No."

Jackson began to uncinch the saddle as if Moria were not aboard. "Do you love me?"

"Okay, okay. I might as well die on the trail if I have a choice," and she slid off the chestnut horse into Jackson's arms. The couple mounted their bareback steeds and turned toward home.

Maxine waved goodbye and called out the window, "See ya in the AM."

"Well, this is a fine kettle of fish," Moria grumbled as they started down the trail. Dusk darkened into night as they walked cautiously on the rocky path. Silver took the lead and marched along as if he did bareback night rides for entertainment. Rainbow peered into the bushes at the slightest noise but kept a steady pace behind his partner.

When they reached the bridge, Jackson looked at Moria, the bridge and the ravine.

"Surprise. Follow me." Rainbow moved forward as if crossing the bridge in the dark was no big deal. Silver agreed and they emerged on the other side.

"Let's take a break," Jackson said with a sigh of relief, moving over to a grassy area nearby. Standing close to Moria, with his arm around her, he whispered, "Here they come."

The horses' ears perked up, lifted their heads from grazing and peered into the darkness. The vision appeared on the other side of the creek, this time, a figure on horseback.

Mesmerized by the sound of hoofbeats on the bridge, the horses and riders became as statues, waiting. Then, the sound faded away as the vision chose not to meet them.

Moria leaned into Jackson, "I need a beer," she sighed, gazing into the night. "More than that, I need a leg up."

Maybe I'm gettin' old," he muttered, looking for a mounting block.

"Here's a rock. It'll work," Moria replied. "I need to do some research and see who these ghost people are. I don't think they mean any harm and I'm pretty certain they're here to stay. Maybe I can do it when we start our Georgia History project." She drifted off into her thoughts of school and the peaceful night sheltered the riders' way home.

"Man, I need a shower in the worst way," Jackson commented after they tended to the barn tasks, settled the horses, and headed to the house. "One more day at the crossing and we'll just keep an eye on it. I want to see how it's going to hold up in a heavy rain, but not this week. We've got to work on the camp, pick up the generator and whatever else. What's your tomorrow like?"

"I need to get organized for our meeting at Richard's and be sure the house is clean. No telling who'll be in and out during the weekend. Sarah and Will could stay in the house or the trailer."

Jackson grinned, "Sarah and Will ... together?"

"Yeah, I gave up on that a while ago. What about us?"

Jackson left his pile of muddy, horse sweat clothes in the kitchen near the laundry, saying, "We need to stay in the trailer in case anything happens in the night. It's parked out of the way. Guess we'll decide closer to the time."

"Works for me," Moria said. "I'm exhausted," smiled, dropped her clothes and followed her cowboy into the shower.

~ ~ ~

Saturday morning Moria poured a second cup of coffee and stared out the window, lost in thought. *This time next week the ride will be under-way. Are we ready? What have we forgotten? When should we move the horses to Maxine's? I need to check the weekly weather report. Food for Jackson's parents. Will and Sarah. Thank goodness, most of the food will be served on the grounds. Marking the trails. What else?*

The answer to her question arrived in a phone call from California. *Doris Weaver. What now?*

"Hi, Doris, you're up early. How's everything going?

"That's what I'm calling about. Could we possibly arrive on Wednesday?"

No. Hell no. Take a breath. "Sure, as far as I know. Let me check with Jackson. We're in the process of getting the camp ready and we have to move our horses across the road."

"I called Jackson and he said talk to you, but he thought it'd be fine."

Okayyy. Moria hackles went up, but she said, in her well trained bless your heart voice, "Of course, you all are welcome anytime." *Not.*

Jackson opened the door and took a step back, seeing Moria's flushed face and her tight smile. He turned to leave.

Moria waved him in, saying to Doris, "Keep us posted on your progress and safe travels." Moria cradled her head in her arm face down on the table.

Jackson came over, rubbed her shoulders, lifted her face and gave her his best cowboy smile. "You can do this, Missy. If early visitors are the worst thing that happens to us …"

"We're lucky, I know. In the meantime, we need to make a plan. Call The Diner for their private dining room for Wednesday night and give them a heads up for a full house. No telling who will want to join us. We'll need the generator by Wednesday so they will have water."

Jackson puzzled, "Why do we have to feed them when they get here?"

Moria smiled and gave her cowboy a hug, "Because that's what we do."

Jackson reached for his phone to call The Diner and waved goodbye as he went outside to continue his tasks.

Moria phoned Maxine. "Guess what?"

"Doris and her crew want to get here on Wednesday."

Moria began to pace the floor. "How did *you* know?"

"Jada said Doris called to see if they could camp at her house so they wouldn't bother you, knowing how busy you'll be. Richard and Jada have no camping room and our pasture is full of horses. So, what's the latest?"

"They're coming here," Moria answered in despair.

Maxine laughed, "Don't worry. We'll put them to work. This is not their first rodeo."

"Well, it's a done deal, as far as I know. We've reserved the extra room at The Diner for Wednesday night. I guess we need to bring our horses over to you on Wednesday morning if it's okay. I'll get their hay and grain over there first of the week."

"No problem. Our horses will get conditioned running the fence line during the day when the riders pass. Why don't you come over so we can work on the final list? Between the camp and the water crossing, the guys are going to be busy. Maybe this afternoon we can check the trail from Rutherford's to the power line. We need to call Jada and see if she wants to go with us."

"Okay, I'll be there shortly.

The two women sat at Maxine's table, deciding what they needed to do. Moria said, "Let's check on the trail from Rutherford's to the power line first. It's my understanding that it's been cleared enough to get through. That's the start of the ride. "I'm pretty sure some people will have to camp at the Rutherfords. It's going to be dangerous for those who are racing," remembering the ride where Rainbow swerved into camp and flung her into the bushes.

"That's where the finish line is. I can't believe we haven't thought about this before now," Moria wailed.

"Check your speed, Missy. We can move the finish line down a ways. Then, block the driveway for the ones that are racing."

"Block with what? Saw horses? That won't work."

"Calm down. No, we'll block the drive with a truck."

There's got to be an answer." Moria began to chew her fingernails.

"Don't do that." Maxine scolded.

Moria frowned, "I have to," switched hands and continued her habit.

"Whatever," Maxine replied. "We'll figure this out. When we ride, we'd better check the Rutherford's pasture and be sure there's no danger-ous stuff lying around."

"We've kept horses over there, but better to be safe than sorry. Maybe I'm just tired or distracted about all the happenings with school. I'd like to think we've covered everything we need to, or anything that could possibly go wrong for the ride. At least we're free for the week." Moria smiled, "Let's ride."

"Sounds good to me. Lunch first, then call Jada and get on the trail. Are we blessed …"

"Or are we lucky?" Moria said, finishing their encouraging thought and spreading peanut butter on her bread.

Soon the three riders met at Maxine's driveway. Jada rode Mayhem, her latest 'go to' horse. The gray stallion tossed his head, announcing to Rainbow Chaser and Catch On Fire that he was in charge. Catch laid her ears back and bared her teeth. Rainbow took a stance for whatever was about to happen. The chestnut gelding reared and pawed the air as a reminder to back off. Mayhem gave Rainbow no mind as he focused on Catch.

The scene took place in seconds. Catch On Fire whirled, throwing Maxine into the ditch. Mayhem, intent on the mare, gave no thought to his rider. Catch raced back to the barn, followed by Mayhem. Jada fought him desperately, knowing what was going to happen. Halfway up the driveway, she bailed off and Mayhem thundered on, in pursuit of his newfound love.

Moria hustled Rainbow over to Maxine, who crawled out of the ditch. "Get the horse!" she shouted. "Lunge whip is at the barn. Whip him if he tries to mount her."

"Guardian angel, grab on and let's go." Moria yelled, caught up in the moment. She raced past Jada who was running toward the barn. Gravel peppered like gunfire as it hit the fence. Rainbow skidded to a stop. Moria did her best emergency dismount ever and threw her horse's reins over a fence post. Dust flew in the driveway as the gray tried to claim the bay for his own.

Catch On Fire would have none of Mayhem's attention as he tried again and again to mount his prize.

Moria remembered seeing the lunge whip hanging on the wall in the aisleway, snatched it and ran back to the two horses.

By now, Catch On Fire was done with this encounter and kicked Mayhem where it hurts. The gray stumbled back. With blazing eyes, he lurched toward the mare again. Moria raised the whip and laid into the stallion. The horse's saddle had slipped to the side and the reins tangled around his front legs. Without thinking, she whipped at the horse's hind-quarters and back legs.

Jada ran up behind her, snatched the whip, and threw it to the ground. "Stop!" she screamed. "Can't you see he's hurt?"

Moria took hold of Catch On Fire just as Maxine, out of breath, reached the scene of the aftermath. She took Catch's reins and glared at Jada. "What the hell were you thinking to bring your stallion out with us? You didn't even ask if my mare was in season." Maxine began to examine the horse and in a huff of breath, said, "She's okay," then turned to Jada who was trying to hold Mayhem still and check about the blood running down his leg. "Take him to the crossties so you can get a better look."

Without a word, Jada led the gray to the barn, put him in the cross-ties and began to examine his injury. In a dejected voice, she concluded, "His leg's got a bad gash. That's where the blood's coming from." Then she laughed, "At least it wasn't his family jewels. Poor baby," and rubbed his face.

Moria and Maxine looked at each other and knew without a word between them, this was not a time to lecture their misguided friend. Maxine put Catch in the wash rack, saying to Jada, who looked like a lost child, "What do you want to do? Do you want to call the vet?"

Jada, startled out of her daze, replied, "Yeah, probably so. I need to call Richard. Can I wait here? I don't think it's a good idea to ride him home. I'm guessing he'll need stitches. Richard can bring the trailer."

Maxine looked at her watch, then at Moria. Less than an hour had passed. "We could go on and check the trail since time is of the essence. Jada, call Richard and the vet. They can come and help you. Good thing he's not out of town."

Jada nodded and reached for her phone in the cantle pack. "Guess this is why you should keep the phone on yourself instead of on the horse," and dialed Richard's number.

Maxine went in the house and brought out water bottles. "Wish this was something stronger." She handed Moria a bottle and said, "Are you okay to go about our business?"

"Sure,"

Turning to Jada, who was securing the phone in her pocket and then putting Mayhem in a stall to wait for Richard, Moria continued, "Take care. We'll check with you this evening."

Arctic Cat, forgotten until now, appeared at the gate. *What's happenin'?* Maxine looked at the horse, saying, "You stay in the pasture."

Mayhem hung his head over the stall door and snuffled on Jada's shoulder, as she sat on the bench beside him. "Richard's on the way and he called Dr. Barr. Sorry I messed up your day," then turned her face toward her horse.

"Could'a been worse," Maxine answered, remembering her climb out of the ditch. Leading Catch On Fire out of the wash rack, she continued, "Hose Mayhem's leg if you want to."

Two riders moved at a walk down the driveway, leaving behind one rider, an injured horse and an atmosphere of discouragement.

Moria glanced back over her shoulder to the barn and said, "Guess we should give her a little space and grace. Hope she learned a lesson. This was traumatic for all of us ... and the horses. What a way to start our day."

On the Rutherford's Road they puzzled about the finish line again. Stopping at the farm's driveway and silently studying the road in both directions. "Let's move the finish past the Rutherford's," Moria said. "A quarter mile can be added to the trail measurement."

"About extra camping space, here's a thought," Maxine offered. "Most trailers will be hauling at least two horses. We've been counting each entry as a trailer, we don't know for sure, but I'll bet you all the trailers will fit in your pasture. Just in case, my front pasture is fairly level for a few hundred feet so we could take the overflow and put our extra horses in the back field."

"Problem solved. Thanks for the offer! Uh, better check with Jeremy about your insurance."

The two women now faced the trail that suffered the pine tree disaster. "Looks better than I expected. The guys did a great job," Moria said, "but it's still going to be tight since this is the beginning of the ride. Let's see if we can get a few volunteers who have time to cut this back some more. Maybe the 4-H kids and the hikers can throw brush." Laughing, she continued, "Wonder how many of our volunteers are paying their entries with rider bucks? I'll call around tonight and see who can come on short notice and finish it up." She looked at her watch, saying, "It's too late to do the rest of this loop. What do you think?"

Maxine grinned, "We could gallop up the powerline and back, now that you can race," thinking back to Moria's race to rescue Catch On Fire that morning, then gathered up her reins as if this was not a question.

I can do this. "Sure, let's go. Guardian Angel, ready for another ride?" A breath of wind answered, *Heels down, Missy. I'm on board.*

Rainbow's flaxen mane streamed into Moria's face. Her auburn hair tumbled out from the helmet and blew out behind her. Joy sang in her heart as Maxine and Catch came up beside her. "Bring it on." she called.

Maxine doubled down, "Race you to Pete's."

The chestnut and bay ran neck in neck until they neared the Deer Trail. "Hold hard," Maxine called, bringing her horse to a trot. Rainbow followed Catch's lead and the riders slowed to a walk. "Let's go up to Pete's gate and see if we can annoy him."

Out of breath, Moria laughed, "That was fun. As long as my Guardian Angel doesn't take another job, I'm good to go. Now I know how Dumbo felt when he flew with the feather. It's all in your mind."

Maxine smiled to herself, "I'm going to be sure you have a feather before the next ride."

"Works for me. Maybe all I need is an Angel and a feather," she leaned over and stroked Rainbow's neck, "and a damn good horse."

As the riders reached Pete's gate, he came to meet them. "What in tarnation? I thought those old soldiers from the bluff was coming to get me. Sounded like the cavalry, for sure."

Pete's friend ambled up beside him and nodded a greeting.

Why is that guy still hanging around? Moria wondered, but said, "Thanks for clearing the Deer Trail. Just a few more days and we'll be out of your hair."

Pete grinned, "Wal, I'll kinda miss y'all disturbin' my peaceful life."

"You are welcome to come to the ride on Saturday evening for some dinner. There might even be an award for your service." Moria said, giving them her best sweet Magnolia honey chile smile.

Pete's eyes lit up and his friend gave a broad grin. "Shore thang," he answered.

Maxine said, "Do you miss your dogs?"

"Naw, I'll get 'em back soon a nough. Rodney allowed them young'uns been behavin' better lately." Then, glancing over his shoulder at the chicken house, he gave a glum look, "Besides, I don't need any guard dogs right now. Nothing to guard."

Not being able to resist, Maxine said, "What about the poinsettias you were growing? We'll need them to sell for a fund raiser at Christmas."

"Make a deal with Piggly Wiggly. They buy 'em wholesale. I'm out of the gardenin' business for a while," scuffing his boot in the dirt, and muttering under his breath, "maybe forever." He looked at the lowering sun and concluded, "Y'all better git along now or those cowboys are gonna be lookin' for yu." Then smiled and waved, "See yu Saturday."

Moria's phone rang as the two women turned toward home.

"We're on our way," she answered.

"Where are you?"

"On the powerline. It's going to be about dark when we get home."

Jackson laughed, "Don't even ask. Yes, I'm on the way to The Diner for our supper. Tell Maxine Jeremy's got her's, too. What's your ETA?"

"I'm guessing about forty-five minutes. I owe you," she answered with a smile.

"Count on it. Hustle."

As the last rays of sun crept through the trees, a light breeze scattered autumn leaves onto the path. They picked up the pace and Maxine said, "Looks like we're going to get some night riding, without glowsticks. You want to lead?"

"Why not? I don't have a feather, but maybe this will do," as she reached out and broke off a Maple leaf twig, waved it over her head and called with delight, "Let's roll."

The remnants of downed pine trees brushed against the horses and riders as they trotted with purpose, homeward bound.

Soon they parted company and Maxine looked up the rise to her house. Light shone from the windows, a welcome sight after a very long day. She called to Moria, "Enjoy your evening."

"You, too," Moria answered, turning Rainbow toward her lighted barn.

Jackson opened the gate saying, "Come to me, Missy," and held his arms up to her.

She leaned into his arms and hugged him. "You're the best."

Rainbow whinnied and nudged his mistress, *'Scuse me? I've toted you around all day. What about some dinner?*

The cowboy took the chestnut's reins, saying to Moria, "Hit the shower, Babe, I'll be there in a minute."

Thunder echoed across the valley. Moria stopped in her tracks, turned to Jackson, who's stricken face said it all.

He began to unsaddle the horse, saying, "Not surprised. Showers are predicted for tonight and tomorrow. What is it Maxine says? 'It's not what happens that matters, it's how you react to it.' Get along, now."

Moria ran to the house just as rain began to fall. Hero and Dixie leapt off the porch to meet her and the cats hovered near the door. "Come on, guys, I know you're hungry." Dixie gave a doggie grin, *no, we're not, he fed us. but more is better.*

Noticing their bowls were on the floor instead of on the shelf, she laughed, "Tricksters." and continued to the shower.

During supper the couple caught up on each others day, ending the conversation with Jackson saying, "Dad and Mom will be here Tuesday evening …"

Before he could finish his sentence, Moria put her head in her hands. "We're not ready for company. I'm glad they'll be here but …"

"You should be grateful they're here early, otherwise I'd be gone two days this week to the job at Drapersville. I'm their attorney, if you remember. Dad has been keeping up with the case and he's going to represent our firm, so I can herd cats here."

Moria sighed with relief. "Molly's really nice and they are staying at the B&B. She can help us, I'm sure."

Thunder and lightning encouraged fireworks in the bedroom at Peace in the Valley Farm. Later, the moon shone through the window, *so this is what endurance is all about* and winked goodnight to the farm.

~ ~ ~

The next morning the daily phone conversation set the plan. "My house," Moria suggested, "since most of the maps are here." Fortified with coffee and muffins, they spread the maps out on the table.

Moria picked up the yellow legal pad and smoothed the wrinkled pages. "Why would I ever need a laptop?" she grinned, hugging the pad close.

Maxine opened her laptop and answered with a smile, "Never say never. Glad we heard from Jada last night. Sounds like Mayhem is going to be okay. Guess he'll have a different attitude when he recovers from the vet's attentions. I think it was Richard's idea to geld him since he has to be sidelined for a while with his leg injury."

"Yeah, when I talked to Jada, she didn't sound too happy. Somehow, Richard's got her number. I think this ride and all that goes with it, has snatched her around more than she expected," Moria said.

"Well, she's still got Chaos. At least he's got a lick of sense, if she doesn't lame him, or worse. Okay, let's tackle the ribbon escapade."

Moria wrote, *Start line to the bridge.* "Why don't we let Rodney mark that section? We're going to need people to do this who have done rides and can also look through the eyes of someone who has never seen this trail. Maybe our early arrivals can ride out and bring back questions or, we'll send them with ribbons, too."

"Uh, no." Maxine answered in alarm. "They could ride out but not carry ribbons. We already have enough monkeys in our circus," she sighed and typed in, *Rodney, start to bridge.* "We need a spotter with a horse at the bridge to be an encourager in case we have spooked horses. I'll bet most of the horses have never crossed a covered bridge."

Moria added, "And there's always the ravine crossing, if all else fails. Why don't we let Jada mark from the bridge to the water crossing?"

Maxine frowned, "Well, she is experienced and would know how to sight the ribbons. Surely, she won't pull some stunt at this stage of the game … you think?"

"Just let her do the marking," Moria said, turning back to her list. "There will be plenty of people riding that section ahead of time. You or I can mark the Ridge Trail and the Deer Trail/Logging Road. Which job do you want?"

Maxine studied the map. "I'll take the Ridge Trail. Are you okay to do the Deer Trail/Logging Road?"

"Sure. Let's do this tomorrow." Also, we need to remind everybody to mark in the direction the map shows. Do you think Cassie would help us? She could borrow one of Rodney's horses. I think she took off this week, knowing we'd need an extra hand. She does have trail experience," remembering their surprise at seeing Cassie's Tevis buckle. She typed in, *Call Cassie.*

"Okay, that takes care of the Red Loop and part of the Blue," Moria said. The powerline and pine stretch won't be too hard. I would trust Wilton, Cade and the 4-H guys for that, once we show them how we want it marked. What do you think?"

Maxine studied the map. "One more section on the Blue Loop, the last stretch before the finish line. It is at the bottom of the ridge, not too wide, though. People can pass but it can be a train wreck when they are racing. I'm guessing the people who think they will be front runners will probably scope the last mile of it to check the footing and space. There could be a problem at the water crossing when riders realize they're going to stack up on the trail once they cross the creek. I'm guessing on their last loop the horses will probably not even get to drink." Then she laughed, "Our cowboys will jerk a knot in them if they are tearing up the bank. Maybe Cassie and the Saddle Club people can mark the 'coming home' section. We're going to have a hell of a race on Rutherford's Road."

"That reminds me," Moria said, reaching for her pen, "We need to have the EMT's here. We should feed them, too. You know, if our horses were fit, you and I could race the trail a couple of days early to see what could happen."

Maxine grinned, "You'd better have the EMT's on speed dial if that were to happen." Then giving a wistful glance out the window, "Our day is coming, girl. You might need to carry two feathers."

In all seriousness, Moria replied, "Do you think that's why the Native Americans had so many feather headdresses?"

"Enough, already. Let's make some calls and plan for people to meet at Jada's tomorrow night. I'll call her first," Maxine answered, reaching for her phone.

"Why don't we sit on the porch to make our calls?"

Moria settled in the swing and Maxine chose a rocking chair. Pounce and Pandora chased acorns across the weathered boards while Dixie and Hero stood guard against squirrels who ventured too close. Autumn leaves spiraled down from the Maple trees, scattering a red and gold carpet onto the porch.

After an hour or so, Jackson and Jeremy's trucks pulled into the driveway. Startled, Moria checked her watch and looked at Maxine. "Dinner?"

Maxine laughed, "Did you mean Diner?"

Jackson observed the 'porch office' and called to them, "Let's wash up and eat at The Diner. We can feed the critters when we get back."

Soon the four friends were seated and ordering their favorites. Darla said, "We're getting extra food for Wednesday night and Lee is coming in to help. Are y'all excited?" Her smile lightened the long day for her customers.

Moria said, "We can give you a fairly close head count Wednesday morning. I think everyone who's planning to come early has let us know."

"That's fine. Also, we're helping out the church people with the meal for Saturday night. I think they're a little overwhelmed." Then she grinned, "Don't worry, we got this."

As dinner progressed, Maxine and Moria shared their day, ending with the planned meeting at Jada's Tuesday night.

Moria said to the guys, "You all might want to be there, too. Some of these people will be our volunteers during the ride."

Jeremy said, "I'll go. Jackson needs to meet Ben and Molly, get them settled at the B&B and go over the latest issues on the case." Then he laughed, "That Ben, he's a brave guy to go off to Drapersville on his lonesome. They'll be impressed that we've brought the 'big dogs' to settle this case."

Between bites of fried chicken, Jackson said, "Dad's looking forward to this new territory." Then, he brought them up-to-date on the water crossing. "We've done about all we can for now. Jeremy or I will stand guard at the creek so nobody races through. That could do some damage. Tomorrow we're going to spend the day working on our pasture for the camp, picking up the generator and marking off parking spaces. When people start arriving one of us is going to need to park people or it will be a helter-skelter mess."

Jeremy then reminded his friends they could bring their horses over anytime. Moria looked at Jackson, "Early tomorrow morning?"

"You take the horses, Missy. I'm going to start my chores."

Jeremy said, "I need to bush hog the front part of my pasture in case we have an overflow, then I'll come over to your place."

As they left the restaurant Moria asked the others, "Do you think it's too early to start trail marking tomorrow?"

Jackson said, "Give it a try. The more we get done early, the better."

"You know, we need some caution tape…," she said looking at Jackson with a 'would you' look.

He grinned, "Yes, when I pick up the generator."

~ ~ ~

At Peace in the Valley Farm the couple dished out feed to the horses, filled the watering trough and sat down on the barn steps to take a breath. Dixie and Hero wandered up and sat for ear scratches.

"Oh, my God. The dogs? They can't stay closed up in the house or barn for five days. Why didn't we think of this?" Moria said, with angst in her voice and hands covering her face.

"Calm down. You're right. Why wasn't this on your list?" he joked.

She gave a laugh, saying, "And if this is the worst thing that happens to us...," she looked at Jackson.

"We're lucky, for damn sure," he said, finishing their favorite saying. "There's a good kennel on the other side of town. Why don't you book them there? Might as well take them over after you move the horses. I've heard it's a well-run place and they have a fenced acre of woods for turn out."

Not us. Pounce growled as he and Pandora hid in the hay bales.

"What about the cats?" Moria puzzled, watching them scurry into hiding. Then, answering her own question, "They'll be fine in the barn or in the house. Speaking of the house, I've got plans for you."

As they raced up the path Moria dropped her shirt.

"So, that's how you want to play?" Jackson laughed, tossing his shirt into the bushes.

"And there's more." Moria stopped, kicked off her boots, dropped her jeans and stepped out of them. Then, looked over her shoulder when she heard Jackson scuffling around with a few choice words.

"I'm way ahead of you," he called as he chased her, now only in his birthday suit.

Moria stopped short. "Did you hear a car?"

"Huh?"

Just then, they heard a voice. "Anybody home?" Around the corner came Jeremy.

"'Scuse me." He threw up his hands and gave a whoop of laughter. "Sorry I missed the show."

Caught! Moria froze on the spot.

Jackson said, "We charge admission." and held out his hand.

Embarrassment finally dawned on Jeremy and he said, "Sorry. I just came to get Maxine's laptop. She left it on the porch."

Moria gave a wicked smile, "Well, at least, you've got a story to tell."

Jeremy grinned, turned toward the house and said, "Hope y'all haven't worn yourselves out before you get to the second act."

In the meantime, unnoticed by the 'performers' and their 'audience', Hero and Dixie trailed behind the 'show' picking up clothes.

Hero said, *they'll have to get their own damn boots. These pants with belt buckles are heavy enough.*

~ ~ ~

Early the following day Jackson left for town to pick up the generator and caution tape. Moria called Maxine. "I've fed the horses and I'm on the way with Rainbow. I'm just bringing them one at a time. Somehow, it seems safer."

Eventually, both horses were moved and when Moria went to her truck, she saw that Jackson had loaded hay and grain for the next several days and Rainbow's tack.

Gathering up the food and vet records for the unsuspecting dogs, she called, "Come on, guys. Let's go for a ride."

At Maxine's the two women unloaded the truck and Moria said, "When I get back from the kennel let's pack a lunch and get out to the trails."

"Okay," Maxine answered, turning to the gate to check on the horses.

When Moria returned home after delivering the dogs, a roll of caution tape lay on the table. She could hear Jackson cranking the tractor. "I love you, Cowboy," she said aloud and walked out to the pasture, flagging Jackson down. "Dogs are settled. They were surprised at first, but took to the other dogs, raced away and never looked back. Also, I left your lunch in the fridge. We're going to the Logging Road and the Ridge Trail in case you have to come get us."

"Don't even say it," waving her away. "Get outa here."

As they left Maxine's, she said, "I hear shots at the firing range. Let's stop on the road and say hi. Rodney said he'd be at the meeting tonight."

When they reached the fence, the youngsters held their fire, laid down the rifles and came over. Rodney and Rita followed, glad for a break.

With a big smile, Sassy said, "We're getting damn good." Then, glanced at Rita. "Sorry."

Mousey reached up to stroke Rainbow's forehead. The chestnut lowered his head and moved closer. Lost in her own world, the child continued to rub and scratch his ears, leaning her face against his muzzle. The adults and Sassy waited in silence until Moria said, in a cartoon voice, "Mousey, I hate to leave, but I have work to do. You know, the trail."

Mousey answered back in a playful voice, "Take care and don't get lost."

Cartoon Rainbow said, "Don't worry, we have the ribbons. You all have some work to do, too."

Mousey looked at Rodney. "When?"

"Tomorrow," he answered with a broad grin. "See you ladies this evening."

The horses crossed the bridge, picked up a trot and soon reached the water crossing. Both horses stepped in, pawed, splashed and drank, then turned back to the trail.

"I think these dudes are glad to be out and about, or maybe it's just us. Why don't we have lunch now?" Maxine suggested.

The riders tied the horses and climbed up on nearby rocks to eat. The peaceful setting brought Moria to say, "I love this forest. It's so steadfast, always here." Her thoughts drifted as she looked up into the trees where two blue jays scrapped with each other. Leaves rustled and feathers glided to the ground.

"Well, lookie here, Missy," Maxine said, reaching for a blue tail feather and handing it to her friend. "We'll call this one 'courage.'"

"A meant to be." Moria smiled, accepting the feather. "Where to put it? I know." Getting up from the rock, she went over and tucked the feather into Rainbow's bridle and picked up another feather, handing it to Maxine. "Bet you might need one, too."

"Thanks, you never know. Okay. Here's where we part company." Looking at the map, she said, "Oh, no. You'll be marking the trail from the wrong direction. What do you think?"

Moria frowned, "Well, I probably can since I know the trail. I could mark it and ride back, changing what I might need to. I'm going to have to get home one way or the other. Might as well backtrack when I finish. I can make good time once I get here."

The 'trail ladies' mounted up and rode their separate ways, Maxine, crossed the creek to tackle the Ridge Trail and Moria turned in the other direction.

Where the Logging Road came out near the creek she stopped and thought, *three ribbons here since they'll be making a turn into the creek.* Looking back, she saw that Maxine had tied three red ribbons at the bank.

The next stretch was open with no side trails. A few bedraggled pines led the way. Remembering to mark on the left, which would be on the right for the riders, she hung a couple of ribbons and changed her plan. *It's way simpler to go all the way to the powerline and start from there.*

As she reached the kudzu section, she noticed that the sneaky vines had begun to creep out again. *I'm going to trot this part. If I can do it, anybody can.* Soon she was free of the vines and cantered the level stretch for a distance. Reaching the embankment, she stopped to catch her breath and Rainbow pricked his ears, searching for horse getters. Sure enough, a figure appeared, walking up the Jeep Trail toward them.

"Hey, Miss Moria, whatcha doin' up there?"

"Well, hey yourself, Pete. I'm out marking this trail for the ride. What are you up to?"

"Jest been down to th cabin to be sure everthin's okay. Yu know, vandals." Then he laughed, "Did ya notice? Yore vines are a growin' back. Kinda' dangerous for a horse race."

"Yeah. I managed to get through. It's not the best footing." *Pete, would you help us out here?*

As if reading her mind, or perhaps her worried face, Pete said, "K… uh, my friend and I can get up here and do a little work in the next coupla days."

She breathed a sigh of relief. "We'd really appreciate it if you all have time," and gave an almost too friendly smile.

Pete grinned, "Since I'm outa th poinsettia business, we'll have time."

"Thanks. That would be great. I've got to hurry along. Thanks again for your help."

Another meant to be. Thanks feather, she whispered, reaching up between Rainbow's ears to touch the feather tucked in his bridle.

Easing down the embankment, she trotted through the Deer Trail to the powerline. Reaching into her bag, she retrieved a roll of blue surveyor's tape. Walking down the powerline a little distance she hung three ribbons around one of the poles, then three more at the turn into the trail.

Marking the trail back to the water crossing seems like a reward for the months of work we've put in, she thought. "Homeward bound," she called to her horse.

Moria set her mind and vision as an unfamiliar rider would be, in a hurry and watching for ribbons in advance of their progress. She became a Cherry Valley endurance rider as she travelled the trail at a steady pace. Stop, tie, move on. The rhythm of her task soon brought her to the embankment. Stop. Tie a wide piece of yellow caution tape. Climb the hill and move on. She reached the water crossing, let Rainbow drink and sponged his neck.

"Okay, dude. Let's roll," and the horse and rider journeyed on, soon reaching the bridge. The sun's slanting rays through the bridge openings caused alarm in the horse and he skittered to a stop. Moria gave him a strong reminder with her heels and they moved on.

Soon Rodney's farm came into view. The lighted windows of the house gave a message of peace and comfort. *Rodney's going to miss his visitors,* she thought. Then smiled. *His sister? We'll see! I'm betting Rita will be back when the trial is over, and the girls are with their parents again.*

~ ~ ~

The barn lights were on at Peace in the Valley Farm to welcome her home as she passed through the gate. Ben and Molly sat on the back porch and walked out to greet her. Jackson came out of the tack room with a rake. Pounce and Pandora sat under a bush guarding two deceased mice.

Moria dismounted, looped the reins over her arm and greeted her in-laws. "Hey, glad you all made it."

"We're at your beck and call," Ben said. "Jackson's been bringing us up-to-date."

"Here, Missy, let me help you," Jackson secured Rainbow in the crossties and began to untack him.

Moria prepared her horse's feed, and said, "I'll take him back to Maxine's in the morning. I did get the Logging Road and the Deer Trail marked. Just hope it holds."

"Your dinner's on the table," Jackson said. "I know you're due at Jada's soon. Molly wants to go with you if that's okay. Dad and I have some work to do. Would you take Molly back to the B&B when you all are finished?"

Jackson's being mighty accommodating. Never hurts to impress your parents.

"Thanks, will do. Come on Molly. Keep me company for a few minutes while I eat and soon you'll have better entertainment than TV."

Molly shared happenings on the Wyoming ranch, ending with, "We really enjoyed meeting Jeremy on their earlier visit this year. He and Jackson are a good team." She smiled, "You and Jackson, too."

It's always great to have approval from your mother-in-law, remembering her trip to Wyoming to meet Jackson's parents and Molly's very polite third degree about her background.

On the way to Jada's, after a quick clean up, Moria shared a brief version of the last few months preparing for the ride.

Molly said, "Jackson's been keeping us in the loop." She laughed, ending with, "He thanked us for our 'no nonsense' parenting efforts which have stood him well with the unexpected turns his life has taken since moving to Cherry Valley."

The parking area at Jada's was crowded with vehicles, signaling a good turn out of volunteers. As they went to the door, Moria said, "Now, you'll get to meet Jeremy's other half, Maxine. She's been my lifeline through all this. I owe her, for sure."

Jada greeted them at the door. "You must be Jackson's mom and gave Molly a hug. "Welcome to Cherry Valley. Come on in and meet the crew."

Moria introduced Molly, who received a welcoming round of applause from the group and the meeting began.

Jada took the floor and Richard sat attentively at his computer. The room quieted. Jada gave an encouraging smile and cast a gaze over the brave hearts who had stuck together through the long summer months.

"We're almost to the finish line, folks." She pointed to the table behind her and continued, "Pick up your rider bucks and add ten more because I know you all have some trail marking to do in the next couple of days. I'm not going to be surprised if most of you have paid for your ride entries with the bucks." For the hikers and others who would not be riding but have earned bucks for your trail work, she reminded them, "The vendors are expecting a lot of business. They'll turn in the rider bucks for reimbursement. Shop till you drop."

Laughter followed her declaration, and she added, "How many of you will be first time riders?" Ten smiling volunteers raised their hands. Jada gave a thumbs up and a final word of advice, "Just remember, to finish is to win."

Yeah. Get that advice tattooed on your arm, Moria thought, remembering the discontinued endurance horses living at Jada's farm.

"Okay, now let's get down to business," Jada concluded, nodding to Moria and Maxine.

Moria took the lead. Laying her yellow legal pad in the chair, she stood and faced the group. *This is my class. I need to teach them about marking the trails.* "Thanks so much for your dedication to an endeavor most of you knew nothing about until this summer. Our reward will be your success in the ride, or, looking toward some of the non-entries, "knowing you can enjoy these trails long after our event is just a memory."

Then, reaching into her bag, Moria pulled out rolls of red and blue surveyor's tape and the caution tape. "We're lucky to have some experienced endurance riders to help us. Before you all leave tonight, we'll go outside and demonstrate how to tie the ribbons." Picking up one of the rolls, she pulled out a piece, ripped it off and said, "This is about the length you'll need. Tie a double knot and tie it high."

"Yeah, the deer," someone commented.

"A plus," she said, smiling at one of the saddle club riders.

"Cassie, your section is the Blue Trail, beginning at the creek to the finish line. Folks new to this job, as you're riding, focus on looking ahead where you would expect to see a ribbon. Cassie, after you've hung a few ribbons, maybe let your people leapfrog, going ahead and tying. Those following can decide if the ribbon is in a good spot. Remember, this is the 'coming home' trail. Don't spare the ribbons. The good news, It's a straightforward path."

The Ranger smiled and said, "Looking forward to it. Saddle Club folks, see me afterward so we can make a plan."

Moria then turned to Wilton and Cade. "Would you all flag the pine tree stretch? What I said to Cassie's group and remember to begin at the start line. Hang ribbons on the right except for a left turn. At the power line, three ribbons together for that turn. In fact, hang several groups of three. Hopefully, we'll have a spotter there." She paused to see if the two guys were tracking with her directions.

Wilton grinned and said, "I love learning a new skill. Thank you for this opportunity."

A split second of silence followed. People glanced at each other, *is he for real*? And then, laughter bounced off the walls.

Moria replied with a straight face, "You always were a prankster. I guess some things never change. Maybe you can go to work for a surveyor in your spare time." More laughter. Maxine tapped her watch and caught Moria's eye.

"Okay, moving on. 4-H riders," looking to the moms, dads and kids, "the powerline won't take too long. Same suggestions as we've given the others. You will see turn ribbons at the Deer Trail. I marked that section earlier today. If you get to Pete's house and miss the turn because the ribbons are gone, I'll have to go to time out, because the deer...," and everyone chimed in, "ate the ribbons."

"Back to the red loop. Maxine has marked the Ridge Trail today. Rodney, if you'll mark from the start line to the bridge and Jada, from the other side of the bridge to the water crossing?" The two nodded with understanding. "Questions?"

"What's our timeline to get this done? One of the volunteers asked.

"By 'O dark thirty' on Thursday, if not before. Also, please carry clippers for any face branches we might have missed." Moria scanned the group. No further questions. "Maxine, your turn," and she took a seat with a mental sigh of relief.

Maxine turned toward Jada asking, "Can you please turn on your outside lights? We're going to hang a few ribbons." Jada obliged and the volunteers trooped outside.

"Before you all leave tonight," Maxine said, "each group will have enough ribbons to get the job done. Call one of us if you do run short. There's pretty good cell service on most of the trail. We'll come to you. If, by chance, there's a tree down let us know ASAP."

She walked to a nearby tree, pulled off a strip of ribbon, reached for a branch and tied the ribbon securely. As she let go of the branch, a breeze blew and the ribbon wrapped around the branches above. Maxine said nothing. Then, moved to the next branch, tied and let the branch go, flinging the ribbon around the branch above. Still, she said nothing and moved to the third branch. By now, people were looking worried. She reached, tied again and let another branch hide the ribbon. Turning to her friends, she said, "Who can right the wrongs, here?"

A Saddle Club member walked over the first ribbon and broke off the branches around it. Then she grinned and said, "That's why we need clippers."

"Good job. Who's next?"

Cade stepped forward. "Wal, if it was me, I'd do this." He untangled the ribbon and tied the loose end to a branch below, securing the ribbon at both ends. "I guess you'd only do that if the situation looked pretty sketchy."

Maxine looked at Moria, saying, "You learn something new every day. Good idea, Cade."

Pointing to the last branch, she looked at the group with puzzlement. "What now?"

"Clippers. They shouted."

Maxine gave a huge smile and added, "If any of you need clippers, I think we have some extras. Okay. Here are the ribbons. Be sure I give you the right color for your trail."

Cassie, Wilton, Cade and the 4-H people all checked to be sure they had blue. Rodney and Jada picked up the red.

Rodney said, "Thanks, ladies for the marking y'all dun. Guess it's up to us now. Then, he winked at Jada, "See yu at the finish line."

The volunteers met with their groups to plan for the next couple of days and looked forward to adding the most valuable pieces of the puzzle to the event.

As Moria, Molly and Maxine prepared to leave, Jada said, "The tents and all other equipment are arriving early tomorrow. The people bringing them will also set up. Will you all be around the campground? Not sure exactly what time they'll be here. I'll come over, too."

Moria answered, with tiredness in her voice, "Tomorrow we'll be there all day unless something unexpected happens on the trails. Are you all going to camp during the ride or go back and forth?"

"We can stay at home to save space here. Would it be okay if I bring Chaos over Friday night and put him in your barn?"

"You're riding Saturday?" Moria questioned in surprise. "Is Chaos fit?"

Jada smiled, "Oh, yeah, we've been training on the powerline... to Drapersville and back."

"Huh? Are you kidding?" Moria flashed a look at Maxine, who took over the conversation.

"Well, tell us about the powerline. We haven't had time to go there."

"Oh, it's great. Hills, but not too steep. Some boggy places. Just needs a couple of bridges." She paused, as if considering what to say next. "Maybe after the ride we can go out there together."

Moria laughed, "Give us a few days to recover and we'd love to go. It's always fun to see new trails and ride ... to Drapersville."

On the way home Moria called Maxine from her truck. "You know where she's going with this, don't you?'

Maxine's answer, "Yeah, another ride. Bet she'll change her mind before this is over."

As Moria drove Molly to the B&B, Jackson's mom said, "You were right. Plenty of entertainment. Jada doesn't seem as bad as Jackson painted her."

Moria answered grimly, "It ain't over till it's over."

Molly responded with a laugh, "I love soap operas."

"Tune in tomorrow for the next episode," she said, walking up the steps to see Molly safely inside. "By the way, you're hired. Low pay, but we'll feed you well. Have a good night," and gave Molly a hug.

Chapter Twenty-two

A short time later, she trudged into the house, fell on the bed and slept until morning.

"Howdy, cowgirl," Jackson said, standing at the foot of the bed with a cup of coffee.

She sat up in a daze, "Is that for me?" she asked, reaching out for the welcome brew. Throwing the covers aside, she looked at herself, "I slept in my clothes? How did this happen?"

"I was outside when you came in and went to bed. No response when I spoke to you. I figured you'd had a hard day … or too many beers, so I decided to let sleeping girls lie." Then, he grinned, "I did take your shoes off."

"Thanks, buddy. Yeah, we had a long, but good, day." She started to elaborate when a truck pulled into the driveway.

Jackson answered her unspoken question. "It's Jeremy. Maxine's coming over soon. I need to get outside." Doris and her tribe will be here mid-afternoon."

"She called you?" Now, Moria was wide awake.

"Yes, and let's get something straight, right now, Missy. "I'm going to hug Doris and the others when they arrive. No cat fights, you hear?"

A wicked smile crossed her face as she got out of bed, stripped off her clothes and headed for the shower. "No problem. Sorry you can't hang around for a while. See you back *here* tonight, for sure! Wait a minute. So, this means I can hug Kam?"

Jackson whipped around at the door, "You rascal! Have at it," he laughed. "Hustle, we've got a lot to do outside."

As Moria finished her shower, she glanced at the steamed over mirror and wiped it dry. "I need to put out a little extra effort today for myself, and you, Doris," digging in the drawer for her 'going out' make up. "What to wear? Not too fancy," she mumbled. "Okay, a tee shirt is always good. Here's the Ridge and Valley completion shirt and a decent pair of jeans. It's doubtful that I'll change clothes before dinner tonight."

Soon Maxine tromped up on to the back porch. Opening the door, she called, "You awake?"

"Yeah, for somebody sleeping in their clothes, I got a pretty good night's rest."

Maxine laughed, "I fell asleep on the couch." Jeremy covered me up and that's where I stayed. Guess we'd better get busy. Bring your white board and some markers. Let's set it up at the barn for a parking map and for the vendors.

Jackson handed Moria a crumpled sheet of paper with the numbered parking spaces. "We staked out each spot depending on trailer size and how many horses they'll have. Jeremy or I will be the parking police and we'll roam the camp to be sure nobody needs anything. We're going to deliver horse water and hope they've got enough people water. I don't want trucks in and out all day."

Moria nodded, *good luck with that!* But said, "We're posting the parking map at the barn. Guess we need a runner to guide them to you. Managing the board would be a good job for Rose. We'll find some kids for runners. I know she wants to spend time with Rodney and the rest of his circus. She wants crew for them on Saturday. Parking is a Friday job, anyway.

"Wow, this looks good," Maxine said, studying Jackson's parking plan and beginning to write on the board.

When Ben and Molly arrived, they walked over to the barn aisle where the women were working. Ben said, "Brought you some help. Put Molly to work and deliver her back to the B&B, if you would," giving her a hug. He proceeded to study the parking design. "Impressive! Hope it works.

What's that saying? 'the best laid plans of mice and men oft go astray.'"
He reached down to rub Pounce, who lingered nearby.

Pounce gave his best cat smirk, meowing, *"Mice never have a plan.
Lucky me!* and ran into the barn on his search. *Hang around a minute
and I'll prove it.*

"You look mighty sharp, Moria commented, observing Ben's well-cut
Western suit and cowboy hat.

Ben laughed, "You'd be surprised what statement an outfit can make,
good or bad. It gets the opposition off guard just long enough for them to
realize they should have put their boots on and turned their caps around."

Moria laughed, "I'll remember that! Could come in handy when we
go back to school. Good luck on your mission."

Ben replied, "Should be back sometime Friday. Good luck to you
guys, too," taking a last look at the transformed pasture/camp, he waved
goodbye.

Moria's phone rang. "Hey, Darla. What's going on?"

"Giving y'all a heads up. Your California people are here."

"What!" Moria shrieked, looking at her watch.

Maxine and Molly came closer to listen. "Where are they? What are
they doing?"

"They're over behind the feed store parked in that grassy area. Looks
like they've walked the horses and whoever's driving the SUV took a
bunch of them to Piggly Wiggly."

"How do you know all this?"

Darla laughed, "I got a few spies out there. Somebody's watching the
horses and the others are taking a stroll down Main Street. My buddy
at the hardware store said Jackson met up with them when he picked up
the generator."

By now, Moria had collapsed on a hay bale. "Okay, thanks."

"You don't sound very happy. What's wrong?" Darla asked, sensing
a problem.

"I guess you're never really ready for the party," she answered in a
forlorn voice.

"Cheer up, you're going to be famous after this event."

"That's what I'm afraid of," Moria laughed and then continued in a determined voice, "to finish is to win! Bring it on!" She relayed the new information to her friends and ended with, "We can't be everybody's act. Let's stay right here and greet them when they arrive."

Jeremy walked up from the other side of the camp. "Jackson called ..."

"Yeah, we know," Maxine answered. "Are they following him here?"

"They're going to stay in town a while longer." Laughing, he added, "Apparently they've fallen in love with our town. They told Jackson they'd be along after they've shopped."

Moria and Maxine looked at each other and Moria groaned and grabbed her phone to call Jada.

"Hey, how's it going?" Jada answered in a chipper voice.

"Not too well. When are the Pottys going arrive?"

"In the morning. What's the matter?" catching the desperation in Moria's tone.

"People will be arriving soon. How could this have happened?"

"Hold on. I'll call them and see if they can deliver today."

Moria paced the aisleway. Maxine and Molly stood by, waiting.

The phone rang and Jada said, "They can bring two this afternoon, and the rest in the morning."

"Thank you, Jesus!" Moria mumbled.

Jada laughed, "And, you can thank me, too. I had to scrounge some of them away from another event. Money talks and ..."

"Thanks, you and Richard are great ride managers," Moria answered, winking at Maxine and Molly.

"Anything else?"

"No. Be sure and come to supper at The Diner tonight and meet some of the folks. Probably around six."

Moria sighed and sat down on the hay bale again. "I will give those two folks credit for taking care of the millions of tasks we didn't have to do. More than likely the travelers emptied their potty tanks where they camped last night." She smiled as Jackson turned into the farm.

"Guess you heard," Jackson announced, "The troops are arriving. They're at the feed and hardware stores to replace what they've used up on the trip. Oh yeah, and Piggly Wiggly.

"Come on, Jeremy, we've got to get the generator running pronto."

Moria started to ask for more details, but Jackson's tense face gave an unspoken message of 'git er dun' as they headed toward the creek.

Jeremy said to Maxine, "See you in a while. Will you feed the horses later? I don't know what we might need to be doing here."

Maxine nodded and said to Moria, "Glad we have plenty of pasture right now so we can feed once a day. We'll be using hay before you know it." Seeing Rainbow's head framed in the stall door, she said, "I'll take him back to my house later."

"Thanks," but Moria's mind was on Doris Weaver. *What happened when they greeted each other?* but she said to Maxine, "Let's get the signs on the road. We can rope off the vet check, too."

"Molly, watch for the Porta Pottys, if you would," pointing to the spot near the barn where they would go. "We'll be in shoutin' distance if you need us. Make yourself at home if you need to go in the house. That reminds me, I've got to clean the bathroom in case it becomes public."

Time passes. The outhouses arrive, signs are in place on the road, vet check is ready for business, generator running, water troughs filled. Darla, from The Diner, surprises the group with a basket of sandwiches.

"Wow! Who ordered these?" Moria asked with a grateful smile.

Darla set the basket on the picnic table, "Just a bonus for having your dinner with us tonight. Thanks for the business."

"We're looking forward to it. See you soon and thanks again!"

"Let's take a break," Moria suggested, wiping her face on her shirt sleeve. "Oh, well, so much for looking nice. You know, we need to go ahead and eat before our company arrives."

"Food's ready!" Maxine yelled to the guys. Everyone sat around the picnic table to enjoy the unexpected treat.

"Who's that flying up the road?" Jackson asked, then had his answer.

Jada's truck skidded into the farmyard. Jumping out of the truck, she raced toward the group.

"This can't be good," Moria muttered.

"Disaster!" their distraught friend screamed, stopping, out of breath, and in tears.

Jeremy guided her to the table. "What's happened? Is Richard okay?"

She leaned on Jeremy's shoulder, took a ragged breath and stammered halting words, "The truck's wrecked, the one with the tents and all ..."

"Maxine said, "Calm down. It's only Wednesday. Surely they can sort this out by tomorrow."

"You don't understand!! The truck went into a ravine. Stuff is scattered everywhere."

Jackson, on alert now, asked, "Where are they?"

"Somewhere on I-75 coming out of Atlanta. Not sure. Richard took the horse trailer to try and recover as much as he can that's not damaged." Then, with a hopeful look at the two guys, she said, "Can y'all help?"

Jackson and Jeremy looked at each other, unspoken questions in the air. *Leave, just as people are arriving at the farm? The women could handle most anything but the back up folks, Rodney, Wilton, Cade and the others are marking trails. They can't be spared from their tasks for a road trip.*

Jackson said, "Let me try to call Richard and see where they are," then looked at Jeremy, who nodded, yes.

Moria clenched her jaws, *It's not all about me. Step back and be part of the solution, not the problem s*he listened as Jackson spoke to Richard, knowing the success of the rest of the day and the evening would be up to her and her friends.

Jackson turned to his cowgirl, who had come to stand beside him. "Missy, we need to go. The wreck is about two hours away. We'll still have some daylight and Richard said the State Patrol will set up lights, if needed." He looked at her with a question in his eyes and waited.

"We've got this, Mister. Do what you gotta do," and gave him a lingering goodbye kiss.

Jeremy and Maxine embraced, and Maxine said, "Safe travels. Keep in touch. Love ya, dude."

By now, Jada was beginning to recover, as her problem was now in capable hands. "Thanks, guys, Good luck." Turning to Moria she said, "What can I do to help?"

"Why don't you move out of the driveway first? It appears they're taking the trucks, not the horse trailers." Sensing these next few hours would be difficult for Jada, returning to an empty house and not knowing the outcome of the day, Moria said, "You can hang out with us and greet the first arrivals if you'd like to."

Jada answered with a smile.

As if on cue, Moria heard Jackson beep his horn at someone on the road. Glancing toward the highway, she saw trailers approaching with right turn blinkers on. Moria and Maxine gave high fives and then to Jada.

Molly, who had stayed in the background and out of the way, signaled a thumbs up and said with a grin, "Show 'em what you got, ladies!"

Moria left the picnic table. "Maxine, if you'll man the generator for water, in case they need to top off their tanks, I'll get them parked.

"Molly, you and Jada welcome them and when everybody's in, come on down to where they're setting up. Is that okay with you all?"

Maxine laughed, "Guess it better be. Here they are." Doris Weaver's trailer turned in first. She stopped at the barn where the women waved a welcome.

Doris rolled down her window and brushed sun-streaked hair from her face. "Hi ya! We're here. Great directions. You must be Moria. Jessie had great pictures of you from the ride last year." Reaching her arm out the window, she shook Moria's hand. "We're glad to be here. That was a long trip."

Moria found herself giving a genuine smile. "Welcome to Peace in the Valley Farm. I hear you all have helped our economy already." *Please still be smiling, Doris, when you roll out of here on Sunday.*

Molly stepped forward to greet Doris. "Remember me?"

"Molly! Good to see you. Didn't know you'd be here."

Jackson's mom laughed, "This an all 'hands on deck' event. Hope you and your Junior have a successful ride."

Jada relaxed as if her world weren't falling apart. "Good to meet you in person, Doris," referring to their previous conversations when Jackson's ex wanted current information about the status of her lost cowboy.

Seeing the other trailers waiting, Moria said, "Come on to your spot. Jackson has them numbered."

Doris released the door lock. "Jump in."

As they headed across the field, Moria said, "Stop for water, if you need to."

"I'm good. Filled up at the feed store. They were great."

At the water tank Moria said, "Stop to meet Maxine. I have to tell you I couldn't have done this without her. Always one step ahead of me." *And if it wasn't for Maxine's encouragement, I wouldn't have married your cowboy!*

Maxine gave her signature grin, saying, "Welcome to Cherry Valley. Let us know if you need anything," and pointed toward their camp sites.

Paul and Ruth followed Doris, with Jessie's excited face framed in the window. Tara and Chris stopped for water and chatted with Maxine for a moment. The two girls pulled away and Kam stopped beside the water trough.

Maxine joked, "Hey, good to see you again. Need some water?"

"No thanks, but I could use a beer!"

"Later, for sure. How does it feel to be back in your old stomping grounds? Do you miss us?"

"Well, I've only been gone a year." He removed his cap, ran his fingers through his hair and looked across the way at the mountains. "Yeah, Sometimes I do. Being a Forest Ranger here was easy … most of the time. Are you and your side- kick staying out of trouble?"

"You could say so," Maxine smiled, remembering their escapades with Pete and sometimes, Jada.

"How's Cassie working out?"

"She's been a godsend. If she doesn't know the answer, she makes a phone call. We had a great night when she made her entrance at The Juniper Tree! For never have lived in this region, she caught on right away and is working on her southern accent."

Their catch-up conversation ended with the sound of a horn calling Kam to add his shoulder to setting up. "I'll be crewing but I'm glad to help out around camp when I'm not busy."

"Welcome to the circus!" Maxine laughed as she hopped in Kam's car and they headed to the first act at the California camp site.

As Moria and Doris reached the designated camping spots, Moria looked back to see the other trailers coming across the pasture. "I'll get out of your way and stand by. I'm guessing this isn't your first rodeo," she added, glad not to be in Doris' shoes right now.

Doris grimaced, "Yeah, that's why I like to get settled early. Okay, let me get parked," all business as she backed into her space.

Like a well-oiled machine, Paul and Ruth eased in next to Doris. Paul's raised voice cautioned Jessie to stay in the truck.

Tara and Chris found the next spot as Moria pointed it out to them.

Kam stopped next to Moria, got out of his car and said, with a twinkle in his eyes, "Hey, Missy. Remember me?" She turned around and Kam swept her into his arms.

Returning his embrace, *uh oh, here we go again* and looking into his mischievous brown eyes, she said, "Welcome to Peace in the Valley Farm," then her unexpected words whispered in his ear, "I've missed you, you rascal!"

Over Kam's shoulder, she saw Maxine and Molly chatting and coming their way.

Behind her, Jessie called, "We're here! Come see my pony! Remember Friendly?"

Moria broke away from his embrace, like it never happened. *I'm going to get a whooping from somebody if I start fooling around. I'm not in high school!* she told herself and welcomed Jessie's hug.

"Let's go see your pony and welcome your parents to the ride," taking the youngster's hand and walking toward their trailer. "You probably need to help your dad. I'll see you in a few minutes," then turned to Molly and Maxine.

Molly's raised eyebrows spoke volumes as she said, "Old friend of yours?"

Maxine winked at Moria, "Let me see if I can be some help over there," removing herself from the conversation and striding toward the trailers.

Moria also began to walk in that direction, as Molly fell in step beside her. "Yes, Kam was the Forest Ranger in our area until last year when he moved to California. He was a big help in getting us a grant to rebuild the bridge. *Keep talking!* That bridge was built by my ancestors. Sometimes I see them … just like at your homeplace in Wyoming."

"You'll have to come back for a visit someday," Molly said, as Moria changed the subject.

"We've talked about doing an endurance ride out West," she answered, thankful to be at the trailers. "Let's see what we can do to help."

Late afternoon sun cast shadows across Peace in the Valley Farm. The California contingent had settled their horses in the electric corrals and gathered around Moria.

Doris dipped her hands in a water bucket and dried them on her pants legs, "Moria, what did you say about dinner this evening?"

"We're going to The Diner. They're expecting us and you all will get to meet some of our volunteers and riders." Seeing everyone look at their clothes from the day, she continued, "Don't worry, it's just us. Besides, I don't think they would recognize us if we were cleaned up. Why don't you all relax while Maxine and I go across the road and feed our horses."

Moria breathed a sigh of relief, *So far, so good!* with a relaxed smile, she said, "Listen for the horn when we're finished feeding and meet us on the road."

Paul said, "That'll give us time to unhook and at least wash our hands," he grinned. "Jessie, you behave."

"Yes sir," the youngster answered.

~ ~ ~

If anticipation were a color, red and gold confetti would be scattered over the reserved room at The Diner. Jessie spotted Sassy and Mousey, who would forever be Alyssa and Teresa in Jessie's world and those who would meet them in the next few days.

Moria raised her eyebrows at Rita, who responded in a quiet voice, "We're out of here right after the ride to our next destination. I figure the girls deserve their last hoorah as a goodbye to Cherry Valley, the fun they've had, life lessons they've learned and the forever memories ... me, too," she grinned. "This gig is the most fun I've ever had."

Don't speak too soon, the breeze blowing through the windows whispered an omen to Rita. You will need all your skills before you leave Cherry Valley.

Cassie came in, followed by Wilton and Cade who sat beside Rodney.

Kam hurried over to his Ranger friend saying, "Cassie, good to see you," giving her a hug. "Come over and sit by me so we can catch up."

Molly, sitting next to Moria, commented, "Guess he's the friendly type, a hug for everybody."

"Yeah, that's him," Moria answered, then stood up to introduce everyone and explain the absence of Richard, Jeremy and Jackson and Molly's husband, Ben.

Dinner proceeded with mixed conversation, everyone talking at once. Friends with a history seemed to be in the making. As dessert was served, Moria tapped a spoon on her glass. "I know this isn't a meeting, but I'm dying to know how the trail marking is coming along."

Rodney spoke up first. "Start to the bridge, done."

Jada added, "Bridge to the water crossing, done.

Maxine raised a hand, "Ridge Trail, done."

Wilton gave a thumbs up, "Pine section, done."

Speaking for the 4-Hers, Moria said, "Powerline, done. Maxine and I caught the Deer Trail and Logging Road. Cassie?"

"The Saddle Club people learned more about marking trails, than they ever wanted to know. They got a running commentary from me about thoughts in rider's minds about trail markers. Those of them who ride this weekend will forever see those blue ribbons in their dreams!"

Darla came with the checks and Moria reached for them, handing her a credit card. "This dinner's on Jackson. I know our guys are sorry they can't be here."

Jada handed Darla a card, too, saying, "Split the check."

People rose to leave, thanking Moria and Jada for dinner and saying goodbye to new-found friends.

"Come on, Molly. I can run you to the Bed and Breakfast," Moria said.

Maxine, walking beside Jada, asked, "Want to spend the night at my house?"

Jada laughed, "Who needs the company, you or me? Thanks for the invite. I need to get home and feed my horses. I'm hoping to hear from Richard. See you in the morning."

~ ~ ~

The house was still dark when the phone rang. Moria struggled from that a deep sleep and grabbed for her cell. "Hey, are you okay?"

Jackson's exhausted voice told the story. "I'm okay, considering we climbed in and out of the ravine more times than I can count. Everything's loaded, the tent, and all the tables and chairs that weren't too damaged. The company is sending replacements for the broken things and sending some people to set up for us. They should arrive by late afternoon. We're heading home now. I need a shower and a couple of hours of sleep, then get on with the day. Catch me up on yesterday. Is everyone settled in camp?"

Moria gave the short version of events, ending with, "I'll have some breakfast for you. Be safe. I love you, cowboy."

She squinted at the clock. "4:30? Might as well get up." Pounce and Pandora tumbled off the bed with Pounce whining, *Missy, what's going on? It's dark! Are you going to an endurance ride?*

Sitting on the porch with coffee and the cats curled up beside her, Moria pondered, *Wish I was headed out for a ride today. My time will come. It was my choice to take on this ride s*he gazed across the pasture as a light came on in Jessie's trailer.

Soon the young girl jogged across the dew-covered pasture, climbed over the fence and approached the porch.

"Good morning, Miss Moria! May I join you?"

"Of course. You're up mighty early."

"Couldn't sleep. I'm too excited. Miss Doris says we can ride today to exercise the horses and check out the stretch of trail to the finish line."

Am I even surprised? Moria thought, but said, "Just don't bother the ribbons. If something doesn't seem right, let us know so we can fix it."

"Do you have many Juniors in the 50?" Jessie asked.

"Tomorrow at the ride meeting we'll announce the numbers. Some people probably won't vet out on Friday. That's discouraging when folks have travelled long distances to get here."

"Like us? Miss Doris says our horses are in good shape and we're going to ride like we've trained."

"That's a good rule to follow." By now, Moria's mind began to wander, thinking about the tasks ahead. "Honey, I've got to get ready. You need to go back to your trailer."

"One more thing." Jessie stood to go, then asked in a serious voice, "Do you all do drug testing?"

Moria stopped short and turned from the door, "Why do you ask?"

"Well, sometimes people do take a chance. Not us," she hurried to say. "But maybe testing can get rid of some of the competition."

I need another cup of coffee! "You run along now, and later I'll give you some directions for your ride today. Let me know if you need anything."

Darkness still claimed the coming day when Jackson and Jeremy's trucks turned into the farm, stopping at the barn. Moria went out to meet them and saw the headlights from Maxine's truck heading their way.

"We're going to park here for now," Jackson's weary voice greeted Moria as he climbed from the truck. His scruffy, dirty look said it all.

"You all come on and sit down," Moria gestured to the picnic table, "I'll get the coffee pot."

Maxine arrived and the four friends looked at each other as Jeremy raised his cup, saying, "To the days that follow, please don't make us holler!"

Laughter accompanied his toast and Moria said, "We need to keep it down or we'll have Jessie for company again. She's already visited me this morning and wanted to know about drug testing the horses."

Startled looks flashed between the friends and brought Maxine to say, "Huh? What are we looking at here?"

Moria poured everyone another cup and said, "Wait a minute," returning with a bottle of Old Bailey's to enhance their coffee.

"This is not Jessie's first rodeo on the endurance trail. She's a pretty savvy youngster. I don't know whether Doris put her up to finding out or she just wanted to know." Silence hovers for a moment while everyone considers if 'out of the mouths of babes' will be a forerunner of events to come.

Jackson held his cup out for Moria to strengthen its contents. "Well, that's the vet's problem. We've got to get this show on the road. Remember, there are some more trailers coming in later this afternoon. Most of the vendors want to set up today, too. Jeremy and I need to be here when the rest of the chairs and tables arrive. The tent's pretty beat up, but it'll do. What's the weather for the next few days?" Jackson paused with his directions to finish his splendid coffee.

Moria smiled, "So far, so good. No rain till the first of the week. I can't believe we have to go back to school on Monday! You know, I kinda wonder if God sent the storm to give us a couple of weeks to finish plans for the ride."

"Thank you, God!" they said in unison.

Maxine said, "Seriously, this might be a good time to reinforce our thanks." The four joined hands and she began, "Dear God, lead us on the path you have prepared. Please give us courage and gratitude to follow you in our endeavors. Keep our friends and their horses safe from harm and bad decisions. We ask this in your name. Amen." Amens echoed around the table. A flock of birds flew over the yard and a feather floated down to land near Moria's empty cup.

"Well, there you go! It's a sign, for sure." She picked up the feather. "Guess this means get to work. If you're hungry," she said to the group, "I have some Jimmy Dean's sausage and egg biscuits to get our day started." No one objected.

Jackson said, "I'm going to get a couple of hours sleep." He nodded to Jeremy, "You, too?" Jeremy waved goodbye, halfway to Maxine's truck.

The California horses whinnied and Moria heard trailer doors opening as the horses began their people's day. *Should I go down and see if they need anything? Probably not.*

I need a list. In the distance she heard Maxine returning.

The two women sat at the picnic table, Moria with the yellow pad and Maxine with her laptop.

"Okay, I need to go get Molly. Well, maybe she can sleep a little longer," Moria said, realizing that the sun was just a promise for the day to come. Richard should be over some time today with the rider cards and all the other materials. He said he checked the Ride Manager's Handbook to be sure he had everything. It's worth putting up with Jada just to have Richard's dedication. We're lucky he has a touch of OCD!"

At the sound of hoofbeats, Maxine looked toward the road. "Speaking of Jada, here she comes on Chaos. Wonder how long that horse will last?"

Jada dismounted at the barn and Moria went to meet her. "You did say I could keep Chaos here," she reminded Moria. "That way we can stay at home and not have to bring the trailer. You'll probably need the room."

"No problem," Moria answered. "Our horses are at Maxine's."

"Richard's bringing hay and grain and the paperwork later today. I brought my camera. Seems like this is the happenin' place. I'm going down and film at Doris's. I'm sure she's set a good example of how to have a safe camp."

"Have at it, just don't wear out your welcome. A few more trailers will be coming in later today. Why don't you hang around and welcome them? Check the board at the barn for their numbered spaces and walk them out there. Be sure they know where the water is. This is a sign of a good manager to be on site when they arrive. Maxine and I are getting things together for the vet check and entry table." Moria paused to see if Jada picked up on 'good ride manager'.

Turning to Maxine, she said, under her breath, "That should keep her busy for a while and we'll be close by." She looked at the two trucks loaded with the salvaged goods, "Hope the people get here to put this stuff together soon."

By now, the sun was above the treeline. Supplies for the vet check and the entry table were in plastic boxes on the picnic table.

"What's next?" Moria asked.

"Heads up, here comes Jessie. Wonder what she needs?" Maxine answered.

Jessie trotted up to them, her face alight with joy for the day. "Miss Doris sent me to get a trail map so we can ride this morning."

"Jessie, tell Doris the maps are on the way. The trail is marked. Remember, I told you not to move any ribbons. When you all are ready, come by here and I'll get you started."

"Will do." The youngster said in her 'grown up' voice.

Moria heard Chaos whinny and glanced to the barn. Jada was saddling up, and no doubt planning to ride out with the others.

She walked over and tapped Jada on the shoulder. "'Scuse me? I believe you have a job here?"

"Oh, we won't be out long," the miscreant answered in a chipper voice.

"Jada, cut the crap. Maxine and I have to help the vendors set up and anytime now the guys will be here to set up for your 'party'!"

Moria saw the California folks approaching the barn. Jada unsnapped Chaos from the crossties, "I'm sure you all can manage for a couple of hours." Mounting her horse, she waved to the approaching group, "Come on, let's ride!"

Moria threw up her hands, "Thanks for your five minutes of help." *Good riddance!*

Maxine motioned her friend to come sit. "If this is the worst thing that happens to us in the next few days, we're lucky."

"Or, blessed," Moria finished their well-worn saying.

"While the drama was going on I noticed we don't have any livestock markers to put the numbers on the horses. I checked both boxes."

"Oh, man!" Moria grumbled. "No, we don't have any. What about if I go by the feed store? I need to pick Molly up anyway. Call me if you think of anything else."

"Some breakfast from the Diner? I appreciated your donation of the biscuits this morning, but we need some real food. I'll call in the order and include Molly."

The last quiet moments Peace in the Valley Farm would see for a few days found the three ladies finishing up breakfast. "Listen," Moria whispered, "No horses, no people, no problems to solve."

As she spoke, voices sounded in the distance as a horse race came off the Blue Trail and on to Rutherford Road. Doris and Jada raced neck and neck, followed by Jessie, Tara and Chris.

Jessie's parents and Kam heard the pounding hooves and hurried to the driveway. Not slowing down, the riders wheeled into the farm as if they owned it. Pulling up at the barn, and laughing, Doris called out, "What a blast! This ride's gonna be a piece of cake!"

The horses crowded on one another. Heaving sides and labored breathing spoke to the meaning of 'getting caught up in the race'.

Moria strode over to the group as they started to their trailers, "What the hell?" She made a circular motion with her arm and pointed to the road. "Out!"

Startled, the riders looked at one another, then at Doris.

"Get over yourself! We're just getting warmed up!" Doris answered back, not happy at being challenged in front of her group.

Moria turned to Maxine, "Would you bring a couple of stethoscopes from the tack room and meet me at the gate?"

Looking at the riders she continued, "I suggest you all take the horses back on the road, dismount and walk them until you think their pulses are down to 64. Come to the gate and we'll check you."

"Well, I never!" Doris said, knowing it was time to shape up. She had lost this round. "Okay folks, get out on the road and do what the lady says."

Jeremy walked over from across the road, stood back and assessed the situation. Moria and Maxine's annoyed faces, as they watched the procedure, gave him a clue that all was not well. He continued to the gate and grinned at Maxine, noticing the stethoscope. "Wanta check my pulse?"

Maxine gave him a wink, "Later."

Paul came to the gate. His irritated voice and frown let Moria know he was not pleased. "I need to help Jessie. Let me through."

Moria placed a hand on his arm, saying, "Let her do this."

Paul stepped back and moved down the fence to watch. "What got into them? That's not how they trained!" He grasped the board with both hands. Moria could see his knuckles turning white.

"Not to worry," she reassured him. "Just hope the horses are okay. Running down that trail wide open is dangerous. They'll have plenty of room to race on the road, pointing back toward the Rutherfords.

Doris came to the gate first. "I did a hand check. I think he's fine," she snapped.

Moria moved the loose girth aside and checked for the full minute. "He's good to go. When you get back to your trailers, you all might want to jog them out."

Doris nodded, walked past Paul and Ruth with no words. Tara and Chris came next. Chris said in a low voice, "Sorry. We do know better."

Tara echoed her friend, adding with a grin, "At least we saw the finish line. You all did a great job on clearing and marking."

"Thanks. We had a huge amount of help. You'll meet them this weekend and I'm sure they would appreciate a word of thanks."

"You got it," Tara said, looking back at Jessie. "I'll wait for her."

Jessie trudged up with Friendly. She looked at the ground, then raised her eyes, "Sorry. This was a mistake, a big mistake," then looked at her dad.

Moria unsnapped Jessie's helmet, fastened it to the saddle and ruffled the child's wet hair. "It's hard when you're not the leader." Giving Jessie a hug, she added, with a smile, "Someday you will be."

~ ~ ~

"I can't believe it's nearly lunchtime," Moria said. I've got some tomatoes for sandwiches and chips."

"What about some special iced tea?" Maxine asked with longing in her voice.

"Tonight," her friend answered.

Molly gave a knowing smile and said, "I can fix lunch. You all go on with your business. I'll let you know when it's ready."

"The tent guys will be here soon," Jackson announced. "Darla called from The Diner and said their truck was parked nearby and they asked for directions to our place. She comped their food and thanked them for their help."

"That Darla! We need to do something for her. At least a completion award," Maxine said.

Jackson laughed saying, "Well, they are making a boatload of money this weekend. She needs extra pay for being our lookout. Here comes another truck. I think it's Running Deer. Who's in charge of vendors?" he asked, looking at Moria.

"Guess it's me," she replied. "Molly is going to help with the vendors later."

Just then, Jackson's mom called, "Come and get it."

Moria met Running Deer in the driveway and showed him the vendor section while the rest of the folks trooped inside for lunch. "Since you're here first, you can choose your spot," she offered, pointing along the fence line. That ribbon marks the beginning of the campsites."

"This looks great! We appreciate your offer for the profits to go to the school."

"Well, you did pay for your space. That works for us. Is there anything you need? You're welcome to come in and have lunch with us."

"Thanks, I've got to get back. I'm going bring the goods in the morning."

"No problem. See you in the morning," Running Deer said, turning to his work.

Moria returned to the house, saying, "Between the vendors, tent people and the early arrivals, we've got a wingding of a day ahead of us." Before she took the first bite of her sandwich, a trailer turned into the driveway and stopped at the barn.

Maxine and Jeremy started to the door. Maxine said, "We'll take the first shift parking people."

"Molly and I can watch for the vendors. Keep your phones handy for a change of plans," Moria said with a laugh.

"Jackson?"

"I'm going finish setting up the vet check and Richard's bringing the paperwork down. Where's Jada?"

"I guess she's over with her new best friend. She needs to be filming the setups and narrating the activities."

Jackson started for the door. "Speak of the devil," as he held the screen open for Jada and made his exit.

"We've got a problem," she announced, a worried look clouding her face."

"What?" Moria asked. *This can't be good.*

Doris' horse is lame.

Am I even surprised?

"What does she need?"

"Do you think we should call Dr. Barr?"

Sensing Jada's distress, she answered, "Come on, let's take a look at her horse and see if I have any supplies that might help. He can't have any drugs or shots if he's going to compete tomorrow."

As they crossed the pasture, another vendor pulled in. Molly came out of the kitchen, waved and called, "I've got this," and went to meet the new arrival.

Jeremy, Maxine and the incoming trailer had reached the water tank on their way to the parking space. Maxine appeared to be having a lively chat with the driver as she waved her hand toward the mountains and Jeremy filled their containers.

The California folks sat at Doris' trailer, watching as she walked Straight Arrow back and forth. The bay horse obviously had a 'hitch in his git a long'.

The angst on his owner's face and the tense muscles on the horse's face brought Moria up short. *That could be Rainbow and me. Give it a rest, Missy.*

Doris stopped walking when Moria and Jada approached. Her stance appeared to brace for another dressing down from Moria.

"Jada told me you're having some trouble here. She mentioned the vet, but there's not much he can do right now if you're hoping to compete tomorrow. I do know someone who might be able to help you."

Straight Arrow pushed his head into Doris' shoulder and snuffled, as if to say, *Listen to her.*

Doris softened her stance, rubbed the horse's neck and said, "Anything at this point would help. I might have to find another sponsor for Jessie."

Reaching in her pocket for the ever-present phone, Moria said, "We have an equine chiropractor coming tomorrow. She's from Chattanooga but she's already in town staying with a friend. Why don't we call and see if she's available?"

"I would appreciate it," Doris answered with relief for possible help.

As they stood together, each ring of the phone gave them hope that the equine angel would answer.

"Hello?"

"Hi, this is Moria from the endurance ride. We need some help over here if you have time to come by," and then explained the problem and gave the lady directions. "She'll be here in about thirty minutes. Do you want to bring him to the barn?"

"Sure," Doris said, gathering up the lead rope. Straight Arrow took a few halting steps and stopped. "Or not. Guess we better stay right here."

"Do you have plenty of electrolytes?' Jada asked. "I've got some at the barn since my horse is here. That reminds me, he needs some, too, and I should be walking him around."

Doris looked at her group, saying, "We've got plenty of electrolytes. Dose your horses and walk them. Take them down to the creek and see if they'll drink."

"Moria and Doris' eyes met, with the unspoken thought, *horses first.*

"Thanks," Doris said, turning Straight Arrow toward her trailer. Her relaxed demeanor said it all.

"I'll check with you later. Let me know if you need a stall." As Moria turned back toward the house, another horse trailer turned into the farm, followed by the tent truck.

She caught up with Maxine and Jeremy saying, "Jeremy, why don't you go on over to the tent people. Maxine and I can settle the incoming, watching a new Exiss trailer headed their way.

~ ~ ~

By sunset, the camp seemed to have settled for evening. Three trailers had arrived from out of state. The vendors came throughout the afternoon to set up their stations, planning to bring their goods the next day. Jeremy and Jackson wrestled the tent into place. Tara, Chris and Jessie helped set up tables and chairs, reporting that the chiropractor had eased Straight Arrow's muscles and would check on him first thing tomorrow. Jada occupied herself with filming preparations for the ride, fed Chaos and left for home. Sarah and Will arrived and became useful parts of the puzzle.

"Hey, y'all look hungry," Maxine grinned. "I've got some pork chops, just bought, and enough potato salad for all of us. Donation to the cause."

The bedraggled group perked up and Moria said, "I've got corn. Hope it's still fresh and there's plenty to drink."

"I'll feed the horses while I'm home," Maxine continued.

Jeremy eased off the picnic bench, "I'll come with you."

Jackson groaned as he got up, saying, "I'll start the grill."

Sarah started to help Moria in the kitchen, but her mom said, "You and Will sit with Molly and get better acquainted. She's got some good stories about Wyoming and Jackson's escapades."

During dinner, everyone learned their assigned tasks for Friday. Moria said to Will and Sarah, "How would you all feel about checking the ribbons tomorrow? You could ride Rainbow and Silver. That would start some conditioning on them. Check one loop, come in for lunch and do the other one in the after a break."

Sarah looked at Will who nodded and flashed a wide smile. "We're on it," she said. "By the way, where are we going to sleep?"

"Ben will be back tomorrow. He and Molly can have the guest room."

"What about the trailer?"

Sarah smiled at her mom, "Do you even have to ask?"

Molly said, "We can stay at the B&B."

"No, we need you all here for the next couple of days. The guest room is ready."

Jackson, who had been listening to the arrangements, said to Molly, "I'll run you over there tonight and come pick you up first thing in the morning."

Moria gave Sarah the necessities for life in the trailer, saying, "You all can shower in the house since the water tank's not filled." Then, as an afterthought, "The potty in the trailer has no water either."

"I know," Sarah laughed, pointing to the two Porta Pottys by the barn.

Moria sat in the porch swing, waiting Jackson's return. Pounce and Pandora jumped up to sit with her and Pounce had his say, with a forlorn meow, *this is a fine state of affairs... locked in the house all day... what's going on?*

She picked up the gray cat and held him close. Pounce licked her neck and wrinkled his nose at the dirt and sweat. Moria stroked him, saying, "Remember, it's not all about you. This weekend is a big deal. Lots going on. I don't want you two to get hurt." She brought Pandora close. "You can roam around tonight and sleep in the barn. But in the morning, back in the house. Scoot!" The delighted cats dashed away into the night.

Moria closed her eyes, pushing the swing gently back and forth. *A million things can go wrong,* but her endurance spirit challenged her, whispering, *and a million things can go right. Put your boots on, Missy. Stand tall and be the 'cowgirl' you're blessed to be.*

Jackson's truck turned in the driveway, the headlights rousing her from the message she would remember during the hard times.

"All's well?" he questioned glancing toward the trailers.

"I let sleeping dogs lie. It appears that they're all getting along and no more emergencies. You know, this is the last night we'll have the house to ourselves..."

"I'm ready if you are. Let's get this party started!"

~ ~ ~

Friday morning Moria awoke in the dark. Glancing at the clock, she muttered, "Might as well get up. I'm going to need every minute I can salvage today… starting at 4 AM!"

Jackson joined her in the kitchen, pouring himself coffee and refilling Moria's cup. She looked at it, studying the design and tracing the image of a racing horse and the words, 'to finish is to win'. You can never have too many completion mugs."

Jackson grinned, picked up a magic marker from the table, reached for Moria's hand, turning her arm over and wrote *to finish is to win.* "Here's your motto, Missy."

"Wow!" she laughed, "Now I can't take a shower."

Jackson winked at her and said, "Better to have a plan than a shower." Reaching for his key chain, he added, "Remember this guy?" unhooking it from his keychain and handing her a tiny charm.

"St. Jude? Oh, my gosh, I'd forgotten all about him!"

Jackson gave her a hug and whispered in her ear, "He hasn't forgotten about you. Keep the faith, baby. I'm going out to walk the property to be sure everything's okay." He placed his hand on the box in a chair beside him. "Here's Richard's paperwork. He said check and be sure he hadn't missed anything."

Moria picked up the tiny metal person and said, "Okay, St. Jude, I'm counting on you to be your best self and protect us from desperate times." Reaching in the nearby bag for her keys, she unhooked St. Christopher from the ring and held him for a moment, saying, "Protect our travelers on their way here today and tomorrow on the trails," then placed him beside St. Jude.

Staring out the window into darkness, Moria thought back to her purchase of the Saint icons for Jackson, Maxine and Jeremy when they first banded together as an endurance team. She set the metals on the windowsill and leaned her head against the cool glass. In the stillness of the morning she prayed that she and her friends would survive and be better people for their endeavors.

Pounce and Pandora peeked through the screen door, reminding Moria, *It's breakfast time! Brought you a snack!* The cats laid two mice on the doorstep, *payment for breakfast,* they meowed.

Scooping up the mice with a paper towel and throwing them in the outside trash container, she let the cats in the house, "We'll have the mice later. Okay?"

The wind blowing across the farm brought the smell of horses, cut grass and pine needles A fresh inscription on her arm and the Saints riding along in her pocket gave her courage to meet the day once again.

Jada appeared from her horse's stall with an empty feed bucket. "Good morning, Sunshine. Chaos is ready to roll. Me, too."

Moria frowned, "Are you sure you should ride tomorrow? After all, you are the ride manager."

Jada grinned, "That's why I chose you and Maxine to be co-managers. This can be your crowning glory. In the meantime, I'm going to be busy filming today. Mind your manners now so you all don't accidently get recorded at the wrong time."

"You can kiss your camera goodbye if that happens," Moria replied, in a tone that got Jada's attention. "Why don't you help me set up the check-in table? Molly said she would take care of it and help the vendors if needed. We're going to use a table under the tent. People can see the vendors as they pick up their ride cards so maybe they'll wander over and buy something. Well, here they come," she said as two vendor trucks pulled in and a horse trailer behind them. "If you're going to film stay close by in case, I need you."

Jada grinned at Moria, "You don't need me, Teacher. See you at the ride meeting," then turned away and began to film the incoming trailers.

I need to stay close to Molly. The check-in table is going to get hectic. Here they come. The California folks arrived first and picked up their ride cards and maps. She gave Jessie a hug, "Stay safe and good luck," she said, waving goodbye to them. A grateful moment surprised Moria as she looked out over the camp and across the road to the pasture with the overflow.

Maxine arrived and took charge of the campers, being sure they were in their assigned spaces. Returning to Moria for a moment, she said, "They can get refills on water and Jackson said he would fill his big tank and drive around from time to time. Also, the chiropractor is tending to Doris' horse one more time. The doctor has her trailer and plans to stay until Sunday morning. No doubt she's going to be busy."

The vendors were in place by noon and most of the riders had arrived. Moria circulated around the camp sites to welcome the distracted riders and answer questions. Most of the people were seasoned endurance riders and knew what was required to prepare for the next day. The first-time folks settled in and most of them quietly observed their neighbors, groomed their horses and prepared for the vet check.

Dr. Barr and his assistant arrived, followed by an out-of-town vet with a mobile unit. "Glad to see you," Jackson greeted them with a genuine smile. "This is unexpected," he said, admiring the unit.

Dr. Simone jumped out to shake Jackson's hand, saying, "I just picked this beauty up last night," she answered, patting the side of the truck.

"Let's get you all parked and then take a look at the vet check to be sure you have everything you need. You all will be staying in the Rutherford's guest house across the road. Hey, here comes the food truck. What about some lunch?"

Peace in the Valley Farm appeared as a movie set, each actor doing their assigned part as the afternoon progressed. Moria watched the vet check as horses and their anxious riders came and went. Seeing Dr. Barr taking a break for some water, she asked,

"How's it going? Do you all need anything?"

Taking a moment to sit down, he answered, "We probably could have used another vet, but things are moving along okay."

"Have you had any non-starts?"

"Just two so far. One from a bang up in the trailer and the other one a slight colic. We'll check them in the morning."

"Doris Weaver's horse?"

"He passed the vet-in. She's done about all she can do. By the way, some youngster was questioning me about drug testing. She seemed intense for a kid."

Moria laughed, answering, "Jessie. She's wise beyond her years. I think Doris sent her. Don't be shy about checking whoever."

Dr. Barr held Moria's gaze, saying, "You know me better than that. Well, I need to get back to work. You all have done a great job with the camp. See you at the ride meeting," waved and returned to his task.

Glancing toward the vendors, Moria saw Sassy/Mousey aka Alyssia/ Teresa and Jessie over at Running Deer's tent. Dale and Rita stood close by enjoying the interactions of the girls with Running Deer. When the children saw Moria they said a quick thank you and raced over to show her their treasures.

"Wow! Looking sharp, girls," Moria said with a smile. "Let's see what you've got."

"These are charms to fasten to our horses' bridles so we'll have good luck and be protected from harm," Alyssia beamed, showing Moria a tiny eagle on a horsehair braided keychain. Teresa and Jessie held theirs out also.

"Now we can ride fast," Jessie smiled, bouncing up and down.

Teresa stroked her charm then looked at Jessie, "Slow and steady wins the race, so I've heard."

Jessie dangled her charm over Teresa's head, "Wish you were riding 50. Then we could race."

Alyssia interrupted, "Not our style. Do your own thing." She took Teresa's arm, "We need to go check on the horses. See ya later," and the two turned away.

Taken aback, Jessie looked at Moria. "Doesn't everybody race?"

"You've got a lot to learn. Just remember, tomorrow, take care of your horse."

"I will," the child answered with a smile, "We're ready!"

Heading back to the check-in table, Moria noticed that Ben had returned and was chatting with Molly. "Hey, Mr. Ben, how was your trip to Drapersville?"

Ben tipped his Stetson back and looked at her with a smile. "It appears that the issues are resolved to everyone's satisfaction. Jackson and I are going back on Monday to assist in signing the final papers." He reached in a bag beside him. "Here, I brought you something," and held out a folded tee shirt.

"Thanks! I could use a present today," smiling and accepting the shirt. She unfolded the light green material to reveal the design of a galloping herd of horses etched in black, surrounded by the words, Follow Your Dreams!

"Oh, Ben, thank you so much. I'll wear it tomorrow. This ride has become my dream… by happenstance." She draped the shirt over her arm and turned toward the house. "I'm putting this in a safe place. Thanks, again," giving Ben a hug.

"Molly, I'll be back in a minute to give you a break." Reaching in her pocket, she handed them tickets for the food truck.

"You don't have to do that," Molly answered. "We can pay."

"I'm sure you can but I want to treat you all for your hard work."

Molly laughed, "Well, the rider bucks threw me until the volunteer who first presented them, explained their purpose. I took him at his word."

"No problem. We're not going to lose money on this ride," Moria said, gazing out over the crowded pasture and across the road to the overflow.

~ ~ ~

Encouraging music welcomed the riders to the evening meeting.

"Come Saturday Morning" flowed across the field as Moria hummed along… *I'm going away with my friends, dressed up in my rings and my Saturday things.* The music repeated, as she gathered her notes then laid St. Jude and St. Christopher on the table beside her. Then smiled to herself with the song's ending… *and then, we'll remember, long after Saturday's gone.*

Excited chatter filled the tent as the riders settled into their chairs. The mellow notes of the music brought their attention to the realization that, "Come Saturday Morning" was tomorrow!

Jackson, Jeremy, Maxine, Jada and Richard sat over to the side. Jackson winked at Moria giving her a thumbs up as she turned off the music and faced the group. *This is it! We're as ready as we'll ever be.*

"Good evening, folks. Welcome to Peace in the Valley Farm and the Cherry Valley Endurance Ride!" Her deep breath drew in a peaceful easy feeling and her voice strengthened. *I know my teachable moment is here.*

"I would like to introduce our manger, Jada Deavers and our secretary, Richard," smiling and gesturing to the couple. Now I'll turn the meeting over to Jada."

Caught off guard, Jada stood and welcomed everyone. Then waved to Moria and Maxine, saying, "These are the ladies and gents, pointing to Jackson and Jeremy, who have put this ride together. In addition to many of you who explored and cleared trails. Enjoy the ride!"

Moria proceeded to give an overview of the trail. "Take a look at your map. Fifty milers will start on the Red Loop at 7:00 AM. Twenty-fives will follow at 8. Sarah and Will be an hour ahead of you to check the ribbons. Your first possible obstacle will be the covered bridge. If your horse is spooked, you can go down beside the bridge to cross. We will have a spotter there. Next is the water crossing. That's where the Red and Blue Trails meet. There are plenty of ribbons and a spotter will be there. There's room for the horses to drink and be sponged. This is the only water on this loop unless you go in the ravine by the bridge. Please give your horse time to drink."

A voice from the back of the group interrupted, "That's all the water?" he complained.

One of the 4-H dads spoke up. "We're spotters on the Blue Loop at the turn off at the powerline. We live nearby and I have a small generator. We can get water from the creek behind the school."

Moria gave the volunteer a grateful smile, "Wow, thanks so much for your quick thinking!"

Then, she glanced back at the 'voice'. "As I said, you can also go into the ravine for water. You'll be about three miles out."

"Okay, moving on. On the back side of your map you will see the start/finish and hold times at the vet check listed for your distance. The Blue Loop is well-marked with a spotter at the turn into the Deer Trail. When you're coming home on the Blue, we don't recommend racing until you come out of the woods. Use your own judgement!"

"The Intro. Riders meeting will follow shortly. Remember, your horses have to be vetted in. You all won't start until 11:00. You can vet in the morning if you haven't already. Your loop will be the 10 mile Red. Jeremy will meet with you all in a few minutes," nodding toward her friend. "If your horse is fit and you want twenty-five to be your ride, that's fine, but you must go to the Intro. meeting if you're a first time rider."

Jeremy stood and motioned the new riders to come over as the meeting drew to a close.

With a sigh of relief, Moria announced, "See you at the Awards Meeting! I'm available for questions," she concluded, as several riders came forward to speak with her.

~ ~ ~

Later, Moria and Jackson sat with Will and Sarah in the barn aisle after the ride meeting, watching riders walking their horses, off in their world of tomorrow, wondering what the day would bring. Evening shadows reached across the farm, encouraging the horses and riders to bed down for the night.

"Mom, be sure and send ribbons with us in the morning in case something has happened to what's out there."

Moria went into the tack room, returning with rolls of red and blue surveyor's tape, yellow caution tape and a map. "Hope everything's okay.

You know these trails, Sarah, I don't think vandals will be about. Everyone here and all the volunteers have a stake in this ride for it to go well."

A thoughtful look crossed Sarah's face. "What about Jada? I can just see her running in the front and pulling ribbons down."

"Hush yo mouf, honey chile," Moria laughed. "I'd be more worried that Pete and his friend would figure out some way to disrupt things. He's been too nice lately. Watch out for the bear when you're out in the morning. She's been prowling around near our farms."

Will said, "I'm looking forward to riding Silver," and grinned at Jackson.

"He could use some exercise. Watch him. He's got a spooky streak."

"Yes sir," Will answered, "We'll be careful."

As they got up to leave, Moria added, "If you all are out an hour ahead of the start time to check on things you'll probably be able to stay in front of everyone. Bring the horses in for a check and if they're doing okay go on to the second loop. I'll bet Rainbow's going to be hard to hold!"

Sarah and Will headed to the trailer and Moria and Jackson started for the house. Moria stopped and took Jackson's hand. "Let's take a walk," and tugged him toward the campsites.

As the couple took one last look at the trailers, listened to horses snuffling in their hay and the low voices of the riders saying goodnight, all seemed well on Peace in the Valley Farm.

The screen door creaked as they entered the house. "Let's not wake Ben and Molly," Moria whispered, removing her boots at the door.

Jackson smiled, "Yeah, let's not wake my parents with bedroom noise. Come on, I've got an idea."

"I'm not surprised," she answered as Jackson captured his favorite cowgirl and brought her to the carpet. Stealth pervaded in the night.

Pounce and Pandora sat outside the bedroom door. Pounce clawed at the door, meowing to his friend, *Something's wrong! They've fallen to the floor!*

Oh Pounce, get over yourself. Be patient. They'll get up in a few minutes.

The gray cat continued to scratch the door until Molly came out, scooped the two cats into her arms and deposited them at the foot of her bed. Molly smiled to herself, *goodnight, you furballs.* as she snuggled up to Ben.

Chapter Twenty-three

Saturday morning. It's ride day, at last! Moria headed for the shower and noticed that Jackson had already gone prowling around outside. She could hear Molly and Ben stirring across the hall and called out, "Be there in a minute. Have some coffee and could you please feed the cats? Give them some extra 'cause I don't think we'll be seeing them much till tonight."

"Sure thing," Molly answered. "Jackson said he was going to help Sarah and Will tack up Rainbow and Silver so they can get started on the trail. Then he and Jeremy are going over to the vet check to see if there are any last minute needs."

Taking one last look in the mirror, she was surprised to see a sparkle in her eyes and the pink on her cheeks telling the tale of the coming day. Scooping up Saint Christopher and Saint Jude, she wedged them in her pocket. "I'm counting on you guys to watch over us today."

"Speaking of help," Molly said, as Moria walked into the kitchen, "Put us on speed dial. We're up for whatever."

"Please take charge of the food tickets and be sure the volunteers and vets are covered. Hold on to them and you can be the 'go to' person to keep everybody fed. Ben, if you would help Richard check the horses' numbers on the call out. We need to know who's starting."

Ben reached for his Stetson and gave Moria a hug. "This will be your finest hour, Missy. Enjoy the day, a day in history. Next year, you'll ride!"

She laughed, "Yeah, to hear Jada tell it, all the way to Drapersville and back. We'll see! Let's just get through this day first!"

Opening the screen door and turning the next page of her life, Moria took a moment to savor the familiar smell of horses mingled with the pine scented air. A light breeze blew across the valley and dawn welcomed the day. Shadows of horses, riders, crews and volunteers blended into the early morning mist, a puzzle with a deadline.

Maxine waved from where she'd parked near the barn. "Is this an okay spot?"

"Sure. Actually, we need someone near the gate. That could be you. Also, if you can relieve the pulse takers for a lunch break and I'll be there, too. Let's go see how everybody's doing at the trailers." She looked up at the mountains, still covered with mist. "I do wish I was riding today."

"So do I," Maxine replied, "but I guess we're boots on the ground since our manager will be on the trail." Frowning, she continued, "Speak of the Devil, here she comes."

"Hey, ladies," Jada chirped, jumping out of her truck.

"You can't park here," Moria said, pointing toward the pasture. "There."

Jada took a stance, hands on her hips, and tossed her hair, saying, "Seems like you could cut me a little slack here."

Maxine walked over to the truck, let down the tailgate and started to unload all the ride necessities Jada had brought. "Lucky for you, you might as well crew at the barn since Chaos is *boarding* here. I'm putting your stuff in the next stall. Try to stay out of people's way and move your truck to the field."

"Aren't you all going to wish me luck?" Jada whined.

"Sure," Moria grinned, "and don't get lost." With those parting words she and Maxine hurried out to the field.

Rodney greeted them with a smile. "So far, so good," he laughed, eyeing his horses saddled and tied to the trailer with Sassy and Mousey hovering nearby. "These young'uns are about to drive me crazy. I should let them run with the fifty milers!"

Moria walked over to the girls. "Okay, cowgirlies, this is your chance to shine. Are you ready?"

"Yes ma'am," they answered in unison.

"So, what do you need to remember?"

Sassy smiled, "Stay with our sponsor and don't argue about the pace."

"What does that mean?" Moria questioned.

"It means we can't go faster than Miss Rita," Mousey piped up.

"And, what's the motto?" Maxine asked.

"To finish is to win!" both girls called out, jumping up to give high fives to each other and to Moria and Maxine.

Rose and Dale approached the group. Rodney waved them over, saying, "Here comes our crew. They came by yesterday to check out the scene and get instructions. That Rose! She's beside herself about leasing Dillon."

"I'm glad that's going to work out. Let us know if we can help," Maxine answered, turning to her teacher friends.

"How's it going?"

"We have news from school. We will be in session Monday. I went by yesterday to get the latest. There are still some things to be done but they can work around us." Rose's expression softened as she walked to Dillon. "You got this, buddy," she whispered and stroked his neck. Next year, it's you and me, going on adventures. Take care of yourself today!"

Moria walked ahead to the California camp. Thirty minutes away from the start time and the riders are mounting up to head to the road. The far-off look in Doris' eyes gives no doubt that she'll meet the day with one goal, finish first with a sound horse and bring her Junior Rider safely home.

"Hey," Moria said, breaking Doris' train of thought, "How's Straight Arrow?"

"He jogged for the vet early this morning and he said good to go, but they'll keep a close eye on him." She frowned, "They better not single me out! This horse is sound."

Moria didn't think this was a time for warm and fuzzy well-wishes. "Enjoy you ride. See you at the vet check."

Doris nodded, gathered her reins, motioned for her posse and they headed to the start line.

Playtime is over for Jessie as she gives Moria a brief, half smile and turns Friendly to follow Doris. Tara and Chris come around from the other side of the trailer, mount up, both wave to her and Moria gives them a thumbs up in return.

Paul, Ruth and Kam stand by the corrals in a daze watching their riders depart. Then, they begin to gather scattered items and prepare for riders returns. Paul greets Moria with a frown. "I'm not sure Doris needs to be running in the front today. We reminded her that Jessie didn't need to win, just finish and to add to her miles. She's already qualified for the Championship Ride next month."

Moria chose her words with caution. "You all have travelled a lot of miles with Doris, or by yourselves. Remember last year when you let me race with Jessie? You didn't know me from Adam's house cat!"

Ruth joined in, saying, "We trusted Doris." Then she laughed, "She knows more about you than you think. Jada's her new best friend and has kept her in the Cherry Valley loop. She even sent Doris a copy of the map."

"I'm not surprised. I think they're riding together today," Moria commented, picking up a towel from the ground and hanging it on a chair.

Ruth reached for her camera as group turned toward the road. "I will say Jessie's wised up over this past year and doesn't take everything Doris says as gospel. I can't tell you how many times she's called AERC to verify something or done research on her on. Yes, this sport is dangerous, but any athletic endeavor has its risk."

"Ruth, I'm glad you and Paul are Jessie's parents. She'll go a long way in this world and not just on the trail, thanks to her raising. *Wow sounds like I'm on the Lifetime Channel!* Hey, we better get to the start line."

Looking toward the road she saw flashes of bay, gray, spotted, black, chestnut and gold horses topped with an array of colors from the riders' outfits. The sides of the road were crowded with crews, vendors, families and friends.

Laurie, the timer, stood near her table with the vets. "Three, two, one. The trail is open!" she called, and the thrill of the chase began!

Moria watched as friends, old and new, trotted and cantered away into the unknown day. A tap on her shoulder brought her back to the moment as Maxine said, "Wake up, Missy," and handed her a walkie-talkie. "Keep in touch with Jackson at the water crossing. I'm on stand-by for the bridge. I'll stay near the gate 'cause it can get crowded with riders in and out. Also, Sarah and Will are on the Red Loop. Said all was well, so far."

"Thanks, I'll hang out at the vet check unless I'm needed somewhere else. I want to be sure and watch the twenty-five milers take off." It seemed like no time before Jackson radioed her. "No surprise, Jada, Doris, Jessie, and a pack of others just splashed through. If I remember, the Ridge Trail is pretty narrow. Guess they'll sort it out. I'd love to see how that works out."

"Yeah, I can only imagine. When they clear the vet check it might be a different arrangement going out. I just hope no one gets hurt. The EMS truck is parked in Maxine's driveway."

The twenty-five mile riders began to crowd Rutherford Road. Moria stood near the timer, watching Rodney's group, who appeared to be all business. He trotted out first, followed by Sassy, Mousey and Rita. Their horses doubled down on the trot as Rodney placed them in the middle of the pack and … they were off!

Shouts from the crowd, "Here they come!" brought Moria over near the water trough so she could see through the trees to Rutherford's Road. To her surprise, four out-of-state fifty milers led the way, followed by Doris, Jessie and Jada. The group came to a stop at the timer's table, gave their numbers and hurried to the trailers and vet check. As she watched, ten more riders appeared, still determined to out ride the front runners before they would reach the finish line.

Moria made her way to the vet check to see if they needed anymore pulse takers. Standing to the side, she watched the riders and crews approach. Two of the out-of-state riders checked through first. "Clear!" announced the vet for both competitors. Doris, Jessie and Jada next in line, cleared also. Doris motioned to Jessie back to the trailer to care for the horses.

Next came the group of ten, plus Tara and Chris. Stress radiated off the two California women and their horses had a pokey trot.

"Need some help?" Moria asked, seeing trouble lurking just around the corner if the two girls chose to stay near the front.

"Yeah, thanks. If you've got time," Chris answered as Moria took their horses.

"Go potty or whatever you need to do. Kam and I can take care of these guys."

Just then, Kam ran up and took Tara's horse. The rider said, "We're set up with everything we need for them. Thanks for helping. Paul and Ruth are trying to calm Doris down. She's fit to be tied because those other guys managed to slip by on the Ridge Trail. Jessie's in a dither because she thinks it was her fault that the others got by. Damn soap opera if you ask me!"

Moria and Kam took the horses to the other side of the trailer, away from Doris and her antics. The horses' crewing needs were laid out in an orderly manner and soon they had their noses buried in piles of Alfalfa hay.

Tara and Chris returned, coming straight to their horses. Tara sank into a chair, saying, "Thanks so much for your help. I thought we were going to get killed up on the ridge. Doris and the two front-runners kept leapfrogging each other. Jessie and Friendly were caught in the middle. Stupid crazy! It's a wonder we didn't all fall over the edge."

Chris checked her horse's legs and filled his water bucket. "I'm backing off the pace. I just want to finish. This is getting to be dangerous shit!" Lowering her voice, she continued with a grin, "I think Doris wants to impress you and Jackson, especially Jackson."

Moria gave a sigh, saying, "I'll be impressed if everyone in your group finishes. Looks like it's going to be a scrappy go on the next loop."

She stopped talking when she heard Paul's raised voice, "If winning comes above my daughter's safety I'm going to get her another sponsor before she leaves this check!"

"Cool it, Paul . We'll be fine. Mount up, Jessie!"

Moria rolled her eyes, "Jesus! I don't have a good feeling about this. Come on, let's watch them leave," she said to her friends.

At the timer's table the two out-of-staters who had come in first gave a smug look at each other as the timer announced for them to go. Doris, Jessie and Jada moved up a few feet, waiting for their out time. Others, who had come in soon after, waited a little farther back on the road. Now, the riders from middle of the pack could be seen heading to the timer, also.

"Looks tight, right now," Maxine said, as she joined the group. "What's going on?" nodding to Paul and Ruth standing away from the group, distress clearly on their faces.

Moria explained the drama that occurred at the trailer and noted that Tara and Chris were dropping back. "Smart move for them," Maxine said, then walked over to console Paul and Ruth.

The vets were checking out the last of the fifty milers as Moria approached the group, joined by Maxine. "What's the damage?" Moria asked Dr. Barr.

"Not too bad, so far. One lameness and one Rider Option." Then he laughed.

Startled, she said, "What's so funny?"

"Well, maybe not funny," nodding over to the EMS truck where a rider lay on the ground. That lady had a hysterectomy a few weeks ago but decided she could ride today. Bad choice, I'd say. Horse people, you gotta love 'em!"

"Thanks for your support ... guess we are a little 'different.'"

"You, dog and cat people ... not so much cow and snake owners. Guess it's in your DNA."

Just then, the walkie-talkie chirped. "Hey, Missy, the last of the twenty-fives cleared the water crossing. They were packed tight. Hope no one gets hurt," Jackson said.

Moria stepped away from the vet check saying, "They need better luck than the fifties, for sure!" and proceeded to tell him about the scramble on the narrow Ridge Trail. "When are you coming back?"

"My relief person for the water crossing should be here soon. Jeremy has help coming, too. That Richard, he's solid gold! Remember when he said he'd arrange for the spotters and the change overs?"

"Yep, and I agree about Richard. Who knew what a help he'd be? See you soon."

The twenty-five milers made it through the vet check with only one discontinue for a horse whose pulse wouldn't reach the 60 beats per minute criteria. As Rodney's group cleared the check, he said to Moria, "Come on over to the trailer if you have time. We can use the extra help."

Kam joined in, taking Mousey's pony while Moria took care of Sassy's mount. As they let the ponies graze and cool down, Kam said, "Sometimes I wish I'd never left," winking at Moria.

"Kam, you're going to be a catch for some lucky girl. It's just not your time."

"Yes, Mother," he answered with a laugh. "You know, Cassie's quite a catch herself. I might end up back in Georgia. Where is she today?"

"She's at the powerline water trough, taking numbers and being sure everyone makes the turn. I'm going to call and see how Doris' group is doing."

Cassie answered saying, "This is gettin' to be quite a horse race! The front runners blew by, not even stopping to offer the horses water. Jessie flashed me a grim look as she glanced over her shoulder at the water tank when they passed by."

"Thanks for the info. I'll be glad when this is over."

"Don't worry," Cassie answered. "There's always going to be pressure at the front of the pack. How they manage it is what matters."

Moria laughed, "Yeah, tell it to those dudes when they come through next time! Keep us posted if you see anything we need to know about."

"Will do. See you at dinner."

"Are you okay to stay where you are?"

"No problem. The 4-H moms are bringing us lunch. I'm just sittin' in the shade visiting with the folks who brought the water trough and learning the town secrets."

Sassy and Mousey came over to get their ponies and Sassy said, "Thanks. This ride is a blast! I hate to leave here. Maybe we can find some more endurance people when we head to our next stop. Rita's looking into it. Oh, by the way, we're leaving right after the ride. I'm not sure we'll even stay for the awards. The van is packed and ready to roll. Do you think we can get our completion awards ahead of time?"

"Of course. Your ponies are doing great! Enjoy the rest of the day."

Mousey stepped close to Moria as the young rider walked back to the trailer to saddle up. "Did you know Rodney gave us the rifles we learned to shoot with? He said we earned them. They're put away in the van."

"Who knows, Mousey? You might come across another bear."

The youngster frowned, "I'd just chase her away. Her life matters, too. Do you think she'll be on the trail today?"

"I doubt it. Too much going on out there. Don't worry. See you at the finish line!"

Jackson and Jeremy drove into camp on the ATV and met Moria at the timer's table. "I waited until the Red Loop cleared before I started back and picked Jeremy up at the bridge. No problems this morning. A few people chose to take the ravine path but no issues. The water crossing's a mess. Our reinforcements to the banks held up for a while but there's other things we can do before … the next ride."

"I didn't hear that," Moria laughed. "Come on and get some lunch before the fifties get back from their second loop."

Maxine walked up, giving Jeremy a hug. "Lunch? Good idea before the horde arrives again."

"After hearing the adventures of the morning," Jeremy said, "maybe I'll go back to the bridge for the rest of the day."

"Uh, no," Maxine said. "We need to relieve the pulse takers at the vet check. That'll be a good excuse not to get mixed up with the California people this round."

As the four friends finished lunch and started to the vet check, they could hear voices from the road, mingled with pounding hoofbeats signaling the arrival of the front runners. Dropping their saddles on the grass near the check Doris, Jada and Jessie headed to the vets. Paul and Ruth, waited with a small wagon, loaded the tack, and pulled it over to the side.

"This is not going to end well," Moria muttered. "What is she thinking?"

Doris presented first to the pulse takers. Moria heard the vet say, "Come back in ten minutes." Doris stalked away, leaving Jessie behind.

Paul and Ruth hurried over as the vet asked Jessie to return in ten minutes also. Paul said, "Come on to the trailer. Let's get Friendly cooled down and get some electrolytes in him. He needs to drink."

Jada met the same fate, as Richard led Chaos to their crewing place at the barn.

The out-of-state riders who had been in the front weren't so lucky either. Nobody cleared the vet check the first time. "What's the matter with these folks?" Jackson grumbled. "This is not their first rodeo for sure." Laying his hat aside, he picked up a stethoscope and stepped into the pulse box with his friends. By now, several other riders who were close to the front-runners, appeared, pulsed down and with smiles, left the vet check.

Doris and Jessie returned, walking past the cleared riders without a glance. Jackson checked Doris' horse. She watched his face closely, taking a breath of relief as the scribe recorded the pulse. She walked over for the trot out, paying no attention to Jessie.

Moria checked Friendly, saying to Jessie, "Hang in there, honey. Take care of your pony."

Jessie walked away, saying in a forlorn voice, "This is not fun anymore. I wanted to stop to water the horses and Doris just kept going. What's the matter with her today?"

Moria gave an encouraging smile, "Some days are diamonds, some days are stones. Looks like this might be a stone day, but the day's not over yet. Remember, diamonds come from stones."

As the fifty milers left out on the third loop, four ran in the front. Doris, Jessie and Jada about ten minutes behind, and the other fast group followed them. In the meantime, Tara and Chris still rode in the middle of the pack, seeming to be glad they'd separated from the front madness.

Maxine's walkie-talkie rang. Answering with a frown, her face wrinkled into worry. "Do you need us up there?" she asked, stepping out of the vet check.

Maxine motioned to Jeremy. "There's been a crash at the bridge. They need some help. One of the vets can go with you."

"What happened?" he asked. By now, the riders in the pulse box waiting for their pulse checks, grew anxious.

"Come on, guys, get a move on," one rider complained.

Maxine moved closer to her friends, putting the speaker on loud as they continued with their tasks. The bridge spotter's anxious voice told the tale. "The front runners didn't slow down at the bridge. Tried to trot through. One horse slipped on some manure and fell. Two others fell, also. They're pretty banged up. That girl from California, the kid and Jada crossed through the ravine. I guess they went on their way. The people involved in the accident can't continue, so I told them to pull over and wait for help."

Jeremy motioned to the vet with the mobile equine unit. "There's room on the road for your van and horses can still pass. Let's get up there and see what we can do."

Cassie, at the powerline trail, radioed Moria. "Last of the twenty-five milers just passed this check. Waiting on the second pass by of the fifties, then we'll head back to camp." Moria shared the accident at the bridge and said, "Check with Laurie to get an up-dated list of who'll be coming through at the timer station."

Moria continued working at the vet check but kept an eye out for the twenty-fives to finish. Caught up in checking the horses, time flew by and before long she heard a call from the finish line. "Here they come!"

After crossing the finish line, the first twenty-five milers dismounted, loosened their girths and walked the horses slowly to the vet check, stopping to water at a trough near the barn. Moria smiled and said, "I see Rodney and his posse. Let's see how they do," Moria said.

Rodney's group cleared the check with flying colors and relieved smiles. "Come on, gang," he said, "Got some donuts to celebrate and some liquids too."

Rose took Dillon and Dale took Timex. The girls followed behind with their ponies, grateful to be finished with sound horses.

"No riders were pulled on the third loop," Laurie reported as Doris, Jada and Jessie left out with the front runners on the final loop, a six pack of frazzled horses and riders.

Time crept slowly for the crews, volunteers and others who crowded at the finish line to see who would come in first. The spotter called Laurie from the water crossing, "Looks like you gotta a horse race comin' in. Doris' group and three others were all over themselves to get through the water and in the lead. "If I was y'all, I'd run that loop in the other direction next time. I see some more 'hot shoes' coming up the trail. I'd better get out of the way!"

Time now seemed to stand still. Moria gripped the fence rail, mesmerized by the sound of on-lookers voices… and then the sound of hoofbeats. *Something's not right* and gave Maxine a questioning look.

The answer came flying down the trail. Chaos and Straight Arrow, without riders, skidded out of the woods and onto the road. Friendly, running wide open behind them with Jessie clinging to his mane, followed as they raced toward the finish line. In an unspoken movement, on-lookers stepped onto the road, forming a human chain to stop the runaways. Seeing the wall of people, the two horses swerved into the Rutherford's driveway. Friendly slowed to a trot, then walked toward the wall of people.

Paul ran to the youngster and her pony, lifting her off the saddle. "Jessie, what happened? Where are the others?" A by-stander took Friendly's reins and stepped back, not sure what to do next.

"The bear! The bear!" Jessie choked out and looked for her pony. The man brought Friendly over and Jessie leaned onto his sweaty shoulder. The pony, sides heaving, dropped his head and stood quietly.

Kam and Ruth took charge of Doris and Jada's horses and came close to hear the story.

"They need help," Jessie cried out in a frantic voice. "A bear spooked their horses and both of them fell…"

Three out-of-state riders trotted up together, unconcerned at that moment about their placings. Dismounting, one of them said, "Injured rider on the trail about half a mile out. Where's the kid?" Then, seeing Jessie, asked, "You okay?"

Jessie nodded and said, "Somebody needs to go help them!"

The EMT's gathered supplies and started toward the trail. "We'll take the ATV. There will be horses running toward us so we'll keep blowing the horn and hope the riders pay attention. We'll radio back as soon as we can."

Paul guided Jessie to the timer's table, where she sat down and Friendly stood beside her.

"So, what happened?" Laurie asked, bringing Jessie back to the moment and handing her a bottle of water.

The young rider looked back toward the trail. "The bear ... it leaped off the bank onto the road, right in front of the horses ... they spun and dumped Doris and Jada. I was back a ways but saw what happened. I was looking to see if they were hurt and Friendly must have smelled the bear 'cause he took off after the other horses ... and I couldn't stop him."

One of the riders added to the story. "We stopped to see if we could help, and Doris said to go on and send the EMT's because Jada was hurt. That's about all we know. Hope everything will be okay," as an afterthought, she turned and said to Jessie, "Sweetie, if you want a completion, I'll sponsor you and ride out however far if it's okay," she said, looking at Laurie. "I'll get you across the finish line and at least, you'll get your completion."

Jessie managed a smile, "Thanks." Then rubbing Friendly's head, said to her dad, "I think we're done for the day. This boy needs some extra care tonight." With those words, she gathered the pony's reins and led him to camp.

Moria and Maxine remained at the timer's station as more riders crossed the finish line and reported that Jada was being tended to. No sign of the bear. The final group of riders trotted behind the ATV as it chugged down the trail.

Laurie recorded the last finisher, saying to Moria, "Everybody came back that left out on this last loop, so I guess we're done. What about the wreck at the bridge?"

"Jeremy said the vet treated the horses and they are able to walk back. They're on the way now." The mobile vet truck rounded the corner by

Rodney's and the riders followed. "Well, I guess dinner and the awards meeting are next on our agenda. Richard drove Jada to the hospital. Seems like she has some kind of a knee injury."

~ ~ ~

Twilight shadowed Peace in the Valley Farm. Trailer lights came on as riders and crews did a last-minute check on their horses. Moria picked up the loudspeaker. Her relieved voice carried across the camp, "Dinner and Awards. Come on down!"

Molly, Ben and Cassie had stepped in and arranged the awards. Molly said, "I know Jada's going to be disappointed not to be here to give out prizes," she winked at Cassie, "and receive praise for her hard work."

Moria heard Molly's pronouncement and added, "Richard called and said they're on the way back. Jada has a torn ACL but they wouldn't miss the finale for anything. Looks like we've got quite a crowd. Even the vendors and the locals wanted to stay. The church people outdid themselves," she continued, observing the steaming containers of food. "I see Pete and his friend decided to take us up on our offer for dinner. At least, they didn't disrupt the ride today."

Rita came up with a worried look, asking, "Have you seen the girls? Too many people here. I hate to go, but I think we need to leave."

"Hold on and I'll get your completion awards. It's been great having you all here. Come back soon." Moria handed Rita three coffee mugs, light green in color with a running horse and rider galloping on a long and winding road. "I guess the girls can keep pencils or hair clips in these until they're old enough to drink coffee."

Rita laughed as she took the mugs, "I'm bettin' on the coffee! If that's the worst, I'm happy." She turned to leave and stopped, "What's going on?"

At that moment, silence hovered over the area as everyone froze in place. Pete and Karl stood on the edge of the grass facing the tent as Sassy and Mousey stepped out from behind the toilets with their rifles pointed at the two men's backs. Nobody moved.

Sensing something was wrong, Pete and Karl looked at each other and then they knew, as Sassy's voice came out loud and clear, "Karl, on your knees! You're under Citizens Arrest!"

The two men spun around and stared at the girls. Sassy took her shooting stance, cocked the rifle and said, "Karl, you're under arrest for killing our friend's father! Remember?"

Mousey stared at Karl and with malice in her voice said, "I'm dying to shoot you! Don't move!"

Pete, trying to smooth the situation over, said, "Hey, little gal, you're just playin' around, ain't you?"

Mousey cocked her rifle and said, "Try me."

The two men whirled, to face the crowd of a hundred people. Sassy stepped up behind Karl and put her rifle hard into his back. "You're going back to Atlanta, dude."

With no words, Mousey followed Sassy's move and prodded Pete with her weapon.

People moved aside as Sherriff Bramblett and his Deputy walked over to secure the suspects. "We've been watching for you, Karl. The Marshal warned us to be on the lookout for anyone suspicious. Guess that would be you. Thanks ladies," the Sherriff continued, as he snapped the cuffs on Karl and Pete.

Rita approached the girls. With her back to the crowd, she grinned and said, "Hand me your weapons, cowgirlies. I think it's time we're moving on." Sassy and Mousey waved to the crowd as Rita ushered them to the van and they drove away in a cloud of dust.

Pete's voice rang out in dismay, "Hey, I didn't do nothin'! Let me go!" The Deputy slammed the door and took the driver's seat.

Sherriff Bramblett walked over to Moria and Jackson, who stood silent, in disbelief. "Sorry to miss a good dinner," he said with a smile. "We'll get back to you all soon and let you know the status of this arrest."

"Wal, I'll be hornswoggled," Rodney said, wiping his face with his bandana. Laughing, he added, "Guess my boarders dun left!"

Everyone began talking at once, looking to Moria and Jackson to clear matters up. After a whispered moment between the two, Jackson waved people to the tent. Removing his hat and running his fingers through his hair, he began. "Some of you have met Sassy and Mousey during this past summer." The 4-H kids smiled and elbowed each other, remembering the night when the girls were going to sneak out with them. Jackson continued, "They did trail work, learned to ride during the summer … and to shoot rifles." Jackson grinned, "Now, I'm going to let Rodney finish the story."

The grizzled cowboy stood, hat in his hand. "I've knowed most of you all my life, so here's the story, believe it or not." He talked about meeting Rita in the Army years ago and that later she became a U.S. Marshal. Going on describe the phone call he received from Rita needing to bring two young girls who were in child protective custody to his farm, to remove them from the Atlanta area. "The girls could identify both shooters. The other shooter was captured but Karl was nowhere to be found."

Someone from the group asked, "How did Pete and that guy become friends? Seems too much of a coincidence to me."

Rodney hesitated and looked at Jackson. *How much do I say?*

Jackson nodded, *Go ahead.*

"Wal, as some of you know, Pete raised other 'plants' among his poinsettias." He scanned the group and saw smiles, perhaps from some of Pete's customers. "Karl and the other guy must'a met Pete through the back and forth of selling his 'goods' to the folks down south."

Jackson stood and said, "Rodney, thanks for filling us in, so not too many rumors fly around. Guess the Cherry Valley Ride will be remembered for more than a great ride. Let's eat!"

As one, the group stood, applauding the day and grateful for the outcome.

Richard and Jada returned in time for the awards meeting. A round of greetings and condolences met them as they settled into their chairs. Jada appeared anxious to begin the ceremony, not aware of the drama that preceded them. In spite of her obvious handicap from the injury and painkillers, she managed to present the hard-earned recognitions and thank everyone for their dedication and support.

"Completions for Rita and her juniors," Jada said, continuing down the list. As no one came forward, she gave a puzzled look and Moria said, "They had to leave early." No one spoke and Jada continued.

"And the hard luck awards go to," Jada looked at the list. "The people from the bridge crash. I'm not sure who you are …" Those unfortunate ones limped forward. "And, sadly, Jessie, Doris and me." She studied the list for a moment and looked at Moria. "Karl and Pete?" The tent shook from laughter and Moria said, "Tell you later."

Maxine and Jeremy stood with Jackson, Moria, Cassie, Richard and Jada as people crowded around to thank them for putting on the ride. One rider asked, "Could you all help me put on a ride where I live?" Moria leaned into Jackson, smiled at her and said, "Sure, give us a call."

Jackson gave his cowgirl a nudge and whispered, "You'll pay for that, Missy!"

With a wicked smile, she said, I can hardly wait!"

Early October ~ Dinner at Peace in the Valley Farm~ Epilogue

The four Cherry Valley friends settled at the picnic table in the back yard. Jackson put steaks on the grill and the friends began to recall the past few months.

Moria gazed out over the field. "Like it never even happened," she commented.

The last of the Autumn leaves drifted down, as if to say, "Done! And Done!"

Jackson laughed, "Movin' on. Glad to hear the trial's over for Sassy and Mousey's part. Rita said their family's moving 'far away' from Atlanta… but the girls are coming back to help at Rodney's summer camp."

"Speaking of the trial," Maxine said, "I'm not surprised, Rita's returning and staying at Rodney's. She did admit they're not brother and sister." Laughing, she continued, "She can live here and still do her job. That's an interesting turn of events!"

Jeremy joined in, saying, "We heard from Jada that the California crew headed home. To hear 'our neighbor' tell it, Jessie's parents are looking for a new sponsor for her. Kam, Tara and Chris are going back to their real lives… from an adventure they'll never forget!"

"Where is Jada?" Moria asked, realizing she hadn't seen her around lately.

Jeremy grinned, "I was savin' the best for last… when I was at the Post Office today one of the workers mentioned that our our neighbor is on a long trip… around the world!"

"So, that's what Richard was holding over her head to make her behave!" Moria laughed. "Well, it was a good try!"

Dusk settled over the farm. Maxine said, "By the way, what do you all think about Pete's arrangement?"

Moria smiled, saying, "Guess we won't be buying any poinsettias for Christmas, not since Pete turned his farm over the National Forest as a rehab place for injured animals."

"Yeah, I heard he's still going to live there, maintain the place and help care for the animals. His only request was to fence off the old cabin and preserve it since his son is buried there," Maxine added.

Jackson said, "Apparently, they searched his farm after Karl's arrest and it was clean. The Sheriff seems to be convinced that Pete didn't know about the murder. They can't prove whether he knew or not. The drug dogs scented on Karl's truck but that was all. Lucky Pete!"

The moon rose over Cherry Valley. Moria and Maxine began to clear the table and Jackson said, "What about a moonlight ride tonight? We need to start conditioning for the next ride!"

Acknowledgements

Where to begin? Thanks to the Ride Managers who rock our world, giving endurance riders an opportunity to enjoy the great outdoors, friends, family, and our treasured horses.

A special thanks goes to Becky Pearman Kichner for the excellent photography on the book cover and to Cindy Young from KY, for the graphics. They were very patient with me.

Thanks to Jennifer Sayers and her lovely mare, Scarlet for gracing the cover of an unknown book. Perfect pictures for Follow the Ribbons, Missy. Your trust was greatly appreciated.

My friend, Ginna Hansen, was one of my first readers and editors. Alas, she moved away, but not before she visited a Broxton Bridge Ride to see what it was all about. She knew "my voice" and would call me out if I was not consistent with the characters.

The Low Country Writers became my next writing support for several years. They were adamant in their pursuit to improve my writing skills. Thanks for your determination.

When the pandemic broke, the writing group went to Zoom and I searched for another writing mentor. I met Sally Murphy and found that she is a published author. Her book, *Turning the Tide*, is an engaging memoir about sea turtle protection in South Carolina. In addition, she is an excellent editor and a 'horse person'. Thank you Sally, for helping me understand more about the writing process and put it to use.

Of course, my endurance friends were a wealth of information about bears, how to harden a water crossing, and rules for "what ifs." Other friends offered many stories of their adventures, also.

To: Cindy S. Young, the bear expert, and a wealth of information about all other forest happenings. Most of all, you're never afraid to 'go boldly forward where no one else has gone.'

To: Joe Schoech, Thanks for your information and expertise about improving water crossings. You were 'spot on' with your advice. Too bad, in the story, Jackson and Jeremy didn't listen to you!

To: Laurie Underwood, you could give me a rule for the most extreme situations I could dream up. Thanks for your entertaining and creative help.

My family! They were happy I was writing a book and not riding a horse! Their support over the years, sometimes crewing for me, and always encouraging my dreams will be remembered with love.

My granddaughters, Rachel and Anna. As I wrote about Sassy, Mousey and Jessie in the story, I remembered the thousands of miles travelled with Rachel and Anna when they were Junior Riders, 'the thrill of success" and… yes, 'the agony of defeat.' I am forever grateful for their courage and adventuresome spirits.

Thanks to Dean Elder, my computer support person and friend. At first, I was paying him. Finally, he said, "No more money. Let's just get the book done."

Thanks to Palmetto Publishing Company for their patience and expertise in bringing my dream to reality.

CPSIA information can be obtained
at www.ICGtesting.com
Printed in the USA
LVHW050757130122
708279LV00008B/333